Peter Lucantoni

Cambridge IGCSE®
English as a Second Language
Coursebook

Fifth edition

CAMBRIDGE
UNIVERSITY PRESS

University Printing House, Cambridge CB2 8BS, United Kingdom

One Liberty Plaza, 20th Floor, New York, NY 10006, USA

477 Williamstown Road, Port Melbourne, VIC 3207, Australia

4843/24, 2nd Floor, Ansari Road, Daryaganj, Delhi - 110002, India

79 Anson Road, #06 -04/06, Singapore 079906

Cambridge University Press is part of the University of Cambridge.

It furthers the University's mission by disseminating knowledge in the pursuit of
education, learning and research at the highest international levels of excellence.

www.cambridge.org
Information on this title: www.cambridge.org/9781316636558 (Paperback)

© Cambridge University Press 2017

This publication is in copyright. Subject to statutory exception
and to the provisions of relevant collective licensing agreements,
no reproduction of any part may take place without the written
permission of Cambridge University Press.

First published 2017

20 19 18 17 16 15 14 13 12 11 10 9 8 7 6 5 4 3 2

Printed in the United Kingdom by Latimer Trend

A catalogue record for this publication is available from the British Library

ISBN 978-1-316-63655-8 Paperback

Cambridge University Press has no responsibility for the persistence or accuracy
of URLs for external or third-party internet websites referred to in this publication,
and does not guarantee that any content on such websites is, or will remain,
accurate or appropriate. Information regarding prices, travel timetables, and other
factual information given in this work is correct at the time of first printing but
Cambridge University Press does not guarantee the accuracy of such information
thereafter.

®IGCSE is the registered trademark of Cambridge International Examinations.

All exam-style questions and sample answers have been written by the authors.

....

NOTICE TO TEACHERS IN THE UK

It is illegal to reproduce any part of this work in material form (including
photocopying and electronic storage) except under the following circumstances:

(i)   where you are abiding by a licence granted to your school or institution by the
      Copyright Licensing Agency;

(ii) where no such licence exists, or where you wish to exceed the terms of a licence,
      and you have gained the written permission of Cambridge University Press;

(iii) where you are allowed to reproduce without permission under the provisions
      of Chapter 3 of the Copyright, Designs and Patents Act 1988, which covers, for
      example, the reproduction of short passages within certain types of educational
      anthology and reproduction for the purposes of setting examination questions.

Contents

Part 1: Leisure and travel   2

Part 2: Education and work   54

Part 3: People and achievements   108

Part 4: Ideas and the modern world   164

Introduction

This new fifth edition is for students who are following the Cambridge International General Certificate of Secondary Education (IGCSE) English as a Second Language syllabus, and follows on from *Introduction to English as a Second Language*. However, this Coursebook can be used independently of the introductory volume.

It is assumed that most of you who use this book will be studying English in order to improve your educational or employment prospects, so it includes topics and themes relevant to this goal. You will find passages and activities based on a wide variety of stimulating topics and about people from all over the world, which I hope you will enjoy reading and discussing.

The book is divided into four themed parts: Leisure and travel, Education and work, People and achievements, and Ideas and the modern world. Each themed part is subdivided into units based on the specific skill areas of the IGCSE English as a Second Language syllabus: reading, writing, listening and speaking. Exam-style exercises are provided at the end of every unit. A new feature of the 5th edition is the inclusion of a short video at the start of every unit. It shows students discussing the unit theme. Speaking skills are practised through discussion activities and pair and group work, which occur in every unit. Furthermore, in Units 5, 10, 15 and 20, there is additional video material of students responding to exam-style exercises. Appendix 1 contains some examples of topic cards, similar to those used in speaking test examinations.

The material becomes progressively more demanding, with longer and more advanced texts used in the second half of the book. This progressive step-by-step approach, including Top Tips, Language Tips and Word Tips throughout the book, will help to build your confidence in all the necessary skill areas, while also developing your techniques for success in examinations.

I hope you enjoy using this book, and I wish you success in your IGCSE English as a Second Language course!

Peter Lucantoni

This book is dedicated, as always, to Lydia, Sara and Emily

How to use this book

LEARNING OBJECTIVES
The title of each unit shows which exam exercise it will focus on. Then there is a short list of the key skills you will learn. In this edition, there are four new Speaking units.

VIDEOS
Videos show real students from around the world sharing their views on the topic of each unit. The new Speaking units also have additional Speaking test preparation videos.

Unit 15: Healthy living Focus on speaking: topic cards

Learning objectives

In this unit you will:

- watch a video of students talking about healthy living, and discuss what they say
- talk about different activities and healthy living
- read about two different healthy foods and discuss them
- watch and listen to students taking part in a speaking role-play, and assess their performance
- read about gardening and make notes and write a summary

A ⊙ Watch, listen and talk

1 Watch and listen to some IGCSE students talking about **healthy living**.
  a What do the students say are the reasons for taking care of our health? Make a note of **three**.
  b What do the students do to have a healthy lifestyle? Could they improve it? How?
2 Talk to your partner/s about how the lifestyles of other people influence your own.

B ⊙ Speaking and vocabulary

1 Look at the pictures (1–7). What can you see in each one?

155

REFLECTION
This feature gives you the chance to reflect on your progress throughout the unit and plan your next steps.

EXERCISE
The exam focus exercises help you to prepare for each exercise of the Cambridge IGCSE English as a Second Language exam. There is plenty of opportunity to practise new exercise types.

Unit 1: Free time

REFLECTION

How well do you think you can do each of these things now?

Give yourself a score from 1: Still need a lot of practice to 5: Feeling very confident about this

In this unit you:	1	2	3	4	5
watched a video of students talking about their free time, and discussed what they said					
read an advertisement about apps and answered questions on it					
thought about the best strategies for providing short answers to questions					
read an online advertisement for a webzine for teenagers and answered questions on it					
practised speaking about your preferences and making suggestions.					

Now set yourself a **personal goal** based on your scores for Unit 1.

Exam focus

Reading, Exercise 1, skimming and scanning

1 Read the following visitor information leaflet about markets in Cambridge, and then answer the exercises.

Cambridge offers you more than you would expect

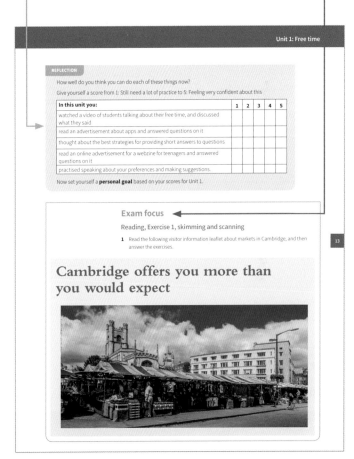

13

v

WORD TIP
Word tips highlight vocabulary which students commonly misunderstand or misuse.

ICONS

 Reading   Vocabulary

Speaking   Video

 Writing   Language

 Listening

LISTENING PRACTICE
There is more listening practice in this new edition.

LANGUAGE TIP
Language tips help with grammar and structure. Sometimes they suggest further practice activities in the workbook.

TOP TIP
Top tips suggest strategies for improving your English and developing your skills.

Overview of Cambridge IGCSE English as a Second Language

Reading and Writing

Students will take either:

Paper 1 (Core) – 1 hour 30 minutes – 60 marks in total – Grades C–G

or **Paper 2 (Extended)** – 2 hours – 80 marks in total – Grades A*–E

Exercise number	Type of exercise	Description	Total marks	
			Core	Extended
Exercise 1	Skimming and scanning	Students read a text and answer a series of questions which require single word/phrase answers.	9	13
Exercise 2	Multiple matching	Students read a text and answer a series of questions testing more detailed comprehension. Students match the correct answer to the question.	8	10
Exercise 3	Note-making	Students make brief notes on a text under a supplied heading or headings.	7	9
Exercise 4	Summary writing	Students write a summary of 80 words (Core) or 100 (Extended) about an aspect or aspects of a text. The text will be a different text from Exercise 3, for both Core and Extended.	12	16
Exercise 5	Writing	Students write 100–150 words (Core) or 150–200 words (Extended) in response to a short stimulus. The purpose, format and audience are specified. This might be a letter, an email or an article for a school magazine.	12	16
Exercise 6	Writing	Students write a report, review or article of 100–150 words (Core) or 150–200 words (Extended) in response to a short stimulus. The purpose, format and audience are specified and will be different to Exercise 5.	12	16

Listening

Students will take either:

Paper 3 (Core) – Approximately 40 minutes – 30 marks in total – Grades C–G

or **Paper 4 (Extended)** – Approximately 50 minutes – 40 marks in total – Grades A*–E

Exercise number	Type of exercise	Description	Total marks	
			Core	Extended
Exercise 1	Short extracts	Students listen to four short extracts of dialogue or phone messages and answer questions on each. Questions require short answers, no longer than three words each.	8	8
Exercise 2	Note-making	Students listen to a formal talk and complete gaps in notes/sentences.	8	8
Exercise 3	Multiple matching	Students listen to six short, informal monologues and match each speaker to appropriate content.	6	6
Exercise 4	Multiple-choice questions	Students listen to an informal discussion between two speakers and answer 3-option multiple-choice questions.	8	8
Exercise 5 (Extended only)	Completing notes	Students listen to a talk and complete short notes. Then they listen to a short discussion based on this talk, and complete sentences using no more than one or two words.	-	10

Speaking

Approximately 10–15 minutes – 30 marks in total (syllabus 0511) or grades 1–5 (syllabus 0510)

Students take part in a discussion with the teacher on a set topic. After a short warm-up which is not assessed, students are allowed 2–3 minutes to read the speaking test card which has been selected from a range of cards. The cards include prompts to guide the discussion. Students are not allowed to make written notes. The conversation itself should last 6–9 minutes. In syllabus 0510 marks for the Speaking component do not contribute to the overall grade. Instead, students will be marked from 1 (high) to 5 (low).

Weighting for qualification		
Assessment objective	0511	0510
AO1: Reading	30%	35%
AO2: Writing	30%	35%
AO3: Listening	20%	30%
AO4: Speaking	20%	Separately endorsed

Skill	Assessment objectives	
AO1: Reading	R1	identify and select relevant information
	R2	understand ideas, opinions and attitudes
	R3	show understanding of the connections between ideas, opinions and attitudes
	R4	understand what is implied but not directly stated, e.g. gist, writer's purpose, intention and feelings
AO2: Writing	W1	communicate information/ideas/opinions clearly, accurately and effectively
	W2	organise ideas into coherent paragraphs using a range of appropriate linking devices
	W3	use a range of grammatical structures and vocabulary accurately and effectively
	W4	show control of punctuation and spelling
	W5	use appropriate register and style/format for the given purpose and audience
AO3: Listening	L1	identify and select relevant information
	L2	understand ideas, opinions and attitudes
	L3	show understanding of the connections between ideas, opinions and attitudes
	L4	understand what is implied but not directly stated, e.g. gist, speaker's purpose, intention and feelings
AO4: Speaking	S1	communicate ideas/opinions clearly, accurately and effectively
	S2	develop responses and link ideas using a range of appropriate linking devices
	S3	use a range of grammatical structures and vocabulary accurately and effectively
	S4	show control of pronunciation and intonation patterns
	S5	engage in a conversation and contribute effectively to help move the conversation forward

The information in this section is taken from the Cambridge syllabus document. Teachers should refer to the appropriate syllabus document for the year that their students are entering for examination to confirm the details. More detailed information about the Cambridge IGCSE English as a Second Language examination, including support available for teachers and students, can be obtained from Cambridge International Examinations, 1 Hills Road, Cambridge CB1 2EU, United Kingdom, and online at www.cie.org.uk

Menu

Part 1:
Leisure and travel

In Part 1: Leisure and travel, there are five units (1 Free time, 2 TV, 3 Food, 4 Transport, 5 Holidays). You will:

- watch and listen to some IGCSE students talking about each unit's topic, and about the opening part of the IGCSE speaking exam;
- think about and discuss what the students said;
- read a variety of texts about apps, television, fast food, methods of transport, and different types of holidays;
- listen to people talking about their travel experiences, and a special kind of taxi;
- practise various exam skills: skimming and scanning, writing for purpose, asking and answering personal questions, and listening.

Before you start Part 1, look at the picture on these pages:

    a   In which country was the picture taken? Why do you think this?

    b   How similar or different is the picture to where you live?

    c   What has the boy in the picture just done, or what is he about to do?

    d   Have you ever done this activity? If not, would you like to? Why?

    e   Imagine you are messaging a friend. How would you describe the picture to them?

skimming and scanning

Learning objectives

In this unit you will:

- watch a video of students talking about their free time, and discuss what they say
- read an advertisement about apps and answer questions on it
- think about the best strategies for providing short answers to questions
- read an online advertisement for a webzine for teenagers and answer questions on it
- practise speaking about your preferences and making suggestions

A 😁 Watch, listen and talk

1 Watch and listen to some IGCSE students talking about their **free time**.

   a Make a note of **three** things that they enjoy doing, and **three** things that they do not enjoy doing in their free time. '

   b Talk to your partner(s) about the things that **you** like and do not like doing in **your** free time.

B 🔤 Speaking and vocabulary

1 What do these pictures show? Discuss your ideas with a partner and write down **at least five** words or phrases that you think of.

Example: *people enjoying themselves*

2   Complete the table with things that you enjoy and don't enjoy doing. Use the pictures above and your ideas from the **Watch, listen and talk** activity. There are two examples. Compare your list with your partner's. Are they the same or different?

Enjoy	Don't enjoy
watching films on TV	tidying my room

LANGUAGE TIP

Remember that the verbs *enjoy* and *dislike* are both followed by *-ing* **NOT** *to*

Example: I **enjoy** watch**ing** movies on TV, but I **dislike** tidy**ing** my room. ✓

   NOT I enjoy to watching movies on TV, but I dislike to tidying my room. ✗

   NOT I enjoy to watch movies on TV, but I dislike to tidy my room. ✗

Complete the exercises in your **Workbook**.

TOP TIP

Skimming and **scanning** are two very different strategies for *speed reading*. They each have a different purpose, and they are not meant to be used all of the time.

Skimming is used to quickly identify the main ideas of a text and is done at a speed three to four times faster than normal reading.

Scanning is a technique you often use when searching for key words or ideas. In most cases, you know what you're looking for, so you concentrate on finding a particular answer. Scanning involves moving your eyes quickly down the page looking for specific words and phrases. Remember that it is usually not necessary to read and understand every word in a text to find the answers to questions.

C ◉ Reading

1   Discuss these questions with a partner.

   a   When you want to find something quickly in a text, how do you read it? Which reading skills do you use?

   b   When you read something for pleasure, such as a book or a magazine, do you read it in the same way as you read a school Chemistry textbook?

   c   What other ways are there to read a text?

2   Look at the advertisement for Datasource products. Answer these two questions. You have ten seconds!

   a   How many different products are advertised?

   b   Which product is the most expensive?

3   Which reading skill or skills did you use to answer Activity C2? Did you read every word in the text? Did you read quickly or slowly?

5

New apps available to download now from **Datasource.com**!

Datasource Puzzle Finder – special discount price of $1 (normal download price: $2 – save 50%!)

This amazing app is the one that sold a million in a month in the USA! If you're a puzzle lover, now's your chance to get the most up-to-date app for finding literally hundreds of online puzzles.

Datasource Photo Squeeze – discount price of $2 (normal download price: $6 – save 66%!)

Now you can create your own amazing images using Photo Squeeze! Take a pic using your smartphone or tablet and then squeeze it into something awesome.

Datasource Trainer – amazing price – it's FREE! (normal download price: $2 – save 100%!)

If you are into keeping fit, you need this incredible app right now! Download onto your smartphone and keep track of your fitness level. This app will even tell you when you're not running fast enough!

Datasource NewsFeed – discount price of $6 (normal download price: $8 – save 25%!)

Keep in touch with what's going on in the world by using this fantastic app! NewsFeed will keep you informed about whatever you choose – sports, entertainment, music … for up to 60 free minutes every day!

Datasource My Movies – discount price of $3 (normal download price: $6 – save 50%!)

This incredible app stores a list of your favourite movies and lets you know about new releases. My Movies also lets you share your list with your friends.

Datasource Comic Fun – discount price of $1 (normal download price: $4 – save 75%!)

Everyone loves comics and this delightful but simple app gives you access to a huge number of titles. And for all you language learners, there are **five** languages to choose from!

$5 OFFER!

You can save even more by signing up to the Datasource loyalty scheme. Download a minimum of **three** apps today and get a voucher for **$5** to use on your next purchase. You also get a 21-day money-back, no-questions-asked guarantee on all our apps, a monthly digital newsletter, and a membership card and number.

4 Answer the following question. Do **not** write anything yet.

Which product has the biggest percentage reduction?

5 Which of the following is the best answer to the question in Activity C4? Is more than one answer possible? If so, why?

a Datasource Trainer has the biggest percentage reduction.

b The product with the biggest percentage reduction is Datasource Trainer.

c It's Datasource Trainer.

d Datasource Trainer.

e Trainer.

6 With your partner, ask and answer the following questions. Do **not** write anything yet.

a How many products have a normal download price of less than $5?

b How can you save an additional $5?

c Which product offers the smallest cash saving?

d How many Datasource Puzzle Finder apps were sold in a month in the USA?

e Give **three** advantages of joining the Datasource loyalty scheme.

f Which product offers you 60 minutes free of charge?

g Which product is available in different languages?

7 Write the answers to the questions in Activity C6. Exchange your answers with a different pair and check them. Use the **Top Tip** to help you.

8 Have a quick look at the second text, *You Write!* Where might you find a text like this? Why? Choose one or more from the list.

> a dictionary   an email   a newspaper   a comic   a TV magazine   a children's magazine
> a blog   a shop window   a leaflet   an encyclopaedia   a website

9 What is the best strategy for addressing short-answer questions? Put the following points into a logical order. Be prepared to explain your order.

a Search likely sections of the text.

b Read the question.

c Underline the key word/s.

d Ask yourself what information the question is asking for.

10 Look at these questions based on the *You Write!* webzine. Do **not** write anything yet. Find and note down the key word/s in each question.

a Who is *You Write!* for?

b When can you read the next publication?

c How many sections are there in the webzine?

d What is the maximum number of words for a creative story?

e If something has made you angry, for which section should you write?

f Which section does **not** tell you how many words to write?

g After you have finished your writing, what do you have to do?

h How long can the title for your writing be?

i If you select the final box, what will you **not** receive?

11 Now write the answers to the questions in Activity C10. Keep your answers short, but remember to include all the information that the questions ask for. Exchange your answers with a partner and check them.

TOP TIP

Often, you do not need to write full sentences for your answers. Sometimes a single word, a few words, or even a number, will be enough. However, you must show that you have understood the question and you must provide all of the information required. If you are writing numbers, be careful to spell them correctly. Also, if the answer is a quantity, make sure you include a symbol or a unit of measurement – for example **$**35, 10 **kilometres**, 2 **hours**.

TOP TIP

Notices, leaflets, signs, advertisements and timetables can contain a lot of information in various formats. The best strategy for answering questions on sources like these is to decide which word or words in the question will lead you to the place in the text that contains the answer. These words are called *key words*.

www.youwrite.eu

The amazing and unique* online webzine for teenagers who want to share their writing!

Send us your writing by 30th June for a chance to see it in the next issue (publication date 31st July) of **You Write!**

Choose which section you want your work to appear in: **MY STORY**, **MY POEM**, **MY OPINION**, **MY REPORT**

MY STORY:
For those of you with a story to tell, this is the section for you! We will consider your funny or serious, original*, creative stories up to a maximum of 275 words.

MY POEM:
What has inspired you to write a poem? An interesting person? An unusual place? A funny pet? Extreme weather? Send us up to 25 lines of your inspired writing in order to be considered for this section.

MY OPINION:
Use this section if you want to get something off your chest! Has something annoying happened that makes you want to put pen to paper? If you are feeling particularly angry, upset, or even happy about something, share your opinion by writing no more than 200 words.

MY REPORT:
Seen or heard something interesting locally that you want to tell others about? Perhaps a new cinema has opened in your town, or your local team won its most recent match? Maybe you want to write about something that you were personally involved in, such as a music or drama festival? Send us your report, up to 275 words.

What do I do next?

Complete and submit the form below. You **must** do this electronically. Do not forget to attach your piece of writing!

UPLOAD YOUR ARTICLE   **SUBMIT**

First name: _____   Family name: _____

Email: _____   Age last birthday: ____   Name of school: _____

Which section are you writing for? Please select.

My Story ❏   My Poem ❏   My Opinion ❏   My Report ❏

Title for your writing (maximum **FIVE** words): _____
Number of words: _____

I have my parent's/guardian's permission to submit my writing to **You Write!** Please select **YES   NO**

Data Protection Act: Sometimes we may wish to send you information about other products that we feel may be of interest to you. Select this box if you do **NOT** wish to receive such information ❏

Need to contact us? **Click here** or email us: info@youwrite.eu

*See the **WORD TIP** in **Section D**.

D Language focus: adjective + noun

1 Notice the use of adjectives in the two texts you have read in this unit:

amazing app   *up-to-date* app   *amazing online* webzine   *creative* stories

   a Copy and complete this sentence.

      Adjectives are used to provide...... about....... In English, adjectives usually come...... the noun.

   b What happens in **your** language? What is the usual order for adjectives and nouns?

2 Quickly read through the two texts in Section C again. Find **at least three** more examples of adjective + noun combinations in each text. Compare your examples with a partner's.

3 Adjectives can often be formed from other parts of speech. Copy and complete the table with the correct words. You may not be able to fill in all the gaps.

Adjective	Noun	Adverb	Verb
amazing	amazement	amazingly	amaze
special	...	...	...
incredible	...	...	...
delightful	...	...	...
funny	...	...	...
serious	...	...	...
original	...	...	...
creative	...	...	...

4 Look back at the two texts in this unit and find **at least five** more adjectives. Add them to your table and then complete the other parts of speech (noun, adverb and verb) where possible.

5 Notice that there are different possible endings for adjectives in English. Using the words from Activities D3 and D4, list some of these possible endings. Then think of **three** more examples for each ending.

   Example: *-ing: interesting, amazing, tiring, fascinating, boring*

6 Choose **eight** adjectives from Activity D5, then combine them with nouns and use them in sentences of your own.

   Example: *That webzine was full of **interesting stories** and **ideas**.*

   Complete the exercises in your **Workbook**.

WORD TIP

original = 1 INTERESTING: not the same as others; 2 FIRST: the earliest form of something

unique = 1 NOT THE SAME: different from everyone and everything; 2 SPECIAL: unusual and special; 3 BE UNIQUE TO: to exist in only one place, or connected to only one person or thing

Use either original or unique to complete the sentences in your **Workbook**.

Adapted from *Cambridge School Dictionary* 2008

9

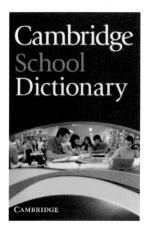

E 💬 Speaking: Showing preferences and making suggestions

1 🔊 CD1, Track 2 Listen to Maria and Christos talking. How many different ways do they use to show a preference or to make a suggestion?

2 Look at the audioscript in Appendix 3 and check the meaning of the phrases that are underlined.

3 Think of more ways to show a preference and to make a suggestion. Copy the table below and add more phrases. Compare your answers with your partner's.

Showing a preference	Making a suggestion
I'd rather go …	Why don't we go … ?
	Let's go …

4 Usually when we **show a preference** for something or **make a suggestion**, we also give a **reason**. What reason does Maria give for wanting to go to the shopping centre later? What reason does Christos give for wanting to go to the shopping centre at the weekend?

LANGUAGE TIP

Look at how **preference** and **suggestion** phrases are followed by infinitive, *to* infinitive or *-ing* forms of the verb.

+ infinitive	+ *to* infinitive	+ *-ing*
Why don't we + do?	Would you like + to do?	What/How about + doing?
Let's + do	I'd like + to do	What do you think about + doing?
I suggest we + do	I('d) prefer + to do	I suggest + doing
Can't we + do?		
I think we should + do		
I'd rather + do		

Complete the exercises in your **Workbook**.

5 Work with your partner. For each of the following examples, one of you makes a suggestion and the other gives a preference. Use a variety of phrases from the Language Tip, and support your suggestions and preferences with reasons.

Example: Buying new trainers or a birthday present for someone.

> **Maria:** *Why don't you buy those new trainers we saw in town?*
>
> **Christos:** *No, I don't think so, Maria. It's my mum's birthday next month and I'd prefer to save my money for her present.*

a Going shopping or staying home to study.

b Eating Italian or Japanese food in a restaurant.

c Watching a film at the cinema or on TV.

d Playing basketball or going swimming.

6 A competition has just been announced. An area of land near your school is going to be developed. For the competition, you need to make a short speech to your school friends, giving your preferences and reasons for the development of the land. Plan your speech. It might be helpful to write down some ideas, like this:

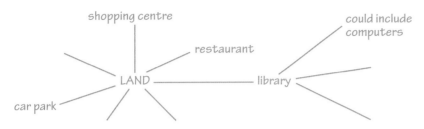

F ◎ Reading

1 You are going to read a newsletter about a sports centre. There are six sections:

Welcome! Opening hours   Membership Facilities Focus on gyms   Personal fitness

In which sections do you think you will read the following information (a–f)? Why?

a Adults

b and make you feel at home!

c Olympic and children's starter pools

d increase your strength

e reach your potential

f Monday–Saturday

2 Write a list of other information you would expect to find in each of the six sections. Write **two** things for each section. Give reasons for your choices.

3 Quickly read the Achileas Sports Centre newsletter and check your answers to Activities F1 and F2.

4 Read the newsletter in more detail and write answers for questions a–h.

a How often is the newsletter published?

b What time does the sports centre close on public holidays?

c What is the cost for a family for a six-month membership?

d How many swimming pools are there?

e What non-sport facilities does the complex offer? Give **two** examples.

f How many different 'fitness goals' are mentioned?

g What do you need to do before the staff can design your personal fitness programme?

h How is your progress assessed?

i What is the main goal of the sports centre?

j What two things do all the 'focus' gyms offer?

5 Follow these instructions and design your own information leaflet.

a Choose somewhere for your leaflet. It could be another sports centre, a shopping mall, an entertainment complex, or somewhere else of your choice.

b Include **four** different sections of information, which could be similar to the ones you have seen here, or different ones.

c Write about **50 words** for each section.

d Write **two** questions per section (total **eight** questions) for your partner to answer.

TOP TIP

Making suggestions and expressing preferences about a particular topic are important aspects of speaking effectively. Although it is important to speak accurately (and using set phrases like the ones in this unit will be very helpful) in order to ensure that no misunderstandings take place, the most important thing is to talk confidently. Also, try to avoid using slang expressions (say *yes* not *yeah*) and vocabulary, and single-word answers to questions.

11

Welcome!

Welcome to the new Achileas Sports Centre and Swimming Pool Complex monthly newsletter! We offer a wide variety of activities for you and all your family and friends. Whether your interest is fitness, football, tennis, basketball or swimming, we can offer you an excellent range of activities to suit all your needs. We hope you will enjoy your visit to the new Achileas Complex and take advantage of the many facilities available.

Opening hours

Swimming Pool

Monday–Friday	07.00–22.00
Saturday–Sunday & public holidays	08.00–21.00

Sports Centre

Monday–Friday	06.00–22.00
Saturday–Sunday & public holidays	09.00–20.00

Achileas Restaurant

Monday–Saturday	12.00–15.00 & 19.00–23.00
Sunday & public holidays	12.00–15.00 only

Membership

	Children (6–17)	Adults (18+)	Couples (2 adults)	Family (2 adults + 2 children)
Annual	$250	$400	$350 each	$1,000
6-monthly	$130	$210	$180 each	$600
3-monthly	$70	$110	$100 each	$330
Monthly	$25	$45	$40 each	$120
Weekly	$20	$40	$35 each	$105
Daily	$10	$20	$15 each	$45

Facilities

Five fitness and special-focus gyms, one children's gym, Olympic pool and children's starter pool, four squash courts, four badminton courts, two basketball courts, eight outdoor tennis courts, two all-weather football pitches, Achileas Sports Shop, Achileas Restaurant.

Focus on gyms

Whatever your fitness level, whatever your age and whatever your fitness goals, we have something to offer you in one of our special-focus gyms! If you would like to lose weight, tone up, increase your strength or improve your health, we have highly qualified staff on hand to motivate you in one of our focus gyms.

All of this takes place in one of our five focus gyms: cardiovascular, resistance training, free weights, general and sports injury. All our focus gyms offer state-of-the-art machines and excellent user-friendly equipment, catering for all your health and fitness needs.

Personal fitness

Whether you wish to work out once a week or every day, for ten minutes or an hour, after an initial consultation, our staff will design your own personal-fitness programme, tailored to suit your individual needs. You will also benefit from regular reviews, where your progress will be monitored and your programme updated or adjusted accordingly.

12

REFLECTION

How well do you think you can do each of these things now?

Give yourself a score from 1: Still need a lot of practice to 5: Feeling very confident about this

In this unit you:	1	2	3	4	5
watched a video of students talking about their free time, and discussed what they said					
read an advertisement about apps and answered questions on it					
thought about the best strategies for providing short answers to questions					
read an online advertisement for a webzine for teenagers and answered questions on it					
practised speaking about your preferences and making suggestions.					

Now set yourself a **personal goal** based on your scores for Unit 1.

Exam focus

Reading, Exercise 1, skimming and scanning

1   Read the following visitor information leaflet about markets in Cambridge, and then answer the exercises.

Cambridge offers you more than you would expect

General market

Cambridge is a market city, and people have been trading at the historic market square in the city centre for hundreds of years. The general market is open Monday to Saturday in the main Market Square opposite the City Hall. Between 10 a.m. and 4 p.m. the market is busy with around 100 stalls selling fruit, vegetables, plants and flowers, but also on sale are books, clothes and even electrical items. Many of these stalls change on a daily basis, so you may not find the same things from one day to the next. You can even have your trousers, shoes, bike or sewing machine mended if you are not in a rush.

Arts, crafts and local produce market

The arts, crafts and local produce market is also situated in the main Market Square, and is open every Sunday. Here you can find a wide selection of produce from the region's finest artists, craftspeople, photographers and farmers. The market is a great mix of everyday items such as organic fruit and vegetables, unique gift ideas, antiques, books, pictures and jewellery. You can also find personalised gifts at this market, which make ideal presents for family members and friends, or even something for yourself as a reminder of your visit to Cambridge.

Street traders' market

Cambridge offers an excellent range of street traders located around the historic centre, along Silver Street and other streets nearby. They include a huge number of food and drink sellers, offering burgers, jacket potatoes, savoury and sweet crepes, and plenty of vegetarian options, so there's no excuse to go hungry while shopping.

Garden art and craft market

This garden art and craft market started in the summer of 1975, and since then has become increasingly popular with locals and tourists. The market encourages Cambridge artists and craftspeople by giving them somewhere to sell the things they make, such as designer jewellery, ceramics, wood carvings, artwork and much more. In the early days, when the market first opened, it was a fair-weather, summer only event. The stalls had no roofs, and if it rained, the artists had to throw plastic sheets over their displays, and then hide under umbrellas or trees for shelter. Nowadays the stalls are protected, not just by the many trees which also provide shade, but by purpose-built covers. Over the years, the garden art and craft market has quickly flourished, not only due to its reputation for beautiful quality arts and crafts but more importantly as a result of its affordable prices. Furthermore, improved public transport links have made it easier for more people to visit Cambridge and the market. However, perhaps the most important reason for the increase in the market's popularity is the chance for people to talk to the makers of the products that they want to buy. The market, just opposite Trinity College, is held every Saturday and some weekdays during the peak holiday season, and is truly not to be missed.

Adapted from www.cambridgebid.co.uk

a Where exactly is the general market located? [1]

b Why might it be a bad idea to delay buying something at the general market? [1]

c What service is offered for people who have time to wait? [1]

d Which is the best day to buy home-grown food? [1]

e Which market would be a good place to buy a souvenir? [1]

f Where would you go to find the largest choice of food and drinks? [1]

g How does the garden art and craft market support local traders? [1]

h What nowadays protects buyers and sellers at the garden art and craft market? Give two examples. [2]

i Why has the market grown so fast? Give **four** examples. **Extended only [4]**

Total: 9 (Core) 13 (Extended)

Unit 2: Television Focus on reading: multiple matching

Learning objectives

In this unit you will:

- watch a video of students talking about television, and discuss what they say
- talk about different types of television programme
- read about 21st-century televisions and answer questions
- practise using *would/wouldn't* in spoken language
- read blogs from different people and match them

A ⊕ Watch, listen and talk

1 Watch and listen to some IGCSE students talking about **television programmes**.

   a Make a note of **three** different types of programme that the students like, and any types of programme that the students **never** watch.

2 Talk to your partner(s) about the TV programmes that **you** like and do not like watching.

B ABC Speaking and vocabulary

1 Work with a partner. Look at the pictures. What type of television programme does each one show? Did the students you just watched mention any of these?

   Example: *1 = cartoon*

2 What other types of television programme can you and your partner think of? Make a list.

3 Discuss these questions with your partner.

   a How much TV do you normally watch each day? At the weekend? How much do you watch each week? What does it depend on?

   b What about your friends? Do they watch more or less TV than you do, or about the same?

   c What would you like to see more of on TV? Why?

4 Work with your partner. Imagine you are responsible for putting together a six-hour TV time slot for next weekend. What would you include? How much variety would there be? Which age groups would you target? Use your ideas from the previous activities to create your TV schedule.

5 Share your TV schedules and decide which TV programmes you are going to watch next weekend.

6 Look back at the list you made for Activity B2. How much time do you spend doing these activities each week? Copy the table below. Complete the first two columns for yourself, then discuss with your partner and complete the third column.

> **LANGUAGE TIP**
>
> Remember the structure: spend time doing something.
>
> **Example:**
> *How much time do you spend watching movies on TV?*
>
> *I probably spend three to four hours watching movies.*
>
> **NOT** *X … spend to watch X*

Activities	Minutes each week (me)	Minutes each week (partner)
Watching films on TV	...	...
...	...	...
...	...	...
...	...	...

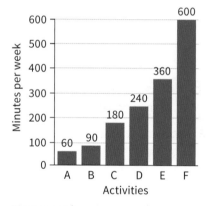

Time spent by young people on activities.

7 Look at the graph and answer questions a–e - Optional.

   a What is the title of the graph?

   b What does the left-hand axis show?

   c What does the bottom axis show?

   d Which axis is horizontal and which one is vertical?

   e What do the small numbers at the top of each shaded column show you?

LANGUAGE TIP

In Unit 1 Section D, you looked at some of the different endings that adjectives can have. When we want to describe the shape or position of something, we often use an *-al* ending, and sometimes an *-ar* ending – for example *horizon**tal*** and *circul**ar***.

Look at the shapes in the pictures. Which adjectives describe them?

Complete the exercises in your **Workbook**.

cylinder

triangle

diagonal

hexagon

symmetry

3D

sphere

angle

8 Work with a partner. Which of the following activities do you think are represented in the graph (A–F) above? Write down your answers. Be careful – there are four extra activities that you do not need to use!

> doing a hobby   doing voluntary work   doing homework   helping in the home
> gardening   playing computer games   doing sport
> reading books and magazines   using social media   watching TV

9 Compare your choices with the ones your teacher gives you. Does anything surprise you? Which activities didn't you choose? Why not?

10 Draw a similar graph using information supplied by the people in your class or school. Your teacher will help you to obtain the information and to draw your graph.

C ◉ Reading

1 You are going to read an internet article: 'What's a television today?' Before you read, discuss the following points with your partner. Decide if you agree or disagree with each other, and give reasons.

    a The television set is the focal point in every home. [1]

    b Television has been completely transformed by technology. [2]

    c Televisions nowadays are designed to provide an experience similar to an evening in the local cinema. [2]

    d Many people predicted that television would soon be gone, but it is very much here to stay. [3]

    e Many people watch television and multitask. [4]

2 Have a quick look at the internet article 'What's a television today?' Find the points a–e from Activity C1 and see if the writer has the same ideas as you and your partner. The paragraph number is given in [brackets] to help you.

3 Do not look at the article again yet. Study these adjectives and nouns. Which adjective do you think describes which noun? Can any adjective describe more than one noun? Can any noun be described by more than one adjective?

Example: b + 1 *focal* + *point*

Adjectives		Nouns	
a	daily	**1**	~~point~~
b	~~focal~~	**2**	televisions
c	high-quality	**3**	programmes
d	high-speed	**4**	viewing
e	top-quality	**5**	sound systems
f	traditional	**6**	availability
g	widespread	**7**	dose of entertainment
h	wrap-around	**8**	wireless internet

17

TOP TIP
When you see a word in a text that you do not understand, you can try several strategies to work out what the word means. First, look at the context (the words around the problem word). Then, try breaking up the word into smaller parts (for example breaking *infrequent* into *in* + *frequent*). Another strategy is to think if there is a similar word in your own language.

What's a television today?

1   The family television set has always been the focal point of every living room in the country, and whoever has their hands on the remote is not to be argued with. But nowadays, every screen in the house, from traditional televisions to tablets and mobile phones, in the kitchen as well as in the bedroom, can access top-quality programmes, twenty-four hours a day, every day of the year. Fighting for control of the remote is no longer an issue, even if the television still remains king.

2   As for the television itself, it has been completely transformed by technology. In fact, many sets are no longer called 'televisions', but have been rebranded as 'smart TVs'. The thing that supposedly makes them smart is the fact that they can be connected to the internet, and they have therefore become extremely large computers, usually attached to your living room wall. Many are no longer flat, but curved, giving the impression of 'wrap-around' viewing, and come with high-quality sound systems. These are designed to provide an experience similar to an evening in the local cinema. The other transformation is of course the television's thickness, or perhaps we should refer to its 'thinness'. Recently a major manufacturer announced that its latest television was 'the thickness of only four credit cards'!

3   But despite changes in what your television actually looks and sounds like, and the fact that there are now other ways to access entertainment and information, it is still not time to say goodbye to the living room centrepiece (nor to the remote). While many people predicted that television would soon be gone, it is very much here to stay. Not only can the television now provide much more than just a daily dose of entertainment, but, due to its size and position, it also acts like a sponge, attracting family members to one focal point in the home. In an age when everyone and everything is so fast moving, the role of the television in stabilising everyone in one place should not be ignored.

4   The interesting thing about television viewing nowadays however is that many people watch and multitask. In other words, although they may be sitting in front of the television, a large percentage of viewers are very openly using their smartphone or tablet at the same time. This could be to stay in touch with friends and family through social media, but it could also be to research further something seen on the television. Coupled with the increasingly widespread availability of high-speed wireless internet, today's television viewing experience has become far more interactive and more sharable.

© Peter Lucantoni

LANGUAGE TIP

Adjectives give more details about a place, a person, a thing or an idea. They describe nouns by giving information about the object's size, shape, age, colour, origin or material. A **compound adjective** is formed when two or more adjectives are joined together to modify the same noun. These adjectives should usually be hyphenated to avoid confusion.

Complete the exercise in your **Workbook**.

4   Read the text again and check your answers to Activity C3.

5   According to the text, are the following statements (a–g) true or false? Give reasons for your answers and say in which paragraph you found the information.

   a   Top-quality programmes are now available from many different sources, not just television.

   b   Televisions are no longer called televisions.

c   Smart TVs have to be fixed to the living room wall.

d   Televisions have become extremely thin.

e   Today's television encourages family members to socialise with each other in one place.

f   Watching television and using another form of technology at the same time is now considered normal.

g   Faster internet speeds allow television viewers to interact more easily.

D Language focus: adverbs

1   Look at these seven phrases taken from the article you have just read. The italic words are all *adverbs*. What is the role of each adverb: to describe a verb, another adverb, or an adjective?

a   … it has been *completely* transformed …

b   The thing that *supposedly* makes them smart …

c   … become *extremely* large computers …

d   … *usually* attached to your living room wall.

e   … your television *actually* looks and sounds like …

f   … viewers are *very* openly using their smartphone …

g   … the *increasingly* widespread availability of …

2   Work with a partner. Choose any ten consecutive letters from the alphabet. Think of an adverb that begins with each of the ten letters and list them.

Examples: *F, G, H, I, J, K, L, M, N, O*

> *F – fabulously, G – greatly, H – horrendously, I – interestingly …*

3   Check your adverbs and then compare your lists.

4   Complete each sentence below with a suitable phrase containing either: *adverb + verb, adverb + adverb,* or *adverb + adjective*.

Examples: *Look at Mario's car. It's been <u>completely destroyed</u> in the accident. His brother, Michael, wasn't injured and the police were <u>incredibly helpful</u>. I'm sure Michael will drive <u>very slowly</u> from now on.*

a   Elena thought the new café would be cheap, but ….

b   Siphiwe usually plays well, but today he's ….

c   When Rasheed and Ranya arrived at their hotel, they were surprised to see that everything was ….

d   The mountains in the interior of the island were ….

e   The room had been painted in a strange way: the walls were ….

f   George did not tell anyone that he was going to visit us. He arrived ….

g   The film was much too long and was ….

h   Only Sayeed agreed with Fiona. Everyone else ….

i   The results of the survey showed that older people ….

j   Tutaleni tried to be independent, but his elder sister Nangula ….

5   Write **five** sentences of your own. Each sentence must include either: *adverb + verb, adverb + adverb,* or *adverb + adjective*.

LANGUAGE TIP

Adverbs can describe verbs, other adverbs and adjectives. They are used to describe *how, where, when, why* and *how often* something happens.

Example: *Maria worked **quickly**, but wrote **very** carefully during the test.*

*When she was **nearly** ready to finish, she rechecked everything.*

In this example, **quickly** tells us *how* Maria worked (verb), **very** tells us *how carefully* (adverb) she wrote, **nearly** tells us to *what extent* she was ready (adjective).

Complete the exercise in your **Workbook**.

19

E ⊕ Speaking: Would/wouldn't do

1 Read this paragraph about the amount of pocket money that young people need. Check any unknown words or phrases.

Do teenagers need more or less pocket money to meet their daily expenses?

Pocket money allotted daily or weekly by parents is the main source of cash for today's teenagers around the world. Depending on where they live, teenagers have different financial needs. They usually use pocket money to pay for public-transport fares, cinema tickets, entrance fees, or to buy some snacks while at school. As the living standards in many developed and developing countries are constantly improving, teenagers need more and more pocket money to meet their daily expenses. In countries that are experiencing financial instability and currency fluctuations, teenagers need increasingly more cash to make up for the effect of inflation. The money they had yesterday may buy fewer things today.

Adapted from www.financialized.ca

2 Work in small groups. Ask and answer these questions.

a Do you think you receive enough pocket money?

b What do you buy with your pocket money?

c What phrases in English would you use to ask your parents or a family member for more pocket money?

d Would you need to give a reason for asking for more?

3 Copy the table and add the phrases below in the correct columns.

> *Cleaning the car is fine by me*   ~~*Cleaning the car is something I'd never do*~~
> *Cleaning the car is the last thing I'd do*   *I can't imagine myself ever cleaning the car*
> *I certainly wouldn't ever clean the car*   ~~*I would be prepared to clean the car*~~
> *I would enjoy cleaning the car*   *I wouldn't have a problem with cleaning the car*
> *I wouldn't mind cleaning the car*   *I'd be quite happy to clean the car*
> *There's no way I'd ever clean the car*

Would	Wouldn't
I would (I'd) be prepared to clean the car	*Cleaning the car is something I'd never do*

4 Suppose you urgently needed some extra money. Would you be prepared to earn it instead of just asking for it? What would you be prepared to do to earn it? What wouldn't you be prepared to do? Discuss your ideas with your partner and try to use some of the phrases from Activity E3.

Examples: *would:* *I'd be quite happy to do the washing.*

wouldn't: *I certainly wouldn't empty the bins.*

LANGUAGE TIP

When you want to ask for something in a polite way, you might use expressions such as:

Is there any chance/ possibility I could have (something)?

Do you think it would be possible (for me) to have (something)?

Would you mind if I had (something)?

Can I have (something)?

Could you let me have (something)?

'Please' is often used before *'Can I...?'* and *'Could I...?'*

Notice the verb forms before *(something)*.

F Reading

1 Here are the first sentences from three blogs about television, written by three different people.

  A Television is definitely not what it used to be.

  B For me, television is an educator above everything else.

  C I'm retired now, but all my life I've never had a television in my home.

Which of the six words in the box below would you expect to read in each blog? Why? Do not worry if you are not completely sure. There are two phrases for each blog.

> … current affairs …　… from science to geograpy …　… is full of books …
> What happened to the days …?　Apparently nowadays everyone is a celebrity, …
> When I was a kid …

2 Decide with your partner in which of the three blogs you think you will find the following conclusions (a–c). Give reasons for your choices. Do not worry if you are not completely sure.

  a But for those people who can only complain about the quality of programmes available, I suggest looking just a little deeper at your television schedule and sure enough you will find something that will not only entertain you, but educate you too.

  b Nowadays it's just a platform for these so-called celebrities to show off and make themselves look far more important than they really are.

  c Sometimes I am involved in three–four books at the same time, in different rooms of the house!

3 Quickly read the three blogs and check your answers to Exercises F1 and F2.

Blog A: Marcos Andreou

Television is definitely not what it used to be. For one thing, there are a lot more celebrities on our screens who, several years ago, would never have even been considered remotely interesting or important enough to appear on a TV show. **Apparently*** nowadays everyone is a celebrity, no matter who they are or what they have done. Every time you switch on the TV there's another supposedly 'famous' person telling us what they think about something. I recently watched a cooking programme which was hosted by a celebrity chef. His one aim seemed to have nothing to do with cooking skills, but with making jokes about football and trying (completely unsuccessfully, I might add) to be funny for 40 minutes. He also promoted his new book, advising everyone to buy it and read it. I learnt nothing about cooking, but I certainly learnt how to tell a bad joke. What happened to the days when television entertained and informed us? Nowadays it's just a platform for these so-called celebrities to show off and make themselves look far more important than they really are.

* See the **WORD TIP**.

TOP TIP

With multiple matching exercises such as the one in this section, the text could be either one continuous text divided into sections, or up to **six** shorter texts (both Core and Extended papers). However, the **content** of the Core text or texts will be different from the content of the Extended text or texts, and **shorter** in length.

Blog B: Alma Dusit

For me, television is an educator above everything else. Today we are incredibly lucky to have access to so many good-quality educational programmes, from science to geography and history, and even cooking and sport. There really is no excuse not to be well-informed about current affairs, or whatever your particular interest might be, no matter how many books you read. **Obviously***, there is also a lot of rubbish on television, but with so many 'free-to-air' channels readily available, we are definitely spoilt for choice, and we can't use money as an excuse not to watch. My biggest problem with television is not knowing what to watch. I often cannot decide which are the best programmes for me, but nowadays many television systems allow you to record programmes or 'catch up' later on something that you might have missed. This of course creates a further problem: finding enough time to watch everything! But for those people who can only complain about the quality of programmes available, I suggest looking just a little deeper at your television schedule and sure enough you will find something that will not only entertain you, but educate you too.

* See the **WORD TIP**.

Blog C: Ali Isfahan

I'm retired now, but all my life I've never had a television in my home. When I was a kid my parents couldn't afford to buy a television, and this was the same for many other families in our street. When I left home and went to university, television was still a relatively new thing in our lives, so once again I didn't have one. After that, I was thinking about my future life, and having a television just wasn't a priority. In any case, I'm a great reader: I'm never without a book, no matter where I am or where I'm going. I even take a book with me when I go shopping in the supermarket, or to the bank, just in case I have to wait in a queue. So for me a home without a television just isn't an issue. My whole house is like a library. It's a school, a college, a university! Every room, including the kitchen, is full of books, so if I need entertainment I simply pick one up. Sometimes I am involved in three–four books at the same time, in different rooms of the house!

4 Read the blogs more carefully in order to complete this exam-style question:

You are going to read three blogs about television, written by three different people. For questions a–h, choose from blogs A–C. The people may be chosen more than once.

Which person:

a always has something to read?

b prefers other entertainment to watching television?

c believes that television can teach us whatever we want?

d thinks television is different nowadays?

e has difficulty choosing a programme to watch?

f is not bothered about their lack of a television?

g mentions money and television?

h thinks that famous people on television are not really very important?

TOP TIP

Some exam questions may require you to identify relevant information and details in one or a number of texts. Some of the texts may say similar things, so you need to read carefully to make sure you understand the content.

WORD TIP

obviously = in a way that is easy to understand or see

apparently = **1 OTHERS SAY**: used to say that you have read or been told something although you are not certain it is true; **2 SEEMING TRUE**: used to say that something seems to be true, although it is not certain

Use either *obviously* or *apparently* to complete the sentences in your **Workbook**.

Adapted from *Cambridge School Dictionary* 2008

REFLECTION

How well do you think you can do each of these things now?

Give yourself a score from 1: Still need a lot of practice to 5: Feeling very confident about this

In this unit you:	1	2	3	4	5
watched a video of students talking about television, and discussed what they said					
talked about different types of television programme					
read about 21st-century televisions and answered questions					
practised using *would/wouldn't* in spoken language					
read blogs from different people and matched them					

Now set yourself a **personal goal** based on your scores for Unit 2.

Exam focus

Reading, Exercise 2, multiple matching

1 You are going to read an article in which four people comment on a television programme they particularly enjoy. For questions a–j, choose from the people A–D. The people may be chosen more than once.

A Andrew Andrews
World at One

This daily news programme is incredibly popular. I mean, all my friends and family members try to catch it if they can, even though the timing can be a bit difficult. The thing that most impresses me is the content, which is always very international. So it's not just home news, which can be a bit boring and repetitive, but news from all over the world, and it's delivered in a very professional manner. The programme lasts about 30 minutes, I think, and starts with the latest headlines and then moves to on going stories. There is some sports content, but they seem to keep it to a minimum, which is good, as I'm not really a big sports fan. Other things that I particularly enjoy are the mix of presenters, so it's not always the same person reading the news.

B Ismaila Martino
My life in Rome
Travel special

If there's one television show that never fails to completely engage me, it has to be this one, because it takes me to places that I will probably never be able to go to myself. Of course, never say never, but sometimes it's actually just as good to find out about places without having to spend any money! Not only is the photography in the programme absolutely stunning, but the commentary by the two presenters has been written so that the whole programme becomes a real eye-opener, a real education. It is definitely not just another tourist holiday show, thank goodness; in fact, it is quite the opposite, as it avoids talking about beach holidays, hotel facilities and souvenir shops. The focus is on the history, culture, people and traditions of the countries the programme visits, their geography, their natural resources, and all the things that make a country unique and inviting to people like me.

C Ken Chang
Know your sport?

There's no way that I'll ever miss this weekly show, even if I'm on holiday. I always record it if I really can't be in front of the TV to watch it. In fact, I've even got the past eight series on DVDs, so that shows you how much I enjoy the show. Just because I know all the answers to the questions doesn't mean that I won't watch the shows again and again. Every week there are different sports people taking part in the quiz, so the show is never quite the same twice, even though the person asking the questions never changes. From time to time they have special editions of the show, to highlight a particular sporting event such as the football World Cup, or the Olympics. These are especially interesting for me because all the questions are based on one area of sport, so you they get to really test your sporting knowledge. Yes, you could say I'm sports crazy!

D Natasha Gassim
Talent spotter

The thing about this programme is that it helps you to forget reality for an hour or so. You can completely switch off, and just sit back, relax and enjoy the show, without taking any of it too seriously. Most of the acts are of course complete rubbish, with people making total fools of themselves in front of a live audience of hundreds, and millions more watching it on their TV at home, just like me. But occasionally there's an act which makes you think 'That person has real talent' and you want them to succeed and become famous. Sometimes you start to feel jealousy at someone's success, but I guess that's only natural, and of course not everyone in life can reach the top. You also have to consider how hard these people must have worked to even get onto the show in the first place, and remember that they are still a very long way from winning anything.

Which person:

a   appreciates the hard work that people have done to be on television?   [1]

b   has a very deep interest in sport?   [1]

c   enjoys listening to different people?   [1]

d   does not think they have much chance to visit other places?   [1]

e   enjoys a programme where people show their skills?   [1]

f   is able to watch their favourite programme as many times as they want?   [1]

g   is happy that there is not too much sport?   [1]

h   never misses their programme?   [1]

i   says that the time of a programme can cause a problem?   [1]

j   thinks that their programme is visually spectacular?   [1]

[Total: 10 Extended]

Learning objectives

In this unit you will:

- watch a video of students talking about food, and discuss what they say
- read and speak about fast food and fast-food restaurants, and answer questions
- look at and comment on sample informal letters
- write an informal letter about a restaurant visit
- practise expressing your opinions

A ☺ Watch, listen and talk

1 Watch and listen to some IGCSE students talking about **food**.

   a Make a note of **three** different types of food that the students like and the **reasons** they give.

2 Talk to your partner(s) about the different types of food that **you** like and your reasons **why**.

B 🔤 Speaking and vocabulary

1 In small groups, discuss the following questions.

   a What is fast food? Why do we use the term 'fast food'? Do you like fast food? Why, or why not? Think about smell, taste, texture, and so on.

   b What would you call food that is not 'fast'? 'Slow food'?!

c Non-fast food is often referred to as 'traditional' food. Put the following foods into two groups: 'fast food' and 'slow [or traditional] food'. [There are no right or wrong answers.]

> hot dog   goulash   sandwich   vegetable pie   rice   moussaka   onion soup
> falafel   samosa   chicken schwarma

d Think of some more types of food that could go in each group. What helps you to decide?

2 You will read an internet article called 'Eight things your fast-food worker won't tell you'. What do you think are some of the things that your fast-food worker won't tell you? Discuss in your group.

Example: *The lights in restaurants are positioned to make food look appetising.*

3 Before you read the article, discuss with a partner whether you think the following statements about fast-food restaurants are true or false. Give your reasons. You will find out later which ones are true.

a A dirty eating area can mean a dirty kitchen.

b A lot of fast food is cooked then repeatedly reheated until it's sold.

c A salad with dressing is always the healthiest choice.

d Asking for 'extra' means you have to pay more.

e At the end of the night, food that is unsold is not thrown away.

f The black grill marks on a burger are not from cooking it.

g Workers don't wash their hands often enough.

h You don't have to accept the food on display – you can ask for something to be cooked fresh.

4 Quickly read the text and check your answers to Exercises B2 and B3. Say in which paragraph you found the relevant information.

5 **Student A:** Work alone. Find these four words and phrases in the article. What do you think they mean? Use different methods to help you.

a cabinet [paragraph 1]

b the timer goes off [1]

c batch [3]

d register [4]

Student B: Work alone. Find these four words and phrases in the article. What do you think they mean? Use different methods to help you.

a sachet [paragraph 5]

b donate [6]

c neglected [8]

d in the back [8]

6 With a partner, discuss the meaning of the words and phrases in Activity B5. Make sure you understand your partner's words and phrases as well as your own.

27

http://www.   C Reader

Eight things your fast-food worker won't tell you ...

These surprising secrets about your favourite fast-food restaurants might make you think twice next time you're waiting in line or at the drive-thru.

[1] After we cook something, we put it in a cabinet and set a timer. When the timer goes off, we're supposed to throw out the food. But often, we just reheat the food. If you want the freshest meal, come between 11 a.m. and 1 p.m. or between 6 p.m. and 8 p.m. More people are in the restaurant then, so we're constantly cooking and serving new food.

[2] Those grill marks on your burger? Not real. They were put there by the factory.

[3] Most of us will cook something fresh for you, if you ask. If you want to make sure your fries come right out of the fryer, order them without salt. Providing you are polite, that forces us to cook you a new batch. Then you can add your own salt!

[4] Avoid asking for 'extra' of something, like cheese or sauce. As soon as you say 'extra', we have to add it to the register and charge you for it. Instead, just say you want us to 'put a good amount on there' and we'll load you up.

[5] It makes me laugh when someone comes in and says she's trying to be healthy – and then orders a salad. Some of those fast-food salads have as many calories as a burger. In fact, a small order of fries contains fewer grams of fat that a packet of creamy salad dressing.

[6] Most of us do not donate our leftovers. I can't believe how much food we throw out every day, especially at the end of the night.

[7] Most of us don't wash our hands as much as we should, even though there are signs everywhere reminding us that it's the law.

[8] Look around to see how much rubbish is in the car park, and if the bathrooms and dining room are dirty. When things that are so publicly visible are neglected, it's likely that even more is being neglected in the back and in the kitchen where the customers can't see.

Adapted from www.rd.com

7 Choose six words and phrases from the eight you have discussed. Use each of your choices to write a complete sentence in order to show its meaning.

C Reading

1 You are going to read a text about fast food in Italy. Answer the following questions on your own. Then work with a partner to check your answers.

  a Find five words or phrases in paragraph 1 that have a similar meaning to the following:

   i 10 years   **ii** company division   **iii** increase

   iv possibility for something to happen

   v use something to an advantage.

  b Look at the five underlined words and phrases in paragraph 2. What do they mean?

  c Use these five words and phrases to complete the gaps a–e in paragraph 3.

   i market share   **ii** sector   **iii** target

   iv workforce   **v** worldwide.

  d Look at the five words [*financial, investment, cultural, provide, dine*] from paragraph 4 in the table below, then copy and complete the table. You may not be able to write something in every gap.

LANGUAGE TIP

Notice these different ways in the text to say *if*:

Providing *you are polite, that forces us to cook you a new batch ...*

Supposing *you want a small order of fries ...*

Complete the exercises in your **Workbook**.

Noun	Verb	Adjective	Adverb	Noun translation/s
…	…	financial	…	…
investment [*thing*] … [*person*]	…	…	…	…
…	…	cultural	…	…
… [*thing*] … [*person*]	provide	…	…	…
… [*thing*] … [*person*]	dine	…	…	…

e Fill in the gaps f–j in **paragraph 5** using suitable words or phrases **of your own choice**.

f What do the following numbers in the text refer to?

  i Paragraph 1: 30%, €350 million, 3,000

  ii Paragraph 3: 450, €1 billion, 10%, 2%, 3%

  iii Paragraph 5: 5,000

Example: *Paragraph 1: 100 = the number of new restaurants that McDonald's is opening*

Fast-food giant tries to convert Italy's pizza-lovers to burgers

[1] US fast-food giant, McDonald's, believes recession-hit Italy will be one of its higher-growth areas in the coming decade and is opening more than 100 new restaurants to convert pizza-lovers to its burgers. In a country where foreign investment has fallen by almost 30% since 2007, the McDonald's Italian arm plans to spend €350 million and hire a further 3,000 people in the coming years to boost its market share. 'We believe in Italy and we are convinced that the Italian market has a potential we can exploit,' McDonald's Italian chief executive Roberto Masi told Reuters in an interview.

[2] The American McDonald's group, which first <u>set foot</u> in Italy nearly 30 years ago and was initially met with <u>suspicion</u> in the land of pizza and pasta, has launched an advertising <u>offensive</u> <u>playing to</u> Italians' patriotism. 'We will create 3,000 more jobs. This is our way to show we believe in Italy,' it says. In the TV version of the <u>commercial</u>, shot by Oscar-winning Italian director, Gabriele Salvatores, three young staff members in trademark uniforms tell how good it is to work for the chain's fast-food restaurants.

[3] Annual sales at the 450 McDonald's Italian restaurants are estimated at around €1 billion and its local **[a]** … is nearly 1% of its **[b]** … staff. But while in Spain and food-conscious France, McDonald's has a **[c]** … of more than 10% of the 'informal eating out' **[d]** … , which excludes top restaurants, its share in Italy is just 2%, with a **[e]** … of 3% in the coming years.

[4] Masi said that since the start of the **financial** crisis, McDonald's had won customers in Italy by localising its offering, making sandwiches with crusty bread stuffed with Parmesan cheese and sliced ham. Still, the McDonald's **investment** pledge met with scepticism in some quarters, showing the group still has a **cultural** hurdle to clear in Italy. Roberto Burdese, chairman of Italy's Slow Food Association, which strives to preserve traditional and regional cuisine, said McDonald's menus could not **provide** a balanced diet on a daily basis. 'We accept it, however, as a sort of theme park where you can go and **dine** every so often,' he said.

[5] The **[f]** … of Big Macs is no stranger to cultural snobbiness. Recently, Milan city council forced McDonald's to **[g]** … its restaurant in the Galleria Vittorio Emanuele II, a tourist-packed shopping arcade 50 **[h]** … from the Duomo cathedral, to make way for a new **[i]** … of luxury fashion brand Prada. McDonald's attracted more than 5,000 takers for its last-day offering of free **[j]** … , fries and drinks.

Adapted from www.reuters.com

2 Work on your own. Read the questions and find the key word/s in each one. Then read the article again and find and underline the answers to the questions. You do not need to write anything yet.

   a Who does McDonald's want to encourage to buy its burgers?

   b What three things does McDonald's plan to do in Italy?

   c How did Italians react to the fast-food company 30 years ago?

   d Which country has the smallest market share of 'informal eating out': France, Italy or Spain?

   e What has McDonald's done to localise its menu in Italy?

   f What does Roberto Burdese compare McDonald's to?

   g Why did the city council close a McDonald's restaurant in Milan?

3 Work with your partner and compare your answers to Activity C2. When you have agreed, write complete answers for each question.

D ⊚ Language focus: *to*-infinitive

Look at these examples of the *to*-infinitive in the text you have just read:

Examples: *… is opening more than 100 new restaurants **to convert** pizza lovers to its burgers.*

*This is our way **to show** we believe …*

*… which strives **to preserve** traditional …*

1 The *to*-infinitive is found in various sentence constructions. Look at these four common uses:

   a To indicate the purpose of something (*to* has the same meaning as *so as to*, *in order to*), for example: She came <u>to see</u> the doctor.

   b After some verbs (advise, ask, encourage, invite, order, persuade, remind, tell, warn, expect, intend, would prefer, want, would like) which are followed by a direct object, for example: They would like you <u>to make</u> a speech.

   c Following a noun or pronoun, to indicate what something can or will be used for, for example: I'd like a sandwich <u>to take</u> to school

   d After certain verbs (ask, decide, explain, forget, know, show, tell, & understand) followed by question words, for example: She asked me where <u>to sit</u>.

   Now decide which of the sentences 1–8 matches each of the four common uses of the *to*-infinitive. There are two examples for each use.

   1 He told me <u>to ask</u> you.

   2 I can't remember where <u>to put</u> this.

   3 I don't have anything <u>to wear</u>.

   4 I'm writing <u>to ask</u> you a favour.

   5 Tell me how <u>to switch</u> on the machine.

   6 Would you like something <u>to drink</u>?

   7 They ordered all the students <u>to leave</u> the building.

   8 Your sister has gone <u>to finish</u> her homework.

2 Reorder the jumbled words in a–f to make sentences which include the *to*-infinitive.

  a appears she hurt to head her have

  b 150 instructions my write are to words

  c immediately we to need leave

  d like eat to would anything you?

  e to calling father your I'm out find about

  f him he with asked come me to not

3 Match the sentence halves [a–g] with [1–7].

a	The McDonald's Italian arm plans …	1	to clear in Italy.
b	The group still has a cultural hurdle …	2	to close its restaurants in the Galleria.
c	Milan city council forced McDonald's …	3	to cook you a new batch.
d	When the timer goes off, we're supposed …	4	to make sure your fries come out …
e	If you want …	5	to see how much rubbish there is.
f	That forces us …	6	to spend $350 million.
g	Look around …	7	to throw out the food.

4 Look at the two texts you have read to check your answers to Activity D3.

5 Complete these sentence halves using your own words. You should use a *to*-infinitive in each one.

  a He arrived too late …   **d** Your brother has gone …

  b Do you understand where … ?   **e** I'd like you …

  c The students need a library …

E Writing: Informal letters

1 You are going to write a letter to a friend about a fast-food restaurant you have recently visited. Before you start writing, discuss the following with your partner. It might help if you concentrate on restaurants that you already know.

  a What is your opinion about fast food taking over from more traditional food?

  b What are the advantages and disadvantages of each type of food?

  c What about the places where you can buy fast food and traditional food? Is one type of place better than another? Why?

2 Now copy and complete the table below, listing the advantages and disadvantages of fast-food and traditional restaurants.

Fast-food restaurants		Traditional restaurants	
Advantages	Disadvantages	Advantages	Disadvantages
quick service	…	…	more expensive

3 Look at these words from an exam-style question: *explain*, *describe*, *write*, *say*. Discuss them with your partner and try to decide what they mean.

4 Look at the exam-style question below and complete the gaps with the words from
Activity E3. Discuss your ideas with your partner. Do **not** write anything yet.

You have recently been to a new fast-food restaurant
in your town. **[a]** … a letter to a friend, telling him or
her about your visit. In your letter you should:

[b] … where the restaurant is, when you went
there, and why
[c] … the restaurant and its atmosphere
[d] … what you ate and what you thought of
the food.

The pictures here may give you some ideas and you
should try to use some ideas of your own.

Your letter should be 100–150 words long [Core] or
150–200 words long [Extended].

TOP TIP

If you are writing
an informal letter
to a friend or family
member, you may
be asked to describe
something or say
what you think
about a suggestion
or a plan. Often,
the question may
give you some ideas
and there may be a
picture to help you.
The main thing is to
show that you can
write in an informal
style.

5 What would be the best way to begin and end an informal letter like the one in Activity E4?
With your partner, make a list of possible opening and closing phrases.

Opening phrases	Closing phrases
Hi Satish!	Best wishes

Letter A [200 words]

Hello friend

I have got your letter some days ago. How are
you? I hope your well. I am well and I am enjoying my
holydays which have started before two days. My
family are well and I am busy getting ready for to
go away on the weekend on the mountains. I have
taken good marks in my school tests, but my mum
and dad as usually they tell me that I must to work
more hard the next year because it is my finally
year at school. I enjoy the school, but I think the
next year is going to be hard for me because I will
have to work hard all the year. Guess what? A new
burger restaurant was opening in my town and I
went there with Marco and Jasper the last night.
We stayed there until very late at night and we had
to walk home because there were no buses! We had
food and the atmosphere too was good. We will go
back there next time you will visit me and I hope to
do very soon. Write to me back when you will have
free time.

Yours faithfully

Felipe

Letter B [163 words]

Dear Adriana

How are you? Thanks very much for your
letter – I was happy to hear that you and your
family are all well. We are all well here too!

I know you will be visiting here soon, so I
wanted to tell you about a new fast-food
restaurant we must to visit when you come
here. It's downtown near the bus station,
so it's very convenient if we take the bus.
It opened last weekend and we went there
together with my class friends for Cornelia's
birthday party.

Inside, they have fantastic music, so the
atmosphere is fabulous too. I know that
you're going to like it like I do. Also, they have
amazing pictures on the walls and really good
furniture – very comfortable! You know I don't
eat meat, but there was loads of choice for other
food with no meat. It was totally delicious and
not expensive like some other places.

Can't wait to take you! See you soon!

Maroulla

6 Look at these two letters written by two students in response to the question in Activity E4. With a partner, decide which of the two letters – A or B – is better. Give your reasons. Think about:

- the language (the vocabulary and structures)
- the information (the ideas) contained in the letter.

You do **not** need to rewrite the letters.

7 Which letter, A or B:

a uses correct opening and closing phrases?

b does not have any paragraph breaks?

c responds to each of the three question prompts?

d contains a lot of spelling mistakes?

e includes information that is not relevant?

8 In Units 1 and 2 you studied adjectives and adverbs. One way to improve your writing is by using more of them. With a partner, talk about how to improve Felipe's letter (A) by using more adjectives and adverbs, where appropriate. You do **not** need to write anything yet.

Example: *We had food and the atmosphere too was good.*
We ate delicious food and the atmosphere was really fantastic!

9 You are going to write your own full answer to the exam-style question in Activity E4. Before you start, make a draft plan. Think carefully about the question and what information it asks for. Draw a 'mind map' like the one you did in Activity E6 in Unit 1.

10 Now write your letter using the draft plan and mind map you created in Activity E9. Exchange your writing with your partner's. Check their letter. What should you be looking for?

F Speaking: Expressing opinions

1 CD1, Track 3 Listen to Anna and Terry talking. In how many different ways do they express their opinion?

2 Look at the audioscript in Appendix 3 and focus on the underlined phrases. In small groups, list other phrases that you could use to express your opinion.

LANGUAGE TIP

Look at these ways of expressing your opinion in both spoken and written English.

		Using the expressions
To my mind, …	… fast-food restaurants are here to stay.	Common in spoken language, also written
In my opinion, …		Very common. Try to use other expressions
If you ask me, …		Extremely common in spoken English
To my way of thinking, …		Emphasis on **my** to show strong opinion
In my view, …		Common in spoken and written English
For me, …		Common in spoken and written English
I'd say …		Very common in spoken English
(Do you want to) know what I think?	Fast-food restaurants are here to stay.	Both extremely common in spoken English, and not impolite
I'll tell you what I think.		

TOP TIP

When you write, use your imagination as much as possible, but remember that your answer must always be relevant to the question. Think about how to improve your writing by using more adjectives and adverbs. Check your work carefully for language errors, and count how many words you have written. Make sure that you follow all the instructions very carefully and write the required number of words.

TOP TIP

Remember that when answering questions, you need to think about both content and language. 'Content' refers to the relevance and development of ideas; 'language' refers to style and accuracy. So, you need to make sure that your writing is relevant, with well-developed ideas, and that the language you use is accurate and appropriate.

3 Earlier in this unit, you made a list of the advantages and disadvantages of fast-food and traditional restaurants. Now imagine that you have to discuss these advantages and disadvantages with your teacher. What is your opinion? Using some of the phrases from Activity F2 and your ideas from Activity E1, write notes to prepare for your discussion.

REFLECTION

How well do you think you can do each of these things now?

Give yourself a score from 1: Still need a lot of practice to 5: Feeling very confident about this

In this unit you:	1	2	3	4	5
watched a video of students talking about food, and discussed what they said					
read and spoke about fast food and fast-food restaurants, and answered questions					
looked at and commented on sample informal letters					
wrote an informal letter about a restaurant visit					
practised expressing your opinions					

Now set yourself a **personal goal** based on your scores for Unit 3.

> **TOP TIP**
>
> When speaking in English, try to focus on the following:
>
> 1 Structure – using spoken language (sentences and phrases) accurately.
> 2 Vocabulary – using a wide range of words.
> 3 Fluency – having a two-way conversation.
>
> Look at some of the speaking-test cards in Appendix 1 and you will see how the phrases you are practising in this unit will help you with more or less any topic.

Exam focus

Writing, Exercise 5

1 You have recently cooked a meal for some members of your family.

Write a letter to a friend, telling him or her about the meal.

In your letter you should:

- explain why you cooked the meal

- say where you ate the meal, and with whom

- describe what you ate and what everyone thought of the food.

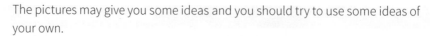

The pictures may give you some ideas and you should try to use some ideas of your own.

Your letter should be 100–150 words long [Core] or 150–200 words long [Extended]. You will receive up to 6/8 marks for the content of your letter, and up to 6/8 marks for the style and accuracy of your language.

2 You recently went for a meal at your favourite restaurant and something unusual happened.

Write an email to your cousin about what happened.

In your email you should:

- explain which restaurant you were in and why

- describe what happened

- say how you felt about what happened.

The pictures may give you some ideas, and you should try to use some ideas of your own.

Your email should be 100–150 words long [Core] or 150–200 words long [Extended]. You will receive up to 6/8 marks for the content of your email, and up to 6/8 marks for the style and accuracy of your language.

Reading, Exercise 1, skimming and scanning

1 Read the text *Hospitality with dates* and answer the following exercises.

a	What two things are offered to guests in Saudi homes?	[1]
b	How many dates does Saudi Arabia produce every year?	[1]
c	Where can dates can be seen in Saudi Arabia? Give **three** examples.	[2]
d	Apart from the nutritional value, what is another benefit of eating dates?	[1]
e	Why are date palms so common in Saudi Arabia?	[1]
f	Which illness might the Ajwa date help to avoid?	[1]
g	How could eating a date help to relieve a headache?	[1]
h	What happens to the vitamin C in a fresh date when it is dried?	[1]
i	What is the date palm tree used for, other than as a source of food? Give **four** examples.	**Extended only [4]**

Total: 9 (Core), 13 (Extended)

Hospitality with dates

A visitor to Saudi Arabia will relish the tradition of Arabian hospitality, which is symbolised by a small cup of Arabian coffee, made with lightly roasted coffee beans and cardamom, and served with a variety of fresh dates carefully arranged on a plate. This offering of coffee and dates is a welcome in almost every Saudi home, as well as most Arabian homes in the Arabian Gulf region.

After Egypt, Saudi Arabia is the second largest producer of dates in the world, with an annual output of more than 1.1 million metric tonnes of dates. The Kingdom has considerable experience in date cultivation and it offers a quality selection, including both soft and dried dates. In fact, there are more than 300 types of date in Saudi Arabia, each having its own taste and texture. These different types of date can be seen in shops and markets, but also in oases, where date palm trees stand tall with their branches outstretched towards the sky and their roots anchored deep into the earth. Saudi Arabia has the highest number of palm trees in the world, with more than 23 million trees accounting for 20% of global date production.

But there is much more to dates … Dates have rich medicinal properties, are highly nutritional, and are considered by many to be one of nature's most perfect foods. Date palms cover 3% of the earth's cultivated surface, giving humans one of the best sources of food, without requiring much effort. Because of this, in Saudi Arabia, palm trees are planted along the sides of every major city street, as well as in every garden and yard. The icon of the beautiful palm tree, representing vitality and growth, is everywhere, including in the national emblem of Saudi Arabia, although it does not appear on the Kingdom's flag.

A number of studies have proved the vital importance of the date fruit in a healthy lifestyle. New research has found evidence that the Ajwa date from Madinah contains active elements useful in the prevention of cancer; furthermore, the fruit contains anti-inflammatory properties, not dissimilar to commercially available painkiller medicines, such as aspirin and ibuprofen. Also, a 100 gram portion of fresh dates is a premium source of vitamin C. However, dates lose their vitamin C content when they are dried. A single date provides about 20 calories and is a good source of carbohydrates, fibre and potassium, as well as some calcium and iron. Dates do not contain significant amounts of fat, cholesterol, protein or sodium and are, therefore, wonderful for normal growth, development and overall well-being.

While everyone appreciates the health benefits of eating dates, let's not forget the date palm itself. The wide branches and leaves provide shade from the strong sun and are also seen as thatching on huts, while the strong trunks are often used as support pillars in buildings as well as for making furniture.

Adapted from 'Hospitality with dates' in *Ahlan Wasahlan*.

Shellfish in Oman

The diverse riches of the sea have always played a significant role in Oman's economy and the lifestyle of her people. The nation's fishing industry continues to increase in importance, as research into its marine life grows stronger.

An animal that is of enormous importance to the south-eastern coast of Oman is the abalone, a shellfish that has become the centre of a multi-million-dollar industry.

Once, abalone shellfish were brought to the surface in the hope that the soft tissue contained beautiful pearls. Today, the shellfish are caught for a different reason – restaurant menus! The fresh white shellfish has a distinctive and much admired flavour and is the most highly valued product from Omani waters. It is fished exclusively along the shores of Dhofar.

This distinctive shellfish has only one shell, unlike other shellfish, which have two. The shell is extremely beautiful. Light is diffracted by geometrically arranged crystals within the shell, creating a wonderful shine.

The shells of several abalone can be used for decorative purposes, and to make jewellery and buttons.

Abalone live in shallow marine waters with rocky-bottom conditions. Young abalone shelter in small groups, holding on to the undersides of medium-sized boulders, whereas the adults live grouped up to a dozen together in rocky cracks. They can only survive successfully in areas where cold, nutritious water rises from the sea bed. There, in the shallow, brightly lit conditions, the abalone shellfish live.

The environmental requirements for cool water conditions are rarely met and, as a result, the geographical occurrence and extent of abalone fisheries worldwide is extremely restricted. Until recently, there was a three-year ban on abalone fishing in Oman and now fishing is only permitted from October 20 to November 15 each year.

The coast of Dhofar in Oman is one of the special environments that support abalone populations. The southern shore of Oman experiences monsoon winds across the surface of the sea from April to September. As these winds skim the surface, the rich cold water from the depths of the Arabian Sea can easily rise and move towards the shore.

Abalone are harvested after the monsoon period, between October and March. Fishermen dive to a depth of 10 metres, assisted only by a face mask and, perhaps, fins. Groups of up to ten men search the sea bed for abalone-encrusted boulders and deftly remove the shells using a knife, before coming up for air. A good diver searches for large adults and will collect up to 600 specimens per day. In order to do this, the diver may have to cover an area in excess of 100 square metres.

Adapted from 'Marketing the mollusc' by Dr Karen Millson, in *Tribute*.

2 Read the article 'Shellfish in Oman' and answer the questions below.

  a Why is Oman's fishing industry continuing to expand? **[1]**

  b Why was the abalone shellfish originally important? **[1]**

  c Where is the only place in Oman that the abalone is obtained from? **[1]**

  d What health benefit does eating abalone provide? **[1]**

  e In what way is the abalone different from other shellfish? **[1]**

  f How do the habitats of young and adult abalone differ? **[1]**

  g Why is modern diving equipment prohibited? **[1]**

  h Why are abalone so rare globally? **[1]**

  i What two pieces of equipment do the abalone divers always use? **[1]**

  j What type of water do abalone need to live in?
    Give **four** examples. **Extended only [4]**

Total: 9 (Core), 13 (Extended)

Learning objectives

In this unit you will:

- watch a video of students talking about different methods of transport, and discuss what they say
- listen to different people talking about their travel experiences, and answer questions
- listen to a Ugandan police officer talking about *boda-boda* taxis and answer questions
- practise using expressions of surprise
- practise listening to short extracts and answering questions

A 🙂 Watch, listen and talk

1   Watch and listen to some IGCSE students talking about which **methods of transport** they prefer and the **reasons** they give.

   a   Make a note of **three** methods of transport that the students mention and the **reasons** they give.

2   Talk to your partner(s) about the method of transport that **you** prefer and your reasons **why**.

B 🔤 Speaking and vocabulary

1 Look at the pictures 1–4. Which of these types of transport have you used? If you haven't used one, which one would you like to use?

2 There are ten different methods of transport hidden in the word snake. How many can you find? Are any the same as the ones you talked about in B1?

bustaxiballooncampervanmotorbikeplanecartraincoachbicycle

3 Which method of transport do you think is the best for going on holiday? Why? Does your choice depend on the type of holiday? Discuss your ideas with a partner.

4 Copy and complete the table. Make a list of the advantages and disadvantages of some of the methods of transport from Activity B2.

Method	Advantages	Disadvantages
car	stop when and where you like	traffic jams

5 In Activities B3 and B4, did you consider the cost of each method of transport? With a partner, rank the methods from 1 to 10, with 1 the most expensive and 10 the cheapest. What factors do you need to think about when deciding on the cost of each method?

C 🔊 Listening 1

1 You are going to listen to four people talking about their experiences of different methods of transport. Which of the following methods do you think you will hear about? Why?

> bus   car   motorbike   balloon   train   ferry   camel
> bicycle   coach   campervan   cab   quad bike   horse

2 🔊 CD1, Track 4 Listen and write the answers to these questions.

a Which methods of transport are being talked about?

b Which of the people enjoyed themselves?

c Which speakers do not mention the name of a country or town?

d What helped you to answer the three questions a–c? What information did you focus on as you were listening? Context? Vocabulary (key word/s)? Something else?

3 🔊 CD1, Track 4 Listen carefully again to each speaker. As you listen, write the answers to the following questions in your notebook.

Speaker 1

a Where exactly did the speaker wait for the train?

b How many people were with the speaker?

c How did the family feel before 8.30?

d What made the speaker and his family become anxious?

e What did the speaker do at 9.00?

f What mistake had the speaker made?

Speaker 2

a Why was the speaker going up in a balloon?

b How old is the speaker now?

c Why did the speaker feel uncomfortable about the balloon trip?

d How long was the balloon trip?

e How did the speaker feel once the balloon had taken off?

Speaker 3

a What **two** advantages convinced the speaker to travel by coach?

b How many disadvantages of travelling by coach does the speaker give?

c How often did the coach stop?

d How long did the coach journey last?

Speaker 4

a At what time of day did the speaker depart?

b What was the weather like?

c Who was the speaker with?

d How fast did they travel?

e What **two** things amazed the speaker?

4 How much can you remember? With a partner, copy and complete the table of information below (not all the gaps can be filled).

	Speaker 1	Speaker 2	Speaker 3	Speaker 4
Departure time	8.30 a.m.	…	…	…
Length of journey	…	…	…	…
Arrival time	…	…	…	…
Weather / time of year	beautiful summer day	sunny, May	…	…
Speaker's feelings	…	…	…	…
Speaker with who?	wife and three children	…	…	…
Cost	…	…	$275	…

5 Read the audioscript in Appendix 3 and check your answers to Activities C3 and C4.

6 Choose a method of transport and write a short paragraph similar to the ones in the listening activity. Remember to include:

▨ information about the time and length of the journey

▨ the weather

▨ the time of year

▨ the speaker's feelings.

Do not mention the method of transport. Write four or five questions about your paragraph for your partner to answer. Read your paragraph to your partner, then see if they can guess the method of transport and answer your questions.

◈ Listening 2

7 You are going to listen to a Ugandan police officer talking about Uganda's famous motorbike taxi, the *boda-boda*. Unfortunately, there are many traffic accidents involving *boda-bodas* and many people are injured as a result.

a Work with a partner and answer the following questions.

 i What type of taxis do you have in your country?

 ii Who do you think rides the *boda-bodas* in Uganda?

 iii What could be the result of having too many *boda-bodas* on the roads?

 iv How could Uganda help young motorbike riders to be safer?

b Work with a different partner. Read the following information and decide which numbers from the box could complete the gaps.

> twice   40%   62%   1800   3343

 i About …… of trauma cases at the hospital are from *boda-boda* accidents.

 ii …… of young people in Uganda do not have a job.

 iii The death toll on Uganda's roads is …… the average across the rest of Africa.

 iv There were …… road deaths in Uganda in 2011.

 v A national scheme has trained …… *boda-boda* riders in basic road safety.

c Work with the same partner. One of you should look at the words in column A in the table below and the other should look at the words in column B. What do the words mean? Using different reference sources to help you, make notes and then explain the words to your partner.

A	B
ubiquitous potholed livelihoods swelled strain trauma	catastrophic fatalities campaigns initiatives participant slogan

8 CD1, Track 5 Listen to the police officer talking about the boda-boda taxis. As you listen, check your answers to the previous exercises.

9 Use the numbers in the box to complete the information below from the listening text. Write your answers in your notebook, then listen again and check.

> 20   25   100   1960s   20 000   250 000   300 000

a Since they appeared on the streets of Uganda in the **(i)**….

b One recent news report estimated that there were more than **(ii)**… bikes operating.

c There are up to **(iii)**… boda-boda-related cases every day.

d Ali Niwamanya, **(iv)**…, a boda-boda driver…

e A monthly fee of **(v)**… Ugandan shillings paid by the city's **(vi)**… motorbike taxis.

f A one-day workshop for **(vii)**… riders.

WORD TIP

catastrophe = an extremely bad event that causes a lot of suffering or destruction

disaster = **1 DAMAGE**: something that causes a lot of harm or damage; **2 FAILURE**: a failure or something that a bad result; **3 BAD SITUATION**: unpleasant circumstances

Use either *catastrophe* or *disaster* to complete the exercise in your **Workbook**.

Adapted from *Cambridge School Dictionary* 2008

41

LANGUAGE TIP

In the text you have just listened to there are some examples of nouns ending in *-ion*, for example *collision, organisation*. The verb forms of *-ion* nouns follow various patterns:

collision ⟶ *collide*

organisation ⟶ *organise*

Look at the audioscript. Find **three** more *-ion* nouns in the text and write the verb form for each one.

Complete the exercise in your **Workbook**.

D ⊚ Language focus: tenses

1 Look at these sentences from the information you have just listened to. What **verb time** (e.g. present) is being referred to by the verbs in bold in each sentence?

a For many years, *boda-bodas* **have been called** Uganda's silent killers.

b Since they **appeared** on the steets of Uganda in the 1960s, …

c They **are** also **injuring** and **killing** thousands every year …

d Some people are warning that in the very near future, the death toll from Uganda's roads **will be** higher than that from diseases such as malaria.

2 Complete the rules for each of the four tenses in Activity D1. What is the function of the tenses in each sentence? The first one has been done as an example.

a present perfect simple   *have/has* + past participle
Function = *to link the past to the present*

b past simple   …
Function = …

c present continuous   *am / … / … + …*
Function = …

d 'will' future   … + …
Function = …

3 Complete these sentences, putting the verbs into the correct tense.

a I'm certain that traffic chaos in big cities … (get) worse over the next ten years.

b This week I … (see) four accidents on the roads in town.

c Some friends of mine … (think) of selling their car because the roads are so dangerous!

d When I was at the police station, a policeman … (tell) me that road cameras … (catch) a lot of speeding drivers last month.

e These days, the government … (try) to improve the situation on the roads.

f In the coming years, there … (be) an even greater increase in the number of road deaths.

g That's the second time someone … (have) an accident at that junction since the traffic lights were installed.

Complete the exercise in your **Workbook**.

E ⊚ Speaking

1 ◖ CD1, Track 6 Listen to how we can show surprise about something.

2 ◖ CD1, Track 6 Listen again and write down the expressions that show surprise.

3 In small groups, discuss the following questions.

a What information from Listening 2 in Section C surprised you? Use the expressions in Activity E2 to help you.

b How does the situation in Uganda compare with the situation in your country? If you don't know, how can you find out?

c What can be done to reduce road injuries and deaths?

4 Work in small groups. Look carefully at these statistics about traffic accidents in the Republic of Ireland, then answer the questions.

🏠 ◄ ► + 🌐 http://www.   ↻ Reader

An Garda Síochána

| About Us | Contact Us | Crime Prevention | Publications | Traffic | Careers |

	Jan	Feb	March	April	May	June	July	Aug	Sept	Oct	Nov	Dec
Fatalities	19	14	15	12	17	13	18	19	17	13	16	17
Section 41 RTA – Detention of Vehicles	1540	1503	1213	1816	2036	1966	1712	1914	1779	1762	1738	
Road Transport Offences	335	312	231	368	296	211	353	430	348	367	506	
Dangerous Driving	33	220	196	211	221	207	146	184	186	215	167	
Fixed charge notices												
Seatbelts	734	865	877	1019	1229	1101	1029	1,002	1071	1050		
Mobile Phones	2210	2108	1513	2427	2335	2094	2057	2113	3058	3167		
Speeding	13,641	12,553	12,111	18,589	19,015	19,425	18,620	19,931	16,815	21,790		

Figures for fatalities are current as of 2 January 2014; all other figures are current as of 5 December 2013 and are provisional figures and subject to change. Fixed charge notices are reported one month in arrears.

Adapted from www.garda.ie

---

a At the bottom of the web page, what does this phrase mean: *are provisional figures and subject to change*?

b What do you think the following mean?

   i Fatalities

   ii Fixed charge notices.

c Find out what Section 41 RTA – Detention of Vehicles means.

d What do you think Road Transport Offences refers to?

e If you were interested in working with Ireland's national police service, which link on the webpage should you click?

f If you clicked on the Publications link, what information would you find?

g Use the information in the table to draw a graph. Choose a single month or a particular set of statistics. Your teacher will guide you.

5 Look carefully at the statistics in the table. Ask your partner **five** questions.

   Examples: You: *In May, how many people got a fixed charge notice for not wearing a seatbelt?*

       Partner: *1229.*

       You: *What surprises you most about the statistics?*

       Partner: *I couldn't believe the number of people caught for speeding!*

6 Does your country, or a country that you know, have a traffic problem? If so, what is being done to overcome the problem? What would you do if you were in charge of solving traffic problems and reducing the accident rate? Discuss in small groups.

F Listening

1 Look at these exam-style questions. With your partner, decide what information each question requires you to listen for.

   a **i** What does Gregory want to order?

      ii What is the product number?

   b **i** What will the weather be like during the late morning?

      ii What is the highest temperature expected?

   c **i** Where does this conversation take place?

      ii What does Marina want to do?

   d **i** For which sport has the price's changed?

      ii How much does it cost for members to book a court on a weekday evening?

2 Here are the answers to some questions. Which of these answers could fit the questions above? Why?

a	$20	**e**	a shirt
b	a bank	**f**	25 degrees
c	very hot	**g**	basketball
d	17 XW 3FG9	**h**	buy something

3 🔊 **CD1, Track 7** Listen to the audio and answer the questions in Activity F1.

4 Compare your work with your partner's. Then use the audioscript in Appendix 3 to check your answers.

> **!** **TOP TIP**
> When listening, you will be given time to read the questions before you listen. Make sure you use this time well. Read **all** the questions and underline the key word/s in each one. Decide what type of information each question requires, for example a number, a place, a street name.

LANGUAGE TIP
Linking words and phrases are just as important in speaking as they are in writing. Make sure you use a variety of them in spoken language. Think about words or phrases that indicate **when** (for example *firstly, subsequently, finally*) as well as **contrast** (for example *but, on the other hand, however*) and **in addition** (for example *also, furthermore, for example*).

Complete the exercise in your **Workbook**.

REFLECTION

How well do you think you can do each of these things now?

Give yourself a score from 1: Still need a lot of practice to 5: Feeling very confident about this

In this unit you:	1	2	3	4	5
watched a video of students talking about different methods of transport, and discussed what they said					
listened to different people talking about their travel experiences, and answered questions					
listened to a Ugandan police officer talking about *boda-boda* taxis and answered questions					
practised using expressions of surprise					
practised listening to short extracts and answering questions					

Now set yourself a **personal goal** based on your scores for Unit 4.

44

Cycle safety

[1] ... Cyclists need to concentrate more than other road users, as you are much more vulnerable. Remember that when you are on a cycle, you have absolutely no protection from dangers around you. Using your mobile phone and MP3 player whilst cycling is extremely dangerous, as you need to concentrate on the road and other traffic.

[2] ... Think about your clothes. Are they bright and visible to others on the road? If bright clothes are not suitable for everyday use, fluorescent and reflective jackets (which will identify you to other users) can be worn until you reach your destination. White front lights and red rear lights MUST be used after dark and in poor light conditions. They will also help you to be seen in the rain.

[3] ... You should always wear a helmet, as this can reduce the risk of head injury in a crash.

[4] ... Keep clear of the kerb and do not ride in the gutter. Don't hug the kerb if a car behind you gets impatient. Don't weave between lanes, or change direction suddenly. Show drivers what you plan to do in plenty of time. Always look and signal before you start, stop or turn. Make eye contact with drivers and let them know you have seen them.

[5] ... Is your bike regularly maintained and checked? If not, why not?! Brakes MUST work well in all conditions: dry and wet. Are lights and reflectors clean and in good working order? Are the tyres in good condition and inflated to the pressure shown on the tyre? Are the gears working correctly? Is the chain properly adjusted and oiled? Are the saddle and handlebars adjusted to the correct height?

[6] ... Traffic laws apply to you as a cyclist, as well as other road users. Cyclists MUST obey traffic signals and signs.

Remember: it is against the law for cyclists to:

• jump red lights, including lights at pedestrian crossings unless there's a sign showing that cyclists are allowed to do this
• cycle on pavements, unless there's a sign showing that cyclists are allowed to do this
• cycle the wrong way up a one-way street, unless there is a sign showing that cyclists can do so
• ride across pedestrian crossings, unless there is a sign saying that cyclists can do so.

Adapted from http://think.direct.gov.uk

Exam focus

Reading, Exercise 1, skimming and scanning

1 Read the internet article about safe bicycle riding for teenagers, then answer the exercises:
  a Why do cyclists need to focus more than other people on the road? **[1]**
  b Why are making phone calls and listening to music hazardous while cycling? **[1]**
  c What is the benefit of wearing a fluorescent or reflective jacket? **[1]**
  d When must cycle lights be switched on? Give **two** examples. **[1]**
  e Give **five** pieces of advice to help cyclists with their position on the road. **[2]**
  f How can you let a driver know that you are aware of them? **[1]**
  g Where can you find information about the correct pressure for tyres? **[1]**
  h Who do traffic laws apply to? **[1]**
  i According to traffic laws, what can a cyclist do if they see a sign giving them permission? Give **four** examples. **Extended only [4]**

[Total: 9 (Core), 13 (Extended)]

CD1, Track 8 Listening, Exercise 1, Part A, short extracts

You will hear four short recordings. Write no more than three words for each detail in your notebooks. You will hear each recording twice.

1 a What is the name of the cinema? **[1]**
  b What time does the cinema open on Tuesdays? **[1]**

2 a What does Daniela want to buy? **[1]**
  b Which is the best place she could go to buy this and why? **[1]**

3 a What job has Jason just started? **[1]**
  b Who is Jason trying to find? **[1]**

4 a Apart from visiting the museum and the markets, what else does the speaker suggest the tourists do when they get off the bus? **[1]**
  b How long are the tourists allowed to be off the bus for? **[1]**

[Total: 8]

CD1, Track 9 Listening, Exercise 1, Part B, short extracts

You will hear four short recordings. Write no more than three words for each detail in your notebooks. You will hear each recording twice.

1 a Where does this conversation take place? **[1]**
  b What **TWO** things does the woman decide to buy? **[1]**

2 a Where did Muna first meet her friend? **[1]**
  b When was Muna's visit to Bahrain postponed? **[1]**

3 a How long did Ali go away for? **[1]**
  b How many matches did Ali's team win? **[1]**

4 a Where does the customer want to sit? **[1]**
  b What is the problem with the table by the window? **[1]**

[Total: 8]

Learning objectives

In this unit you will:

- watch a video of students talking about holidays, and discuss what they say
- listen to someone talking about aerial tourism in China and answer questions
- read about different types of holiday and share the information with a partner
- listen to a winter tour organiser and complete notes about what she says
- practise asking and answering questions for the IGCSE speaking test

A 😊 Watch, listen and talk

1 Watch and listen to some IGCSE students talking about their favourite **types of holiday** and the **reasons** they give.

  a Make a note of **three** favourite types of holiday that the students mention and the **reasons** they give.

2 Talk to your partner(s) about **your** favourite type of holiday and your reasons **why**.

B 🔵 Speaking and vocabulary

1 Look at pictures a–g which show **seven** different types of holiday. What do you think each holiday involves? Discuss with your partner and say **two** things about each holiday.

  Examples: *I think **a** is somewhere cold, maybe in Scandinavia, or somewhere like that.*

  ***c** is a cake, maybe someone is getting married.*

2 Here are the names of the **seven** holidays in the pictures above, but each name has been cut into two. Match the parts to find the names of the holidays.

a Hiking with	**1** training in Mongolia
b Genghis Khan warrior	**2** in Turkey
c Chocolate cake	**3** off Kangaroo Island
d Yoga cruise	**4** in China
e Eco adventure	**5** baking in Hawaii
f Swimming with dolphins	**6** huskies holiday in Finland
g Aerial tourism	**7** farming holiday in Scotland

3 Answer questions a–f with your partner.

  a Which of the holidays would you most like to go on and which of the holidays does not appeal to you? **Why?**

  b Who would you like to be with you on the holiday? **Why?**

  c What types of people might you meet on such a holiday? **Why?**

  d Which of the holidays do you think are 'real' and which do you think are 'fake'? **Why?**

  e Think of a criterion for ranking the holidays, for example *the distance from your home country*, or *the most exotic location*. Then rank the holidays accordingly.

  f Think of another unusual holiday and agree on a name for it.

C ◀ Listening

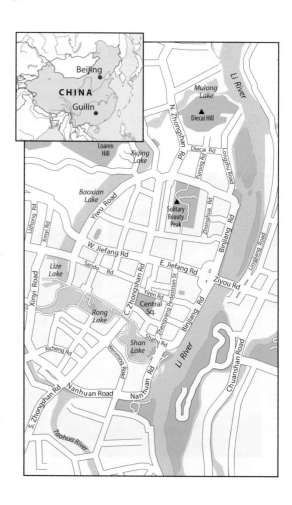

1 You are going to listen to Wang Yanghua being interviewed about one of the holidays in Section B. Wang lives in Guilin, Southern China, where he works as an aerial tourism helicopter pilot.

Before you listen, answer these **two** questions:

  a What do you think 'aerial tourism' is?

  b What things might a tourist see from the sky around Guilin?

2 ◀ **CD1, Track 10** Listen and check your answers to 1(a) and 1(b).

LANGUAGE TIP

*station**a**ry* (adjective) = not moving

*station**e**ry* (noun) = things that you use for writing, such as pens and paper

See CD1, Track 10, Appendix 3

Use either *stationary* or *stationery* to complete the sentences in your **Workbook**.

Adapted from *Cambridge School Dictionary* 2008

3 🔊 CD1, Track 10 Listen again and do **two** things:

   a check the order in which you hear the **eight** adjectives in the box

   b say what each adjective describes.

Example: (a) *1b*, (b) *amazing + job*

a	ground-level	**e**	dramatic
b	~~amazing~~	**f**	static
c	normal	**g**	popular
d	spectacular	**h**	stunning

4 How much can you remember? Work with your partner and complete Chen's notes about her interview with Wang.

> Full name: *Wang Yanghua*
>
> Work location:
>
> Licence obtained:
>
> Normal day starts at:
>
> Takes tourists in Guilin to see:
>
> Popular attractions in Beijing:
>
> Advantages of aerial sightseeing:

5 🔊 CD1, Track 10 Listen again and check your answers.

6 Read the audioscript in Appendix 3. How many more adjective + noun combinations can you find?

D 🔍 Language focus: compound (multi-word) adjectives

> **LANGUAGE TIP**
>
> Remember from Unit 2 that **adjectives** describe nouns by giving information about the object's size, shape, age, colour, origin or material. A **compound** (also called **multi-word**) **adjective** is formed when two or more adjectives are joined together to modify the same noun. These adjectives are usually hyphenated to avoid confusion. Look at this example from the listening text: *ground-level sightseeing*.
>
> Complete the exercise in your **Workbook**.

1 You and your partner are each going to read a different text. **Student A** is going to read **Text 5A** *Hiking with huskies in Finland* in Appendix 2, and **Student B** is going to read **Text 5B** *Swimming with dolphins off Kangaroo Island* in Appendix 2. Before you read, answer questions a–c below.

   a Look at the adjectives (1–12) taken from the two texts. With your partner:

     i Discuss what they mean.

     ii Decide in which text you think you will read them.

     iii Which adjectives are difficult to decide on? Give reasons for your answers.

     There are **six** adjectives from each text.

1	abundant	**7**	memorable
2	advisable	**8**	more intensive
3	comprehensive	**9**	paramount
4	customised	**10**	shock-absorbing
5	husky-trekking	**11**	more strenuous
6	innovative	**12**	sturdy

b Which adjectives (1–12) from the list above do you think describe these nouns and noun and verb phrases (a–l) from the two texts? **Why**? Which adjectives can you use more than once? **Why**?

a	Deep sea excursion	**g**	lead between the hiker and the dog
b	Dolphin experience	**h**	normal hill-walking
c	dolphins, parrots, sea lions and iguanas	**i**	to take a water bottle
d	importance	**j**	tours
e	holiday	**k**	trainers
f	husky-trekking	**l**	way of learning

c Think of **one** more adjective which you could use to describe each of the nouns and noun and verb **phrases** (a–l).

E 📖 💬 Reading and speaking

1 Quickly read your text and check your answers for Activity D1a and D1b.

2 **Student A**: Ask your partner the questions under your text, and make a note of the answers.

Student B: Answer your partner's questions.

3 How much can you remember? Tell your partner everything you can remember about their text. Ask any questions you may have.

F 🔊 Listening

1 You are going to listen to a talk by a woman who organises winter tours to Dali in Yunnan Province, China. Before you listen, decide which adjectives best describe the nouns. Give reasons.

Adjectives	Nouns
complex	attraction
freshwater	event
lush green	experience
natural	guide
professional	lake
snow-capped	landscape
snow-white	leaves
spectacular	mountains
thrilling	seabirds

2 ● CD1, Track 11 Listen and do two things:

a Check your answers to Activity F1.

b Number your answers in the order that you hear them.

Example: *1 = snow-white seabirds*

3 ● CD1, Track 11 Listen to the talk again and complete the details below. Write one or two words **only** in each gap.

Winter tours

Main attractions: beautiful islands, **(a)** … scenery, wonderful wildlife. [1]

Xiao Putuo island in Erhai Lake – **snow-white seabirds**

Erhai means **(b)** …, second largest freshwater lake, area of **(c)** … square kilometres, average 11 metres deep [1]

Important food source. **(d)** … catch fish and return to fishmongers

Small boats available for visiting **(e)** … and lake [1]

Cangshan Mountain: **(f)** … covered by forest, difficult for inexperienced walkers, up to 200 people need rescuing **(g)** … . [1]

Cable-car to the top, 45-minute ride, 4,000 metres above **(h)** … [1]

Mountain landscape changes from green to **(i)** …, weather can be **(j)** … near the top [1]

Better **(k)** …, including air links, increasing number of visitors, as well as events such as **(l)** … shopping festival [1]

Yearly **(m)** … fair has almost 100 000 visitors [1]

4 Read the audioscript in Appendix 3 to check your answers.

G Speaking

1 Work on your own. Write **five** questions that you think you might be asked.

2 Work with a partner. Ask and answer your questions.

3 Unjumble the words to find the questions. Are any the same as the questions you thought of with your partner in G1?

a in town live do which you?

b for weekend what plans next your are?

c me school talk at favourite your to subjects about

d your what's name?

e you name your do spell family how?

f have how sisters brothers and you do many?

g describe how today travelled you here

h career would follow like you to what?

i do did you what weekend last?

j tell you what doing your in free enjoy time

> **TOP TIP**
> In many speaking examinations, the assessment is divided into several parts. The purpose of the first part is to put you at your ease and to help you relax, talking about things which are of a personal nature. These often focus on where you live, your school, and what you do in your free time, and usually last about two to three minutes.

51

4 In what order do you think the questions will be asked? **Why**?

5 CD1, Track 12 Listen to Stefanos's answers. As you listen, check **two** things:

   a your answers to G3

   b the order in which the questions are asked.

6 CD1, Track 12 Listen again and write Stefanos's answers to **six** of the questions.

   a Describe how you travelled here today.

   b Tell me what you enjoy doing in your free time.

   c Talk to me about your favourite subjects at school.

   d What career would you like to follow?

   e What did you do last weekend?

   f What are your plans for next weekend?

7 Which of Stefanos's answers do you think could be better? **Why**? **How** could Stefanos improve them?

8 CD1, Track 13 Listen to Maria answering the same questions. Do you think she did better or worse than Stefanos? **Why**?

9 CD1, Track 13 Maria uses some 'filler' words and phrases at the start of some of her answers. Listen again and make a note of any fillers that you hear.

   Example: *Interviewer: How do you spell your family name?*

   Maria: **_Actually_** *it's quite easy: CHRISTOU*

10 Read Audioscript 5.2 in Appendix 3 to check.

11 In what way is Maria's final filler **Next weekend?** different from the other ones that she uses?

>
> **LANGUAGE TIP**
>
> We often use fillers, like the ones Maria used, to give ourselves some thinking time before we answer. They can help to make your speaking sound more natural and fluent.
>
> Complete the exercises in your **Workbook**.

H 😄 Watch, listen and talk

1 😄 You are going to watch an IGCSE student talking in an exam. The student is answering questions in the first part of the test. Which of the questions you have seen in this unit so far is asked?

2 😄 Now watch a second student. Which of the questions you have seen in this unit so far is asked? Which of the two students do you think performs better? Why?

3 😄 With your partner, take turns to ask and answer questions. Try to practise using the language you have already seen in this unit.

> **TOP TIP**
>
> Questions may not always begin with a question word (e.g. *Where? Why? How many?*). Look at this example: *Tell me about your holiday plans, Talk about your hobbies,* in order to guide you about what they want you to say.

REFLECTION

How well do you think you can do each of these things now?

Give yourself a score from 1: Still need a lot of practice to 5: Feeling very confident about this

In this unit you:	1	2	3	4	5
watched a video of students talking about holidays, and discussed what they said					
listened to someone talking about aerial tourism in China and answered questions					
read about different types of holiday and shared the information with a partner					
listened to a winter tour organiser and completed notes about what she said					
practised asking and answering questions for the IGCSE speaking test					

Now set yourself a **personal goal** based on your scores for Unit 5.

Exam focus

Listening, Exercise 2, note-making

You will hear a talk by a man who is arranging tours to visit five different volcanoes around the world.

🔊 **CD1, Track 14** Listen to the talk and complete the details below. Write one or two words only in each gap. You will hear the talk twice.

Global Volcanoes

a Volcanoes are powerful, prized, beautiful, ... **[1]** Talk is about five volcanoes in Asia, USA, Indonesia, ..., Europe $\left[\frac{1}{2}\right]$

b Mount Fuji .... metres high $\left[\frac{1}{2}\right]$ Many Japanese hope to reach the top during lifetime

c Shape of top of Mount Fuji is like a .... $\left[\frac{1}{2}\right]$ and possible to see it from .... $\left[\frac{1}{2}\right]$ Distance to volcano is .... $\left[\frac{1}{2}\right]$

d Mt Semeru is .... $\left[\frac{1}{2}\right]$ volcano in Indonesia Mt Bromo: wonderful .... $\left[\frac{1}{2}\right]$ views

e Virunga is Africa's first .... $\left[\frac{1}{2}\right]$ Possible to see .... $\left[\frac{1}{2}\right]$ and world's largest .... $\left[\frac{1}{2}\right]$ at Mt Nyiragongo

f Near Naples, Mt Vesuvius, famous for devastating eruption almost .... $\left[\frac{1}{2}\right]$ years ago Volcanology research information from visit to .... $\left[\frac{1}{2}\right]$

g Crater Lake landscape not seen until you reach edge of crater, and lake is different shades of .... $\left[\frac{1}{2}\right]$

h Lake surrounded by cliffs and .... $\left[\frac{1}{2}\right]$ Visitors can drive or hike.

[Total: 8]

Part 2:
Education and work

In Part 2: Work and education, there are five units (6 Learning, 7 Jobs, 8 Communication, 9 Interviews, 10 Education). You will:

- watch and listen to some IGCSE students talking about each unit topic, and speaking in the IGCSE speaking exam;
- think about and discuss what the students said;
- read a variety of texts about school facilities, the work of a cosmetic scientist, spelling and letter writing, effective study methods;
- listen to people talking about NASA, CVs, people in different job interviews, and students discussing the IGCSE speaking exam;
- practise various exam skills: note-making, summary writing, writing for purpose, listening, and speaking.

Before you start Part 2, look at the picture on these pages:

    a   Where do you think the picture was taken? Why do you think this?

    b   What is the girl in the picture doing, or is about to do?

    c   Have you ever done an activity like this? If yes, explain when and where. If not, would you like to? Why?

    d   Imagine you are messaging a friend. How would you describe the picture to them?

    e   How important do you think it is to do practical experiments at school? Why?

Learning objectives

In this unit you will:

- watch and listen to some students talking about school facilities, and discuss what they say
- read and make notes about school facilities
- practise giving spoken advice and suggestions
- read and make notes about teenagers getting up in the mornings
- write notes about a language school

A 😄 Watch, listen and talk

1 Watch and listen to some IGCSE- students talking about **school facilities**.

   a What do the students think are the most important facilities that a school should offer? Make a note of **three**.

   b What **extra** facilities would the students like to have?

2 Talk to your partner(s) about what **you** think are the most important facilities that a school should offer, and what extra facilities **you** would like to have in **your** school.

B 💬 🔤 Speaking and vocabulary

1 Look at the pictures of some facilities in schools. Work in small groups and answer these questions.

a Are any of the school facilities in the pictures the same as you discussed in Section **A**? Which ones do you have in your school? Which ones do you not have, but would like to have? **Why**?

b What facilities would you expect a school to have that are missing from these pictures? Why are they important?

c What are the different facilities that primary and secondary schools need? Why is this? What about a university or college?

2 Work on your own and think about which facilities in your own school are the most important to you. Make a list and put them in rank order, with the most important at the top. Draw a graph illustrating the order. Your teacher will help you.

3 Work in small groups. Tell your group **three** things about the information in your graph, giving reasons for your choices.

Example: *I think a gym is the most important facility because we have nowhere else to play sports.*

C Reading

1 The following words and phrases appear in the text below, which is taken from the website of a language school: LearnFast Language Centre. Discuss the words and phrases with your partner and try to agree on their meanings. Use different reference sources to help you.

a extensive	**e** counselling	**i** welfare
b blended learning	**f** appropriate	**j** self-catering
c 10 000 volumes	**g** intolerant	
d on loan	**h** policy	

2 Skim the text on the next page. Match the headings in the box with the paragraphs (1–5). There are three extra headings that you will not need to use.

> Accommodation and welfare   Social and leisure programme
> Banking facilities   Sports centre   Cafeteria   IT centre
> Library and Multimedia Resource Centre (LMRC)   Counselling service

3 Skim the text again. What specific facilities and services are offered by the school? Are any of them the same as the ones you listed in Activity B2? Are there any that you did not list? Are there any facilities that you would like to add to the school? Why, or why not?

4 Look at the text again. Find the words from Activity C1. Do the meanings you and your partner agreed on make sense?

5 Copy the table below into your notebook. Then look at the text again and complete the information about the opening and closing times for the cafeteria, the IT facilities and the LMRC. Remember that there are different times for some of the facilities at the weekend.

Facility	Time	06:00	07:00	09:00	16:00	17:00	19:00	21:00	22:00
Café		Opens M–F	…	…	…	…	…	…	…
IT facilities		…	…	…	…	…	Closes wkend	…	…
LMRC		…	…	…	…	…	…	Closes M–F	…

57

LearnFast Language Centre

Facilities and Services

[1] ... Our extensive, state-of-the-art IT-centre facilities offer our students a completely new approach to language learning. At **LearnFast**, you can choose between classroom-based lessons with a teacher, computer-based self-study lessons, or a mixture of both: blended learning. The choice is yours! Even if you choose classroom-based lessons, there will still be one weekly timetabled lesson using IT. Our IT facilities are open from 0700 in the morning until 2200 at night (0900–1700 at weekends) for general use and for further practice*, with someone always available to help and advise you. We have special software to help you practise*: pronunciation, listening skills, grammar and examination skills, as well as the chance to improve your speaking skills. However, if you just want to check your emails or send a message on Facebook, the IT centre facilities – including Internet – are free and available for all **LearnFast** students.

[2] ... If you prefer paper to digital, our Library and Multimedia Resource Centre (LMRC) is the place for you. With more than 10 000 volumes, this is the ideal place for some quiet time, not just for language students, but also for our many teachers and trainee teachers. Students can choose from a wide range of graded reading books, from beginner to advanced, many of which also have MP3 audio files, so you can listen, as well as – or instead of – read. If you want to do some studying at home, most items in the LMRC are available on loan, including audiovisual equipment. The librarian (available from 0900 to 1900) can advise you on what materials are best for your level. You may also purchase books (digital and print) and audio files, at a discounted price, from the LMRC. Please note that coursebooks are included in your course fees and are yours to keep. The LMRC is open 0900–1900 every day, but is closed at weekends.

[3] ... **LearnFast** is aware that many students and trainee teachers may need advice on what to do and where to go when they finish their course. We offer free careers guidance, counselling and university placement advice. Using the latest software, we can identify an appropriate career path, as well as locate a course suitable for your needs and abilities.

[4] ... Open from 0600 to 2100 every day (0900–1600 at weekends), our cafeteria offers hot meals, snacks, sandwiches, hot and cold drinks and fruit for all types of diet, from vegetarian to lactose intolerant! It is a policy at **LearnFast** to keep our cafeteria prices as low as possible. Generally, a meal will cost less than half the price of a similar meal elsewhere. The cafeteria also offers free access to online English-language newspapers and magazines by supplying its customers with small hand-held tablets!

[5] ... **LearnFast** understands that different people require different types of accommodation, and our three full-time Accommodation and Welfare officers will help you choose the best for you. Staying with an English-speaking family, a short walk from **LearnFast**, is always a popular option, but self-catering in student hostels is a cheaper option. For those who prefer hotel accommodation, we have many for you to choose from, either budget or more luxurious. However, please note that only one of the hostels and none of the hotels are within walking distance of the Language Centre.

58

* See the **WORD TIP**.

WORD TIP

Notice that in UK English the word practi**c**e is a noun and the word practi**s**e is a verb. In USA English, the word practi**c**e can be either a noun or a verb.
Use either practi**c**e or practi**s**e to complete the sentences in your **Workbook**.

Adapted from *Cambridge School Dictionary* 2008

6 Look at these notes written by a student about the information in paragraphs 3 Counselling service, 4 Cafeteria and 5 Accommodation and Welfare:

Work with your partner.

a Student A write 4–5 notes about paragraph 1 IT centre, and Student B write 4–5 notes about paragraph 2 LMRC.

TOP TIP

In some examinations, you may be asked to read a text and write short notes under different headings. These types of questions require careful text reading in order to identify the most important details to include in your notes.

My notes

Paragraph 3 – students may need advice about career, education counselling service available

Paragraph 4 – open 6 a.m.–9 p.m. but 9 a.m.–4 p.m. weekends, different food options, vegetarian, lactose intolerant, low prices, free online newspapers and magazines

Paragraph 5 – three officers for help, choose from English-speaking family close to school, self-catering in hostel cheaper, hotels not near school

b Exchange your notes and check if you agree. Is there anything you think is missing or should be added?

c Without looking back at the text, use your partner's notes to write the paragraph.

d Give your paragraph to your partner to read and compare with the text in your coursebook.

7 Here are the answers to ten questions based on the text. Write the questions.

a once a week

b from 09:00 to 17:00

c pronunciation, listening skills, grammar and examination skills

d about 10 000

e audio files

f from the LMRC

g the latest software

h small hand-held tablets

i three

j students can walk to LearnFast

8 Compare your questions with a partner's. Are they the same?

D Language focus: prefixes and suffixes

LANGUAGE TIP

A *prefix* is a group of letters added before a word or base to change its meaning. When a prefix is added, a new word is formed. Two of the most common prefixes are *un-* (meaning *not*, or *the opposite or reverse of*) and *re-* (meaning *again* or *back*).

REMEMBER! The spelling of the word never changes when a prefix is added. Also, the spelling of the prefix never changes, no matter what word you add it to.

Examples: ***un**necessary*, ***re**pay*, ***multi**media*. Note that in some cases, a prefix is followed by a hyphen.

Complete the exercise in your **Workbook**.

LANGUAGE TIP

A suffix is a group of letters added after a word or base **to form a new word**. Two of the most common suffixes are *-ing* (for example: *bring**ing***) and *-ed* (for example: *work**ed***). A suffix can make a new word in one of two ways:

1 Grammatical change – for example changing tense: *climb → climb**ed***. The basic meaning of the word *climb* does not change.

2 Meaning change – the word + suffix has a new meaning: *teach → teach**er***, and often a new part of speech: *verb → noun*

59

1 Work with your partner. Look at these phrases from the website article Section C.

… <u>self</u>-study lessons

… facilities including <u>inter</u>net

… lactose <u>in</u>tolerant

… one week<u>ly</u> timetabled lesson

… from beginn<u>er</u> to advanc<u>ed</u>

… suit<u>able</u> for

The underlined groups of letters are prefixes and suffixes. Do they change the grammar or the meaning of the words?

2 Look at these prefixes. For each one, decide what it means and then match each prefix with a suitable word or base to create a new word. Finally, tell each other what the new words mean.

Example: *auto + matic = automatic = without human control*

Prefixes	Words and bases
~~auto-~~, hyper-, sub-, trans-, equi-, bi-, mono-, anti-, ex-, contra-	marine, distant, annual, dote, president, ~~matic~~, diction, lingual, market, continental

3 Look at these prefixes. For each one, decide what it means and then think of more words that contain the prefix.

Example: micro- = *very small, on a small scale:* **micro**chip, **micro**scopic

a self-   **c** inter-   **e** audio-   **g** pro-

b multi-   **d** con-   **f** dis-   **h** tri-

4 Different suffixes can change words into nouns, different verb tenses or parts of verbs, adjectives or adverbs. For example -ed and -ing are mostly used with verbs, -tion with nouns, -est with adjectives and -ly with adverbs.

Match the following words and suffixes to make new words, then say what part of speech the new words are. You may need to change the spelling of the word when you add the suffix.

Example: *happy + ness = happi**ness** = noun*

Words	Suffixes
accident, avail, cheap, excite, guide, happy, imagine, love, luxury, say	-ability, -al, -ance, -er, -ing, -ious, -ly, -ment, -ness, -tion

5 Look at the following noun and adjective suffixes. Use each one to create a word. Then choose five of your words and use each one in a sentence.

Examples: *comfort + -able = comfortable (adjective)*

music + cian = musician (noun)

Marios always chooses the most comfortable chair in the room!

Stella excelled as a musician.

-able -ac -ade -ary -cian -est -less -phobia -sion -ular

E Speaking: Giving advice and making suggestions

1 In Section F, you will read an internet newspaper article called 'Why can't teenagers get up in the morning?' Work in small groups and discuss these questions.

   a Do you have a problem getting up in the morning in time for school? What about your friends or people in your family?

   b Why do you think some teenagers have this problem? Is it laziness, the thought of going to school, or is something else to blame?

   c Do you know any adults who have a problem getting up in the morning to go to work? Why do they have this problem? Is it for the same reason that some teenagers can't get up in the morning in time for school?

   d What advice would you give to someone who has a problem getting up in the morning?

2 CD1, Track 15 Listen to ten people giving advice about how to wake up in the morning. As you listen, match the phrases in columns A and B.

A	B
1 ~~I reckon you should …~~	**a** … to ask your parents to help you.
2 Why don't you …	**b** … change your habits.
3 ~~How about …~~	**c** … to get a new alarm clock.
4 If I were you, …	**d** … get someone to wake you up?
5 I suggest …	**e** … I'd go to sleep earlier.
6 You'd really better …	**f** … to set your alarm clock.
7 I would strongly advise you …	**g** … sleeping with the window open.
8 My advice would be …	**h** ~~… use a louder alarm clock.~~
9 It might be a good idea …	**i** ~~… using two alarm clocks?~~
10 You might try …	**j** … you have an afternoon nap.

3 CD1, Track 15 Listen again. Which **advice expressions** are followed by *to* + verb? Which ones are followed by *–ing*? Which ones are followed by infinitive without *to*? Which advice expression does not follow any of these patterns? What is it followed by?

   Examples: *I reckon you should **use** a louder alarm clock.* Infinitive without **to**

   *How about **using** two alarm clocks?* **–ing**

4 What advice would you give to someone who finds it difficult to concentrate while studying? Work with a partner and give each other some advice. Try to use the advice phrases from this this section.

   Example: *If I were you, I'd find a friend to help you study.*

5 Team up with another pair and tell each other what advice you gave.

   Example: *Myria told me to study with a friend.*

F Reading

1 Look at these five statements (a–e). Do you think they are true or false? Why? What do the others in your group think?

   a During the 'terrible teens' period, all children develop a lazy streak.

LANGUAGE TIP

The words *advice* (noun) and *advise* (verb) are often confused.

Look at these two examples:

My advice would be to revise all the units in the book.

The teacher strongly advised us to revise all the units in the book.

advice is an uncountable noun:

~~*My advices would be …*~~ *My advice would be …*

~~*He gave me good advices*~~ *He gave me some good advice*

advise is a regular verb: *advise, advised, advised.*

Compare with *practice* and *practise* earlier in this unit.

Remember that in US English, the spelling does not change. Both the noun and the verb are 'practice'.

Use either *advice* or *advise* to complete the exercise in your **Workbook**.

61

b Evidence is emerging that teenagers are biologically incapable of going to bed at a sensible time.

c Other studies have shown that sleep-deprived teenagers will smoke less than their well-rested peers and are prone to depression and anxiety.

d Despite the potentially fatal consequences of a shortage of sleep, just one in five teenagers gets the nightly nine hours recommended to keep them in tip-top condition.

e Although it isn't known exactly how our body clock controls our sleeping hours, it is thought that teenagers are around an hour out of sync with everyone else.

2 These words and phrases have been removed from the text *Why can't teenagers get up in the morning?* With a partner, quickly discuss the meanings.

a bleak

b jeopardises

c metabolism

d moan

e out of sync

f sleep deprivation

g succumb to sleep

h trivial matter

3 The following phrases all appear in the text. What do you think you will read about each one? Why?

> a different time zone   chronic jet lag   getting good grades   hormones
> in a car accident   lie in bed for hours   perform very poorly in the morning
> sleepiness   sleeping hours   teenage body clocks

4 Skim the article and do the following. Do not worry about the gaps at the moment.

a Find out what advice Dr Ralph gave.

b Check if the statements in Activity F1 are true or false.

c Check if the article says the same as you about the phrases in F3.

5 Read the text again and complete the gaps i–viii with the words and phrases a–h in Activity F2.

6 Answer the following questions in your notebooks.

a Give three examples of behaviour during the 'terrible teens' period.

b What reason is given for children's inability to get up in the morning?

c What can sleep deprivation put at risk?

d Why have some teachers never seen their students at their best?

e What does Dr Ralph's research on animals show?

f What percentage of people who die in car accidents are aged between 16 and 25?

g When and where do you think teenagers might show symptoms of narcolepsy?

TOP TIP

It is important to show that you can understand information presented in a visual format, such as a graph, table or chart, as well as in a written text. Look out for questions that start with the words: *According to the chart/graph/picture …* , as these will tell you that the answer is not in the written text itself.

62

h According to the pie chart, how many hours are spent sleeping by the largest percentage of students?

i Give two pieces of information about how the human sleep cycle works, and two pieces of information about how teenagers are different.

Why can't teenagers get up in the morning?

[1] They refuse to go to bed at a decent hour, **(i)** … when they have to get up for school and lie in bed for hours at weekends. During the 'terrible teens' period, most children appear to develop a lazy streak. And now it seems that their inability to get up in the morning may not be their fault, with research showing that teenage body clocks may simply be **(ii)** … . A slight shift forward in the body's natural rhythms makes teenagers annoyingly alert late at night and frustratingly groggy in the morning. While this may be irritating for their parents, it could have serious consequences for the teenagers themselves.

[2] *New Scientist* magazine explains: 'Evidence is emerging that teenagers are biologically incapable of going to bed at a sensible time. This is no **(iii)** … . If teens are refugees from a different time zone, then by making them get up and go to school before their bodies are ready, we are not just making school life difficult for them and their teachers, we are also putting them at risk. **(iv)** … **(v)** … their future prospects, their health and even their lives.'

[3] Toronto University psychologist, Professor David Brown, said: 'Adolescents, who are usually evening types, perform very poorly in the morning, which is the time of day that they are usually assessed for examinations. There are some kids whose teachers have simply never seen them at their best and that is a terrible shame.'

[4] However, getting good grades could be the least of their problems, with other research showing that disruptions to our body clock could seriously damage our health. Tests on hamsters* showed that changing their cycle of sleeping and wakefulness had shocking consequences. Dr Martin Ralph, of Toronto University, said: 'Their cardiovascular system was destroyed, they suffered kidney disease and they died much earlier.'

[5] His findings look **(vi)** … for sleep-deprived teenagers. 'These kids are being woken in the night – before their body should wake – and are suffering the equivalent of chronic jet lag,' he said. 'All our animal studies show how harmful this is to health.'

[6] Other studies have shown that sleep-deprived teenagers are more likely to smoke than their well-rested peers and are prone to depression and anxiety. And half of all people who die in a car accident through falling asleep at the wheel are aged between 16 and 25.

[7] Despite the potentially fatal consequences of a shortage of sleep, very few teenagers get the nightly nine hours recommended to keep them in tip-top condition. The situation is so bad that many teenagers exhibit symptoms more usually associated with narcolepsy**, a serious condition in which sufferers can nod off in an instant.

[8] Although it isn't known exactly how our body clock controls our sleeping hours, it is thought that teenagers are around an hour out of sync with everyone else. Our natural cycle is kept in check by two mechanisms – one promotes wakefulness, while the other enhances sleepiness. During the day, the ever-increasing pressure to fall asleep is kept in check by hormones stimulated by light. But, at dusk, our bodies produce the hormone melatonin, which encourages sleepiness. At the same time, the body temperature cools and **(vii)** … slows, and eventually we **(viii)** … .

[9] In teenagers, there are two key changes. The build-up of pressure to fall asleep is much more gradual, making it easier for them to stay up later and be alert later. And their bodies start to produce the hormone melatonin around an hour later than usual. While some researchers are trying to find ways to reset the adolescent biological clock, others favour a more simple solution. Dr Ralph advised: 'Schools and universities should ideally not start before 11 a.m.'

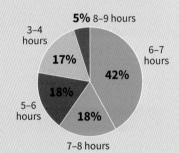

The number of hours spent sleeping by 9–17-year-olds according to a survey of 1,000 people.

* hamsters = small animals without a tail, sometimes used in laboratory experiments

** narcolepsy = medical condition that makes you fall asleep very suddenly

Adapted from www.dailymail.co.uk

63

7 You are going to give a talk about why teenagers can't get up in the morning to your school class. Prepare some notes to use as the basis for your talk. Make short notes under each heading.

Teenagers and their sleep problems
'Terrible teens' behaviour
. . .
. . .
. . .
Health problems faced by sleep-deprived teens
more likely to smoke
. . .
. . .
Natural body cycle
desire to sleep reduced by light
. . .
. . .
Differences in teenagers
. . .
. . .

REFLECTION

How well do you think you can do each of these things now?

Give yourself a score from 1: Still need a lot of practice to 5: Feeling very confident about this

In this unit you:	1	2	3	4	5
watched and listened to some students talking about school facilities, and discussed what they said					
read and made notes about school facilities					
practised giving spoken advice and suggestions					
read and made notes about teenagers getting up in the mornings					
wrote notes about a language school					

Now set yourself a **personal goal** based on your scores for Unit 6.

Exam focus

Reading and writing, Exercise 3, note-making

1   Read the newspaper article about reading from a tablet before going to bed, and then complete the notes.

Tablets versus books before bedtime

People who read from a tablet before going to sleep felt less sleepy and had different electrical activity in the brain during sleep than those who read from a physical book, a recent study found. But the time it took to fall asleep and time spent sleeping were similar under both conditions.

'Since light has an alerting effect, we predicted a lower sleepiness in the tablet condition at bedtime compared to the book condition' said lead author Janne Gronli of the University of Bergen in Norway. But it was surprising that the tablet light did not delay the start of sleep, she said.

Participants

The study included 16 non-smokers aged 22 to 33 who were familiar with tablets and had no sleep, medical or psychiatric disorders. For a week before the study began, they were instructed to keep to a regular sleep-wake schedule and to stay in bed at least as long as they needed to sleep. During the study, in which participants slept in their own beds, the researchers recorded three nights of sleeping patterns: one to collect a baseline of how a person slept, one night of reading from a tablet

for 30 minutes before turning out the light, and one night of reading a book for the same amount of time. On the night they read from a book, the participants used an ordinary reading light in their bedrooms.

The sleep pattern recordings, including measurements of brain electrical activity, provided data on total sleep time, sleep efficiency, and the percentage of time spent in each sleep stage. Other aspects of sleep quality during the time between lights off and the start of sleep were also recorded, as well as the time before the first period of REM (rapid eye movement) sleep.

A light metre measured illumination at eye level while the participants were reading either the tablet or the physical book. Illumination was about twice as high while reading from a tablet compared to the book, and the tablet emitted a high level of blue light, the researchers noted. Participants said they felt sleepier when reading the physical book. After reading from the tablet, recordings showed delayed and reduced brain wave activity, representing deep sleep compared to when the participants had been reading from a book. Bedtime and the time at which people got up the next day were similar in both conditions, with an average sleep duration of slightly less than eight hours.

'We only examined one night using a tablet,' Gronli said. 'It is tempting to speculate that daily use of a tablet, and other blue light emitting electronic devices, before bedtime may have consequences for human sleep and brain performance. To avoid increased activation before bedtime, the bedroom should not be used for work or being on social media.'

A new tablet operating system includes a nighttime mode, which takes into account the effects of too much blue light in the late evening by filtering it out, and thus avoiding making users feel sleepy.

Adapted from, 'Reading from a tablet before bed may affect sleep quality', by Kathryn Doyle, Reuters, in *The Jordan Times*, 17 March 2016

You are going to give a talk about sleep to your Science Club at school. Prepare some notes to use as a basis for your talk. Make short notes under each heading.

Tablets versus books before bedtime
Participants
...   [1]
...   [1]
...   [1]
Data obtained from recordings:
...   [1]
...   [1]
...   [extended] [1]
Possible impacts from blue light:
...   [1]
...   [1]
...   [extended] [1]

[Total: 7 Core, 9 Extended]

Learning objectives

In this unit you will:

- watch a video of students talking about jobs, and discuss what they say
- read and answer questions about the job of a cosmetic scientist
- practise making notes and writing a paragraph
- listen to a careers adviser talking about jobs with NASA and answer questions
- practise writing a summary

A 🔵 Watch, listen and talk

1 Watch and listen to some IGCSE students talking about **jobs**.

    a What jobs do the students want to do in the future?

    b What in particular appeals to the students about the jobs?

2 Talk to your partner(s) about what job you would like to do when you finish your education, and what in particular appeals to you about the job.

B 🔵 Speaking and vocabulary

1 Look at the pictures. Name at least **two** things that you can see in each one.

2 What jobs are the people doing? Would you like to do any of the jobs? Why, or why not?

3 Work with a partner and answer these questions.

   a Think about your answer to A2. Have you always wanted to do this job, or have your ideas changed as you have grown older?

   b Are there any negative aspects to the job?

   c What do you think are the most important aspects of a job: working hours, location … ?

4 Here are seven more jobs, but the letters in a–g are jumbled. What are the jobs? Use the pictures to help you. The first letter of each job is in **bold**. Write the words and be careful of the spellings.

   a dami**c**one   **c** histaca**p**rm   **e** ra**g**enerd   **g** coat**c**atnun

   b re**d**vir   **d** **f**loaterlob   **f** tun**a**ratso

5 What does each person do? Write a short definition for each of the seven jobs you found in Activity B4. Use different reference sources to help you.

   Example: *d A **comedian*** *is someone who tells jokes and makes people laugh.*

6 Which job in Activity B4 would you most or least like to do? Why?

C ◉ Reading

1 You are going to read a newspaper article about how to become a cosmetic scientist. Before you read the article, talk with a partner about what you think a cosmetic scientist does.

2 With your partner, look at the following information about cosmetic scientists and decide if it is true or false. Try to give reasons.

    a Cosmetic scientists usually need a four-year degree in Chemistry or Microbiology

    b It is essential to have a Masters or PhD degree

    c There are few work opportunities for cosmetic scientists

    d 'Formulators' invent and create

    e A résumé or CV is very important when you start looking for a job in the industry

    f You should try to get a temporary position first

    g Social networking sites do not really help you find a job

3 Here are headings (in the wrong order) for the seven paragraphs in the text. Quickly read the text and decide with your partner which heading (a–g) goes with which paragraph (1–7). Give reasons for your choices

    a A temporary assignment

    b Get a job

    c Get your science degree

    d Maybe get an advanced degree

    e Network with other cosmetic chemists

    f Pick a job

    g Research cosmetic companies

4 Now decide in which paragraph (1–7) you would expect to find the information in Activity C2. Give reasons.

5 Check if the sentences in C2 are true or false.

6 Look at the six underlined phrases in the text. Work with your partner to find out what the phrases mean. Which reference sources are you going to use? Why?

> **WORD TIP**
>
> *except* (preposition, conjunction) = not including a particular thing, fact, or person
>
> *accept* (verb) = 1 AGREE: to agree to something that is offered to you; 2 ADMIT: to admit that something is true, often something unpleasant; 3 ALLOW TO JOIN: to allow someone to join an organisation or become part of a group
>
> Use either *except* or *accept* to complete the exercise in your **Workbook**.
>
> Adapted from *Cambridge School Dictionary* 2008

69

D 🔊 Language focus: modals for advice and suggestions

1 Look at these two examples from the text you have just read:

    You <u>*could*</u> **start** your own company

    You <u>*should*</u> **get** a four-year degree

    The underlined words are <u>modal verbs</u>.

2 Which other modal verbs do you know? Are any of these modal verbs used in the text?

could, should	must
WEAKER	STRONGER

Seven steps to becoming a cosmetic scientist

[1] You could start your own company, or work for a family member who has started one, but this is not how most people get into the cosmetic industry. If you are following the <u>traditional path</u>, you should get a four-year degree from a college or university. The most common degrees that cosmetic scientists get are Chemistry, Chemical Engineering, Biology or Microbiology. You also find a few Physics majors too.

[2] While a four-year degree is all you need, larger companies <u>tend to favour</u> students who have Masters or PhD degrees in Cosmetic Science. The truth is that most of these degrees do not help make you a better cosmetic scientist. The training you receive on the job is much more valuable. The exception to this is when you enrol in one of the few cosmetic-science-focused programmes in universities.

[3] There are literally thousands of scientists and chemists working in the cosmetic industry. Fortunately, the number of jobs continues to grow. This is an industry that continues to sell its products, even in uncertain economic times. Everyone wants to look good, no matter how much money they are making. There are various types of companies that employ cosmetic scientists and chemists. A great place to find potential employers is through trade journals and magazines.

[4] In college, you are rarely told what kind of job you might get when you graduate. If you are looking to work as a scientist in the cosmetic industry, there is a wide variety of jobs to choose from. Use the list below to see which one <u>best fits your interests</u>:

- **Cosmetic formulator:** If you like inventing and creating, the formulator is where you should be. Most of these jobs are with finished goods and contract manufacturers.
- **Quality control chemist (QC):** If you enjoy chemistry and physics, and more analytical studies, you might enjoy a QC or QA job. Every company in the industry hires these scientists.
- **Analytical services:** This is the closest thing in the industry to scientific research. Most raw material suppliers and finished goods manufacturers have analytical departments.
- **Process engineering (PE):** Do you like building things and engineering? Then this might be the job for you. Almost any cosmetic company with manufacturing facilities will hire PE scientists.
- **Synthesis chemist:** If you love organic chemistry, then raw material synthesis is the place you should be.
- **Regulatory scientist:** For people who like science, but do not want to work in a lab, a job in regulatory is a good place to go. Nearly all companies hire regulatory scientists and (unfortunately) more and more jobs are being added. I say unfortunately because more governmental regulations make it tougher to create innovative cosmetics.
- **Sales:** If you like talking to people, going out for meals with potential customers and negotiating, a job in sales might be right for you. Plus, these are the people in the industry who usually have the most flexible jobs and make the most money.

[5] To actually get a job, the first thing you are going to want to do is put together a résumé or CV. You should be working on this in the early part of your final year at university. The sooner you have a résumé or CV, the sooner you can start sending it to human resources (HR) departments. You can go the <u>old-fashioned route</u> of looking through advertisements in newspapers or in university careers offices, but you can also use the power of the Internet and search numerous websites.

[6] Sometimes you will not be able to find your perfect job right out of school. Large companies often hire people who worked for them first as temporary workers. Get your résumé or CV to a scientist-focused temp agency and see if you can <u>land your first assignment</u>.

[7] Perhaps the most powerful way to get a job in the cosmetic industry is to get involved with social networking sites. But EVERYONE should create a LinkedIn page. This is where professionals hang out and post their career information. But it is even better because you can <u>strike up relationships</u> with people all over the industry of which you want to become part. Another great resource is Facebook. People often list the names of the companies they work for and the jobs they do.

Adapted from http://chemistscorner.com

3 Where could you put the advice and suggestion modal verbs on this diagram?

could, should,   must

WEAKER ◄——————————► STRONGER

4 For past time, the modal verb is followed by *have* + past participle. What is the form for present/future time?

5 a Rewrite the two examples in D1 in the past.

  b Find four more examples in the text and rewrite them in the past.

6 Choose four advice/suggestion modal verbs and use them in sentences of your own.

E Writing: Note-making and summary writing

1 Work on your own and look at the text again. For each of the seven paragraphs, write two notes.

Example: *Paragraph 1: Get your science degree*

- ▪ *most common degrees are in science areas*

- ▪ *some students get degree in Physics*

2 Work with your partner and compare your answers. Did you both include the same information from the text? For example, in paragraph 1 you could also have written something about starting your own company or joining a family business. Which information in the text do you and your partner think is the most important? Why?

3 Imagine that you are a journalist. You are going to write a short article about becoming a cosmetic scientist. Complete the notes below, using a few words in each gap. Refer back to the article and the notes you made for Activity E1.

---

1 Get your science degree
Science degree essential, usually four–year from **(a)** …
Many science degrees are common, but **(b)** … also acceptable

2 Maybe get an advanced degree
Large companies prefer students with **(c)** … or …
But on–the–job training often **(d)** … than qualifications

3 Research cosmetic companies
Plenty of **(e)** … opportunities and number is **(f)** …
Industry continues to grow despite economic **(g)** …

4 Pick a job
(h) … does not usually tell you what job you will get
Plenty of different jobs available, so best to choose one which **(i)** …

5 Get a job
Important to start preparing résumé or CV **(j)** … and then send it to **(k)** …
Jobs advertised in **(l)** … as well as **(m)** …

6 A temporary assignment
Having a **(n)** … can help find something more permanent in the future
Use a **(o)** … to help you get your first assignment

7 Network with other cosmetic chemists
Create your own social network pages because professionals post **(p)** …
Also best place to begin **(q)** … with other people in the industry

---

TOP TIP

When you are asked to make notes about a text, you will generally be given a heading or headings to guide you. All the marks are usually given for the **content** (**what** you write). Usually there are no marks awarded for your language (**how** you write). You should try to keep your notes brief, but still make sure you have included all the relevant information.

4 You are going to use your notes from E3 to write about becoming a cosmetic scientist. Before you write anything, look at the linking words and phrases in the table. Then decide in which of the three categories the words and phrases in the box belong.

Adding information	Sequencing	Contrasting
In addition (to) … And	Firstly, Secondly, etc	But, However

Also	Although / even though	Apart from	As well as
Besides	Despite the fact that	Finally	Furthermore
In spite of Lastly	Moreover	Nevertheless	Whereas

5 Work with your partner and think of **at least one** more word or phrase to add to each category.

6 Look at how the notes for Paragraph 1 could be joined together:

Firstly, the most important thing is to get your science degree, and this is usually a four-year course from a college or university. There are many common degrees, such as Chemistry, Chemical Engineering, Biology and Microbiology. However, Physics is also acceptable in the cosmetics industry.

Work with your partner. **Student A** look at paragraphs 2–4 and **Student B** look at paragraphs 5–7. Working alone, combine your notes from the previous exercises, using linking words and phrases where appropriate. Write about 50 words.

7 Combine your writing with your partner's to make one longer paragraph. Write about 100 words in total.

LANGUAGE TIP
Linking words are words (and phrases) that help you to connect your ideas together in such a way that the reader (or listener) can better understand you. Commonly we use linkers for: sequencing *(lastly)*, contrast *(in spite of)*, summarising *(in conclusion)*, showing additional information *(furthermore)*, giving a reason *(because of)* or a result *(consequently)*, and so on.

Complete the exercise in your **Workbook**.

F 🔊💬 Listening and speaking

1 You are going to listen to a careers adviser being interviewed about jobs with NASA – the National Aeronautics and Space Administration in the USA. Before you listen, work with your partner and answer these two questions.

 a What is NASA? What does it do? What is it famous for? If you do not know, how can you find out?

 b Decide what type of careers might be available at NASA. Do you think any cosmetic scientists are employed by NASA? Why/not? Try to give reasons.

2 Here are some of the interviewer's questions from the interview. Work with your partner and try to guess what the answers might be.

 a So, what does a young woman need to do in order to work for NASA?

 b But what is an engineer? What does an engineer, actually do?

 c Is there just one type of engineer, then?

 d So is an engineer a scientist?

 e I've also heard about technicians. What do they do? Is it different from engineers and scientists?

 f Most of our listeners are still at school, studying hard, so what should their focus be, if these types of careers are interesting to them?

3 CD1, Track 16 Listen to the interview and answer these two questions:

   a How many careers are discussed in detail?

   b What does the interviewer say one of his listeners might be doing in the future?

4 CD1, Track 16 Listen again and make written notes about questions a–f in Activity F2.

5 Work with a partner. Interview each other, using the questions from Activity F2 and your notes from Activity F4.

6 Read the audioscript in Appendix 3 and check the answers you gave in response to the questions.

REFLECTION

How well do you think you can do each of these things now?

Give yourself a score from 1: Still need a lot of practice to 5: Feeling very confident about this

In this unit you:	1	2	3	4	5
watched a video of students talking about jobs, and discussed what they said					
read and answered questions about the job of a cosmetic scientist					
practised making notes and writing a paragraph					
listened to a careers adviser talking about jobs with NASA and answered questions					
practised writing a summary					

Now set yourself a **personal goal** based on your scores for Unit 7.

Exam focus

Reading, Exercise 4, summary writing, Exercise 3, note-making

1 Read the article about female athletic trainers. Write a summary of how their role in athletic training has changed over the years. Your summary should be about 80 words long. You should use your own words as far as possible.

[Total: Core 12]

Females in athletic training

Athletic trainers play a vital role in sports at all levels, from youth athletics to the professionals, and more and more of them nowadays are women. From giving first aid to implementing programmes for injuries, athletic trainers are health care professionals who are essential to any team or individual athlete. But despite making up nearly half of all certified athletic trainers, female trainers still face challenges.

(a) …

Athletic trainers are not the same as personal fitness trainers. They do not develop training programmes or prescribe exercises. A Certified Athletic Trainer, or CAT, is a health-care provider trained to prevent, diagnose, treat and rehabilitate injuries. CATs work with physicians and other health-care professionals, and can be found in a variety of work situations.

(b) …

The National Athletic Trainers' Association (NATA) is a professional association for athletic trainers with more than 30 000 members, nearly half of whom are women. For its first two decades NATA was primarily a boys' club, until the first female trainer passed her board certification examination in 1972. Four years later, in 1976, the first female trainer joined the US Olympic medical staff. In the 1990s, NATA developed a task force to address the subject of professional female trainers. In 2000, NATA elected its first female president. In recent years, more women have been coming

into the profession than men. In 2005, 47.6% of National Athletic Trainers' Association members were women, but in 2011 that number had climbed to 50.9%. Student memberships illustrate the trend even more, with 60% of those held by women.

(c) …

Despite the increased number of female CATs, today they are still under-represented in professional sports. In 2002, the NFL (National Football League) hired a woman as an assistant athletic trainer and the NBA (National Basketball Association) employs two female assistant athletic trainers. Female trainers have had better luck in women's pro sports and, in 2011, the Los Angeles Dodgers named veteran trainer, Sue Falsone, as the first female head athletic trainer to a professional men's sports team.

Adapted from www.livestrong.com

2 a You have been asked by your teacher to prepare a talk about Indian camels and their breeders. Make notes in order to prepare your talk. Make your notes under each heading.

Official figures for the Pushkar fair

... [1]

... [1]

... [Extended only] [1]

Raikas' relationship with their camels

... [1]

... [1]

... [Extended only] [1]

Impact of modernisation on camel trading

... [1]

... [1]

... [1]

[Total: 7 Core, 9 Extended]

b Re-read the article about camel breeders in India. Write a summary of the decrease in popularity of the camel fair, and the reasons for it. Your summary should be about 80 words long [Core] or 100 words long [Extended]. You should use your own words as far as possible. You will receive up to 6/8 marks for the content of your summary and up to 6/8 marks for the style and accuracy of your language.

[Total: 12 Core, 16 Extended]

Indian camel breeders lament⋆ Pushkar fair's⋆⋆ downfall

As dusk falls on the desert town of Pushkar in northern India, turbaned herdsmen huddle around fires and lament the downfall of one of the world's largest livestock fairs. Like many traders, Jojawa has trekked hundreds of kilometres to reach the decades-old cattle and camel fair, a journey that took him seven days from his village in the desert state of Rajasthan. But the way things are going, he expects to go home with his pockets half-empty and some of the 25 camels that he hoped to sell still in tow.

'This year there are fewer buyers and fewer camels,' says Jojawa, who has been coming to the annual fair for 35 years. 'If it goes on like this, in another four or five years, I'll be finished,' adds Jojawa, who uses just one name.

Official figures for the five-day fair, which has long been a major tourist attraction, show that the number of camels on sale has fallen to less than 5,000, a sharp drop from the 8,000 recorded in 2011, and a fraction of those from previous decades. The Pushkar fair is the only time of year when camel breeders earn a cash income. Camels are normally sold for around 15 000 rupees, or $230 each, and used on farms or as transport.

But as sales decline, breeding is becoming a less viable way to earn a living and, as a result, the traditional values that underpin the market are rapidly disappearing. Rajasthan's traditional Raika farmers are among the most prominent camel herders and they believe it is their religious responsibility to rear these animals. They consider their relationship with camels as sacred and they are unique among camel herders worldwide for not slaughtering the camels they rear. But that is changing.

In the past ten to 15 years, the taboo against the slaughter of camels has changed and now in Pushkar most camels are actually sold for meat. Traditionally, it was also taboo to sell female camels, considered the life-blood of a herd, but these days they are sold for slaughter. But once the females are sold, many camel breeders go out of business.

As modernisation has swept across India, thanks to the economic boom, the country's camel population has dropped by 50% over the last three decades. In 1982, there were more than 1 million camels nationwide, but numbers dropped to just over 500 000 by 2007. Of

these, more than 80% live in Rajasthan, where camels have traditionally been used as work animals on farms or as transport for carrying goods.

But as vehicles and agricultural machinery become ever more accessible and affordable, sons from breeding families see no value in camels. Like tens of thousands of other young Indians, many are seeking a more lucrative income away from the land in India's cities. The herders who are left are mostly from older generations, men like Jojawa for whom life has changed little and is only becoming harder. Most complain about the reduction in grazing areas for feeding their stock, as development spreads to common land and national parks and forests become out of bounds. Another problem is that breeding becomes riskier because a poorer diet makes camels more susceptible to disease and illness.

A government-backed programme in the city of Bikaner in northern Rajasthan is trying to create stronger animals through better nutrition, but herdsmen say that only herders in the large, arid region of the Thar desert benefit. There has been no impact on communities further south. Herders want the government to provide financial help, so that they can invest in camel milk dairies, an industry that has already taken off in the Middle East. It is estimated that the global market for camel milk is worth $10 billion, but India's share is currently just 0.1%.

Adapted from 'Indian camel breeders lament Pushkar fair's downfall', in *Arab News*.

* *feel very sad about something*
** *an outdoor event, with animals or entertainment, or both*

Learning objectives

In this unit you will:

- watch a video of students talking about communication, and discuss what they say
- look at some differences between British and American words, and talk about ways to remember vocabulary
- read a text about why spelling is important
- read about the decrease in letter writing and answer questions
- practise formal writing - Optional

A 😃 Watch, listen and talk

1 Watch and listen to some IGCSE students talking about **communication**.

   a What different ways of communicating do the students mention? Make a note of **three**.

   b Listen for **three** different ways of communicating that the students use with their families and friends.

   c How important do the students think spelling is?

2 Talk to your partner(s) about how important **you** think correct spelling is when you communicate.

B 🔤 Speaking and vocabulary

1 Some British English (BrE) and American English (AmE) words differ in their spelling, such as *colour* (BrE) and *color* (AmE). With a partner, look at the pictures and decide what they show. The first letter of each word has been given to help you. Then write a list of the two different versions: British English and American English. Add any other words that you know are different.

Picture	BrE spelling	AmE spelling
1	colour	color

2 Decide if the following words are British English or American English spelling versions. Try to give a reason.

> fiber   favour   labor   paralyze   fueled   defense   dialogue

Example: *fiber = AmE because AmE spelling often uses -<u>er</u> instead of BrE -<u>re</u>*

LANGUAGE TIP

You may come across differences in British and American English, other than spelling. For example, sometimes BrE uses one word for something, while AmE uses a completely different word.

Examples: *pavement (BrE) = sidewalk (AmE)*
underground (BrE) = subway (AmE)
biscuit (BrE) = cookie (AmE)
lift (BrE) = elevator (AmE)

What others do you know?

It does not matter which spelling system you use, but you must always be consistent. In other words, you cannot write *colour* and then change to *color* later on.

Complete the exercises in your **Workbook**.

3 Work with your partner and correct the spelling mistakes in the following list of words. All the words appear correctly in the text you are going to read in Section C. You can check your answers later.

a becuse   **d** reasonible   **g** univercity   **i** suprising
b compleating   **e** literucy   **h** acheve   **j** extreemly
c desent   **f** especialy

4 On your own, make notes in answer to these questions.

a Which words do you find difficult to spell?
b What method might help you spell these words correctly?
c How do you keep a record of vocabulary items?

TOP TIP

Mnemonic devices are a very effective way to help you remember how to spell words (and they can also be used to help you remember other things, such as the number of days in each month of the year, or the names of the different planets). Look at these three examples:

1 There's **a rat** in *sepa**rat**e*

2 **F**ather **a**nd **m**other **I** **l**ove **y**ou = *family*

3

5 In small groups, discuss your answers to Activity B4.

6 In your group, decide which of the following strategies are the best for recording and learning vocabulary. Give reasons.

   a Writing words in alphabetical order.

   b Putting words into thematic groups.

   c Recording words in a sentence.

   d Writing the translation of words.

   e Writing the part of speech and how to pronounce the words.

   f Having a separate book for recording vocabulary.

   g Using mnemonic devices.

C 🔖 🔤 Reading and vocabulary

Reading 1

1 Look at the words (a–h) which have been removed from the reading text. Work with a partner and match each one with an appropriate alternative word or phrase (1–8).

a	concern	**1**	basic requirement
b	impression	**2**	effect or influence
c	crucial	**3**	match or be very similar
d	effective	**4**	most
e	correspond	**5**	short forms of words or phrases
f	abbreviations	**6**	useful or something which works
g	fundamental	**7**	very important
h	majority	**8**	worry or anxiety about something important

2 The five paragraphs in the text are in the wrong order. With a partner, work out the correct order. Do not worry about the gaps a–h at the moment. Use the following tips to help you with the order.

   a To find **the first paragraph**, look carefully at the title of the article.

   b Look at the final words in the first paragraph, and find the opposite in the first sentence of **the second paragraph**.

   c To find the third paragraph, look at the end of the second paragraph, which mentions the end of a person's school life.

   d Use the idea of poor spelling to find the link to **the next paragraph**.

   e So the final paragraph must be … ?

3 How did you decide on the correct order for the paragraphs? What clues did you find in the text, apart from the ones given in Activity C2?

4 Look at each gap (a–h) in the text more carefully. What type of word or phrase is required to complete each one? For example, does the gap need an adjective or a noun? Use the eight words from Activity C1 to fill in the gaps. Check your answers with a partner.

5 Find the words that you corrected in Activity B3 in the text. Were your corrections right?

Why is learning to spell important?

[1] Despite this, every parent and every schoolteacher knows that being able to spell properly is a **(a)** … skill that young people must grasp as soon as they enter education, although if they can start learning before they enter the classroom, so much the better. But, as every parent and teacher also knows, learning spelling can be difficult for children in the early stages. The problem with English spelling is that the letters do not **(b)** … to speech sounds.

[2] Good spelling skills are an important part of being able to read and write to a reasonable standard. Reading, writing and spelling are important in the first place because they all help to develop an **(c)** … of literacy. Without this, school coursework would not be completed satisfactorily and end-of-year exams would be failed. Obtaining good grades in exams, especially towards the end of a person's school life is **(d)** … if they are looking to go on to college or university before entering the employment market.

[3] Learning to spell is important because being able to spell correctly adds so much to your skills and abilities, especially when it comes to finding a college or university place, or entering the job market for the first time. Writing a decent CV and completing the application correctly is vital in the effort to make **(e)** … . It was reported recently that employers rejected the **(f)** … of 1,000 job applications submitted by graduates simply because of bad spelling.

[4] Could our use of technology be the reason for bad spelling? Although not proven, there have been concerns in recent years that the rise of text messaging and 'chatspeak' used in social media could be leading to a decrease in literacy, as **(g)** … become commonly used by children. Opinions differ on this possibility. Some research suggests that this may not necessarily be true, but other studies have indicated that in some cases it is **(h)** … .

[5] But the end of school education may be too late. Obviously, the prime time for learning is during childhood and most people achieve a reasonable level of spelling to help their overall literacy. But it is perhaps surprising that many adults have extremely poor spelling and struggle with common words such as *embarrass*, *occasion* and *restaurant*.

Adapted from www.vocabulary.co.il

81

6 Find words or phrases in the text that have a similar meaning to the following:

   a understand [paragraph 1]

   b realistic [2]

   c above average [3]

   d how someone remembers someone else [3]

   e confirmed [4]

   f complete [5]

   g have a problem with [5]

Reading 2

1 You are going to read a newspaper article about postal services. Before you read it, discuss questions a–d with your partner.

   a Have you ever sent or received a handwritten letter or card? When? What was it for?

   b Do you think the number of letters written by hand and sent by mail nowadays is increasing or decreasing? Why?

   c When do you think modern postal systems started? Why do you think this?

d Do you think there is a need for post offices and postal services in the 21st century? Why/not?

2 Read the article. As you read, stop after each of the five paragraphs and answer the questions (a–j).

Sunset days for handwritten mail

1 A mail system involves the transportation of a message from sender to recipient, using a variety of transportation methods, from people to aeroplanes to bicycles to trains and trucks and even animals and of course birds! Obviously, people have been carrying messages from one person to another for thousands of years. There is some evidence of this happening in Egypt 4500 years ago, although Rome is documented as having the first postal service, around 2500 years later. Postal services as we know them today were not really established until the 19th century in Europe, and the first adhesive postage stamp was the famous Penny Black, issued in Great Britain on 1 May 1840.

---

a How many different ways of carrying mail are mentioned?

b When did modern systems of sending and receiving letters begin?

---

2 A cold but sunny morning dawns as Jane Jones begins to strap letters, small packages, and other postal items onto the sides of her motorbike before beginning her day-long journey. Every Monday, Wednesday and Thursday she delivers mail to the villages nearby, a job she has held and enjoyed for nearly three decades. Today is Thursday, and Jane, who often has to use a boat as well as her own motorbike to reach remote areas, is interested in only one particular envelope, on which the address has been written by hand. It is the only such envelope today, this week, and even this month, as almost all mail items nowadays are mostly printed, and many are small packages. Jane's job is no longer secure.

---

c For how many years has Jane been delivering the mail?

d Why do you think Jane's job is no longer safe?

---

3 Until perhaps ten years ago, Jane's motorbike would have been weighed down with hundreds of handwritten letters, greetings cards, and sometimes telegrams, but now paper communication has decreased to perhaps two to three items a month. In the digital age, mobile phones and internet-based messaging have taken over, and handwritten letters are vanishing fast. Everyone working in the postal business agrees that communication by writing is a skill of the past, and as a result, the number of post offices is rapidly decreasing. There is simply no longer a need for the personal human contact services that post offices have provided for more than a century, such as weighing a small parcel or simply buying a stamp to put on a handwritten letter. **Fashions★** change, along with technology.

e Why has the number of letters written by hand decreased so much?

f What examples are given of postal services? Name **two** of them.

> **4** The **trend★** of falling paper communication is a global phenomenon, and postal service providers worldwide are beginning to feel the heat. In 2015, worldwide letter–post traffic was estimated at approximately 350 billion items per year, a 3.5% drop domestically and just over 7% internationally from the previous year. However, at the same time, the weight of these items increased by about 30% (and consequently revenue also rose), due to the rapid rise in popularity of online shopping and the need to send and receive purchased items via a postal service. Furthermore, the number of people employed within the postal service all over the world held steady at around five million.

g Which service decreased the most: letters sent abroad or letters sent within a country?

h Why has buying things over the internet resulted in greater financial income for postal service providers?

> **5** Transforming postal services has been easier in some countries than in others, mainly due to competition between service providers, as well as sensible financial investments, and people like Jane may still be needed, even if the job is no longer about delivering handwritten letters to remote villages. Innovation, introducing new services, and embracing technology rather than fighting it, are the ways forward for the traditional postal system. Competition should be seen positively, as it injects new energy into the market, and provides Jane's customers not only with a much wider and more efficient list of services, but also with a choice.
>
> © Peter Lucantoni

83

i Why has changing postal services happened with less difficulty in different countries? Give **two** reasons.

j What do customers receive as a result of competition between service providers?

*See the **WORD TIP**.

3 In pairs, find out what the following words and phrases mean. **Student A** look at a-h. **Student B** look at words i-p. Then discuss with each other what you have found out. Paragraph numbers will help you to find the words and phrases in the text.

Student A	Student B
a adhesive postage stamp [paragraph 1]	**i** phenomenon [4]
b strap [2]	**j** feel the heat [4]
c remote areas [2]	**k** revenue [4]
d secure [2]	**l** held steady [4]
e weighed down [3]	**m** financial investments [5]
f vanishing [3]	**n** innovation [5]
g century [3]	**o** embracing technology [5]
h trend [4]	**p** injects [5]

WORD TIP

fashion (noun): **1 POPULAR STYLE**: a style that is popular at a particular time; **2 MANNER**: a way of doing things

trend (noun): a general development or change in a situation or in the way that people are behaving

Complete the exercise in your **Workbook**.

4 The newspaper article you have just read contains several numbers written as either a word or in figures. For each number, complete the gaps in the table below.

Text numbers	Figure numbers
thousands	*1 000s*
	4,500
	19th
two to three	
	350
	3.5%
five million	

D 🔍 Language focus: passive voice

1 The passive voice is used to show interest in the person or object that experiences or receives an action, rather than the person or object that performs the action. In other words, the most important thing or person becomes the subject of the sentence. Look at these examples from the texts you have read in this unit.

Example: *school coursework would not be completed*

Rome is documented

How is the passive voice formed?

2 Here are some more examples from the texts, but the verb *to be* and the main verb are in the infinitive. Use the tense in brackets and the past participle of the underlined main verb to complete the sentences (a–f).

a It (*be* – past) report recently …

b Although it (*not be* – present) prove

c Postal services as we know them today (*not be* – past) really establish

d the address (*be* – present perfect) write by hand

e all mail items nowadays (*be* – present) mostly print

f worldwide letter-post traffic (*be* – past) estimate

3 Look back at the texts to check your answers.

4 It is possible to use a modal verb in the passive. Look at the example from the first text.

Example: *would not be completed*

Find **three** more examples in the second text (Sunset days for handwritten mail).

E 📝 Writing: formal letters - Optional

1 What should the layout of a formal letter or email look like? What should be included in the introduction and the conclusion? How should the body of the letter deal with the subject? Discuss your ideas with a partner and try to agree on the best layout.

2 How do you begin a formal letter in English? What can you write after *Dear*? Look back at Activity E5 in Unit 3. Would any of the endings be suitable for a formal letter?

3 Look at this email sent to an online newspaper. Does it follow the layout you agreed on in Activity E1?

> **TOP TIP**
>
> A formal letter may give or ask for information, or it may simply state an opinion about something. Remember – a formal letter is the type you write to someone you have never met before, or to someone with whom you have no personal relationship.

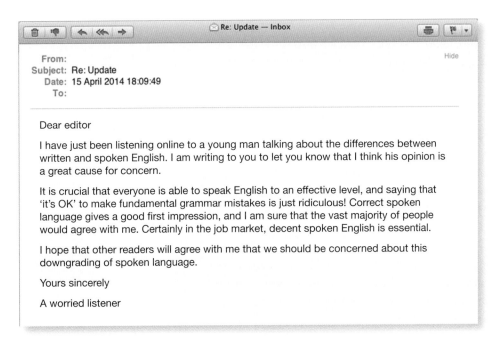

From:
Subject: Re: Update
Date: 15 April 2014 18:09:49
To:

Hide

Dear editor

I have just been listening online to a young man talking about the differences between written and spoken English. I am writing to you to let you know that I think his opinion is a great cause for concern.

It is crucial that everyone is able to speak English to an effective level, and saying that 'it's OK' to make fundamental grammar mistakes is just ridiculous! Correct spoken language gives a good first impression, and I am sure that the vast majority of people would agree with me. Certainly in the job market, decent spoken English is essential.

I hope that other readers will agree with me that we should be concerned about this downgrading of spoken language.

Yours sincerely

A worried listener

4 What information is given in the email? Match parts of the e-mail with the information a–f.

a closing   **c** giving opinion   **e** introduction

b conclusion   **d** reason for writing   **f** opening

5 Could any paragraphs could be joined together? Why/not?

6 Which words and phrases in the email show that the style is formal?

Example: *I am writing to inform you of my opinion about …*

7 Think of a different way to write each word or phrase from Activity E6.

Examples: *I am writing to tell you what I think about … / I am writing to give you my thoughts on …*

8 Look at this exam-style exercise. What exactly do you have to do? Discuss the question with a partner, but do **not** write anything yet.

You have seen a television documentary about language and the importance of spelling. Your teacher has suggested you write a report giving your opinion. In your report describe what you learned from the documentary and explain your own opinion, giving reasons.

Here are some comments from two friends:

'Correct spelling shows that you care about what you write'

'English spelling is so difficult. We need help to avoid making mistakes'

Write the report

The comments above may give you some ideas and you should try to use some ideas of your own.

Your report should be 100–150 words long [Core] or 150–200 words long [Extended]

You will receive up to 6/8 marks for the content of your report and up to 6/8 marks for the style and accuracy of your language.

TOP TIP

In a letter-writing task, you do not need to supply addresses or a date, unless you are specifically asked to. However, you usually need to write the name of the person you are writing to – there will often be a space provided for this.

9 Look at this letter written by a student in response to the question in Activity E8. The writer of this letter has made some language mistakes. There are also some mistakes in the layout and the way in which the student has answered the question. With a partner, identify as many mistakes as you can. Do **not** rewrite the letter.

Dear ESS

January 29

I have seen your advertisement today in my local newspaper magazine and want to get more information from you about the cources you offer people who want to improve their speling. I would like to be able to throw away your dictionary and not worry any more about making speing mistakes. I would like to help your friends and work colleagues with their speling.

I am a student who I am studyng english in college and my speling is not very good so I want to improve and write better english. I need to write compositions in english and I do not have time to use a dictionary all the time at home and at school. Please will you send me some informations about your cources, the prizes and lenth and the materials you will send me and tell me when I can start a cource with ESS. I am look forward to hear from you a.s.a.p.

Best wishes
Bruno

---

10 Look at the following answer to the question in Activity E8. In what ways is it an improvement on the letter in Activity E9? Discuss the letter with a partner. You do not need to write anything.

29th January

Dear Sir or Madam,

I have just seen your advertisement in today's 'Daily Courier' newspaper and I would be grateful if you could send me further information and details about your courses for people who want to improve their spelling and their friends' spelling.

I am a 16-year-old student studying English, Geography and History at a college in Botswana. I am currently in my first year at college. My teachers tell me that I need to improve my spelling to make my writing better. Also, I find that using a dictionary at home and at college takes up a lot of very valuable time, and often it is difficult to find the word that I want. Furthermore, as I sometimes study with my classmates, I would also be able to help them when they have problems with their spelling.

I think one of your courses might be of use to me, and I would therefore appreciate it if you could send me some information about your courses, including full details of your prices, the length of the courses and the study materials available.

I look forward to hearing from you in the very near future.

Yours faithfully,
M. Gaobakwe

> **TOP TIP**
> A formal letter will usually contain at least two paragraphs, and will use formal language and no abbreviations. If the letter begins with *Dear Madam* or *Dear Sir*, it should end with *Yours faithfully*. If the letter begins with somebody's name, for example *Dear Mrs Sanchez*, it should end with *Yours sincerely*.

11 Write your own answer to the question in E8. Use the information in this section to help you.

F  Reading and writing

1 Read the text *Are you a poor talker?* and answer the following questions.

   a In what situations can the new technique improve your conversation skills?

   b Where can you get more details about the method for improving your speaking and writing skills?

   c In what two ways does the text say that you can influence others?

   d In what ways is conversation like any other art?

   e Why have the publishers printed details of the training methods in a book?

   f How can you obtain more information? Give three ways.

2 Using the text *Are you a poor talker?*, give another meaning for each of the following phrases. Use different reference sources to help you. Then use each one in a sentence of your choice that makes its meaning clear.

   a pay dividends

   b work like magic

   c radiate enthusiasm

   d make a good impression.

Are you a poor talker?

A simple technique for acquiring a swift mastery of everyday conversation and writing has been announced. It can pay you real dividends in both social and professional advancement. It works like magic to give you added poise, self-confidence and greater popularity. The details of this method are described in a fascinating book, *Adventures in Speaking and Writing*, sent free on request.

Many people do not realise how much they could influence others simply by what they say and how they say it. Those who realise this, radiate enthusiasm and hold the attention of their listeners with bright, sparkling conversation that attracts friends and opportunities wherever they go. Whether in business, at social functions, or even in casual conversation with new acquaintances, there are ways in which you can make a good impression every time you talk.

After all, conversation has certain fundamental rules and principles – just like any other art. The good talkers, whom you admire, know these rules and apply them whenever they converse. Learn the rules and you can make your conversation brighter, more entertaining and impressive.

Then you could find yourself becoming more popular and winning new friendships in the business and social worlds.

To acquaint all readers of this newspaper with the easy-to-follow rules for developing skill in everyday conversation and writing, we, the publishers, have printed full details of this interesting self-training method in a fascinating book, *Adventures in Speaking and Writing*, sent free on request. No obligation. Just email: admin@effectivespeaking.org.sz or visit our website www.effectivespeaking.org.sz for more information.

3 Read the letter below, which was printed in a weekly newspaper. Write your own letter to the Editor in response to the writer, expressing your opinion of young people today and commenting on the views expressed by Mr Davies.

Dear Editor

I am writing to complain about the crowds of young hooligans who meet outside the 'Café New' in Market Street on a Friday night.

Last Friday, I was walking along Market Street at about 9 p.m. when I noticed a crowd of perhaps ten or twelve of these young troublemakers, standing around talking to each other, smoking and chewing gum. As I approached, they made no effort whatsoever to get out of my way, and I had to go off the pavement into the road to get past them!

Not only is this sort of behaviour totally unacceptable, but it is also an indication of the laziness that we are seeing in young people today. When I was a teenager, we used our free time constructively and we knew how to be polite to our elders and superiors. As for smoking and chewing gum, they were unheard of. These louts should find themselves a responsible job and learn some decent manners.

Yours faithfully

REFLECTION

How well do you think you can do each of these things now?

Give yourself a score from 1: Still need a lot of practice to 5: Feeling very confident about this

In this unit you:	1	2	3	4	5
watched a video of students talking about communication, and discussed what they said					
looked at some differences between British and American words, and talked about ways to remember vocabulary					
read a text about why spelling is important and discussed the format of formal letter writing					
read about the decrease in letter writing and answered questions					
practised formal writing					

Now set yourself a **personal goal** based on your scores for Unit 8.

Exam focus

Writing, Exercise 6

1 Imagine that a new cinema complex has opened in your home town. Here are some comments that have been made by local cinema-goers.

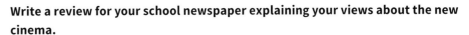

Considering the cost of the tickets, I was expecting a much better experience.

Do we really need cafés and restaurants and shops in the new cinema, as well as six different screens?

Finally, a cinema where we can relax and enjoy a variety of films in comfortable surroundings.

The new cinema really provides so much more than just films – it's a great place to go for an enjoyable afternoon or evening.

Write a review for your school newspaper explaining your views about the new cinema.

The comments above may give you some ideas and you should try to use some ideas of your own.

Your review should be 100–150 words long (Core).

You will receive up to 6 marks for the content of your review, and up to 6 marks for the language.

2 A new supermarket in your town offered all its customers a course about healthy eating and preparing healthy meals, and your school class attended. Your teacher has asked you to write a report about the course. In your report, say what you learned from the course and suggest how other students could benefit from healthy eating and preparing healthy meals.

Here are two comments from other students who attended:

> I didn't realise how easy it would be to change my eating habits and to eat more healthily.

> The course was very enjoyable, but it seems to me that preparing healthy meals is very time-consuming.

Write the report for your school webpage.

The comments above may give you some ideas, and you can also use some ideas of your own.

Your report should be between 150 and 200 words long (Extended).

You will receive up to 8 marks for the content of your report, and up to 8 marks for the language.

Learning objectives

In this unit you will:

- watch a video of students talking about interviews, and discuss what they say
- listen to a careers adviser giving advice about CVs
- write your own CV
- listen to two students being interviewed for a job and answer questions
- listen to six people talking about their interview experiences and match them to different opinions

A 😀 Watch, listen and talk

1 Watch and listen to some IGCSE students talking about **interviews**.

   a What do the students think are the best ways to prepare for a part-time job interview? Make a note of **three**.

   b What part-time jobs do they mention? Make a note of **three**.

2 Talk to your partner(s) about what you think are the best ways to prepare for an interview.

B 🔤 Speaking and vocabulary

1 Many teenagers in different parts of the world have part-time jobs, either after school or at the weekend – sometimes both. Look at the photographs of teenagers working. What do you and your partner think was happening immediately **before** and **after** the photographs were taken? Why do you think this?

2 With a partner, answer the following questions.

   a What particular skills or qualifications do you think are needed for these jobs?

   b What skills and abilities do you think the teenagers are learning?

3 In small groups, discuss what information you think a CV should contain. Make a list of possible headings – Education, for example.

4 Compare your list with the headings below. In what order do you think these headings should appear on a CV? You can check the order later.

- Education
- Hobbies
- Languages
- Qualifications
- Personal information (name, date of birth, etc.)
- Work experience
- Referees (people who will provide a reference for you).

C ◀ Listening

1 CD1, Track 17 You are going to listen to a careers adviser, Janine Mesumo, at a school in Spain being interviewed on the radio. As you listen for the first time, check the order in which the CV areas from Activity B4 appear.

2 Look at the multiple-choice questions and answers below. Read each one carefully and decide which option is correct – A, B or C. Check if your partner agrees. Do **not** write your answers yet.

   a Janine Mesumo's main role is to …

     A advise students who have completed their exams

     B give advice on writing a CV

     C deal with students' problems.

   b Why should CVs not include too much information?

     A Because students do not have time to write very much.

     B An employer only needs a brief overview.

     C Students cannot write very good CVs.

   c What information do some people forget to include in their CV?

     A Contact details.

     B Education and qualifications.

     C Name.

   d The section after 'personal details' is usually …

     A work experience

     B hobbies

     C education and qualifications.

   e Why do some students worry about their work experience?

     A Because they don't have any.

     B Because part-time work is not important.

     C Because they work for charities.

TOP TIP

With multiple-choice questions, make sure you take time to read all the options carefully before you decide which one is the best answer. Usually, at least one of the incorrect options is close to being correct, so watch out!

f What should students not do in the 'hobbies and interests' section?

   A Give details about what they like to read.

   B Give information about playing an instrument.

   C Provide a list of things that interest them.

g The final sections of a CV should include …

   A all the skills already mentioned   **C** anything not already mentioned

   B proficiency in languages.

h A referee is someone who …

   A will write positive things about you   **C** will help you to write your CV

   C will check the content of your CV.

3 🔊 **CD1, Track 17** Listen to the interview again and answer the questions in Activity C2. Were your ideas in C2 correct?

4 How much can you remember? Here are some of the things the interviewer said. How did Janine respond? Work with your partner and write notes to answer each point.

  a What areas should first-time CV writers include?

  b So what information would you say is essential?

  c But often students don't have any work experience!

  d What about hobbies and interests?

5 Read the audioscript in Appendix 3 and check your answers.

D 📝 Writing

1 Look at this CV written by Sophie Labane, an IGCSE student in Swaziland. Unfortunately, she has omitted some important information and has put some other information in the wrong order. Work with your partner and rewrite Sophie's CV. Use the advice in the previous sections to help you.

Personal details
Name: Sophie Labane
Email: labane.sophie@swazimail.com.sz

Referees
My headteacher
My Aunt Millicent

Education and qualifications
2011–today: Manzini High School
Before 2011:   Manzini Primary School

Work experience
None

Hobbies and interests
I love reading books and watching my favourite basketball team, the Bosco Steels

Other skills
I speak Swazi and English, but Swazi is my first language I am a member of the Bosco Steels fan club

2 You now know what information should go in a CV and the order in which it should appear. With a partner, talk about the information you would put in your own CV. Think about the details that you would not include too!

3 Write your own CV. Use the template below. Make sure that you include information in all the areas: try not to leave anything blank. Read your partner's CV. Has your partner included all the necessary information?

Personal details

Name

Address

Email

Telephone

Education and qualifications

(Put your current school or college first and then the one before, and so on)

(Include any qualifications or certificates with the school or college where you obtained them)

Work experience

(Include part-time or voluntary work, starting with the current or most recent)

Hobbies and interests

(Don't forget to give details)

Other skills

(IT, languages, club memberships, etc.)

Referees

(Give two – not members of your family! A teacher and a doctor?)

E 🔊 Listening

Job interview 1

1 You are going to listen to a student being interviewed for the job advertised here.

Before you listen, decide with a partner what questions the interviewer might ask the interviewee. Write down your ideas as notes.

Examples: *Tell me in what way you are interested in sports.*

How up to date with sports fashions do you think you are?

2 What information do you think the interviewee should give the interviewer? Before you listen, decide with your partner and make notes.

Examples: *I love all sports, but, in particular, I really enjoy swimming.*

I think I'm quite up to date – I read online sports fashion blogs.

VACANCY

Are you aged 16–19 with a school-leaving certificate? Want to join a well-known international sports company? Would you like to influence sports fashion over the next three years? Here's your chance!

We are looking for young, enthusiastic people with a real interest in sport and the sports clothing industry to join our Head Office.

Your role will be to decide which new fashion designs should be sold in Winning Sports shops all over the country.

Why not contact us today for more details?

Winning Sports, 246 Arena Lane, Cairo, Egypt

Tel: 246 1234, email: enquiries@winningsports.int

LANGUAGE TIP

Notice how the word *interviewer* changes to *interviewee*. When spoken, the stress on these two words is different: *inter<u>view</u>er, interview<u>ee</u>*. Other examples are *em<u>ploy</u>er* and *employ<u>ee</u>*. There are a small number of other 'person' nouns in English that end in *-ee*.

Complete the exercise in your **Workbook**.

3 🔊 CD1, Track 18 Listen to the interview. What do you notice about the interviewee's techniques in answering the questions? Can they be improved? How? Make notes.

4 🔊 CD1, Track 19 Listen again to four of the interviewer's questions, this time without the interviewee's answers. What would you say in response to the questions? Look back at your notes in Activity E2. Discuss with your partner.

Job interview 2

1 🔊 CD1, Track 20 Listen to Bambos being interviewed for the *Teen Weekly!* job.

Look at the advert, then, as you listen to Part A, note down three positive things that Bambos does or says in the interview.

Example: *He introduces himself politely and gives the interviewer some information about himself.*

TEEN WEEKLY!
New magazine for teenagers all over the world!

Stories, celebrity biographies, sports gossip, competitions, problem page and lots more!

We are looking for people who are interested in these topics to join our team of young writers.

If you think you can write for teenagers, contact us today for more details.

Teen Weekly, 912 Riddle Road, London, SW16 4RT

vacancies@teenweekly.en

2 Compare your notes with your partner's. Did you note down the same things?

3 Before you listen to Part B of the interview, decide what questions you think Bambos will ask Lan Huang. What answers do you think she gives? Work with your partner.

Example: *Question: How much time would I need for this job?*

Answer: It's part-time, only five hours a week.

4 🔊 **CD1, Track 21** Listen to the second part of the interview, then work with your partner and check your ideas in Activity E3.

5 Read the audioscript in Appendix 3 and double check your ideas.

6 Do you think Bambos got the job? Why do you think this?

F 🔊 💬 Listening and Speaking

1 A youth organisation in your home town is looking for young people to join the group. Read the online advertisement and then do the activities that follow.

Youth Club

WE need YOU to join US!

Our club is looking for 16–18-year-old volunteers to help us organise weekend activities with three different groups of young people aged 6–9, 10–13 and 14–16.

We also need a new name!

If you think you have the skills to work with young people in a fun and engaging way and can spare some time at the weekends, drop us an email or click this link NOW!

volunteers@weneedanewname.org.zx

95

2 Work in pairs.

Student A: You are going to be interviewed by Student B for the job above. Using the CV you have already written and the ideas about interview technique from this unit, prepare yourself for the interview.

Student B: You are going to interview Student A for the job above. Prepare some questions, using the ideas from this unit. Refer to Student A's CV during the interview.

3 When Student B has interviewed Student A, change roles. If possible, record or video your interviews.

4 How did you feel while you were being interviewed? Which questions were the easiest and most difficult to answer? Which was the most stressful part of the interview? Why?

5 Now tell your partner how they performed in their interview. Are you going to give them the job? Why/not?

6   CD1, Track 22 You will hear six people talking about their experiences of job interviews. For each of the Speakers, 1 to 6, choose from the list, A to G, which opinion each speaker expresses. Use each letter only once. There is one extra letter which you do not need to use.

Speaker 1	A Being the interviewer was something I did more recently.
Speaker 2	B Having a job interview is something that has never bothered me.
Speaker 3	C I don't recommend spending too much time on the internet preparing for a job interview.
Speaker 4	D I made plenty of mistakes for my first job interview.
Speaker 5	E I think interview preparation is essential, and the internet is the best source of information.
Speaker 6	F I'm happy at the moment, but this is not the only job I'll ever have.
	G They employed me, but I wasn't very happy.

WORD TIP

fault (noun) = **1 SOMEBODY'S FAULT**: if something bad that has happened is someone's fault, they are responsible for it; **2 AT FAULT**: responsible for something that has happened; **3**: something that is wrong with something or with someone's character

drawback = a problem or disadvantage

Use either *fault* or *drawback* to complete the exercise in your **Workbook**.

See CD1, Track 22, Appendix 3

G Language focus: imperative verb forms

1 The imperative form can have many functions: giving an order, an instruction or a command, giving a warning, offering some advice, or making a recommendation or suggestion, or making an offer. Sometimes the imperative verb form can sound as though the speaker is bossing someone around, even if the sentence has a polite tone.

Look at these three examples from the listening texts in this unit. Which is making an offer? A suggestion? A recommendation?

a Start with personal details: name, address, contact details.

b Hello, have a seat.

c Be prepared, and don't copy my example.

TOP TIP
Body language is just as important as spoken language! During an interview, make sure you sit in a comfortable position, but don't look too relaxed – keep your back straight and your feet on the floor! This is true for both the interviewer and the interviewee. Also, try to maintain eye contact with the person you are talking to – this not only shows that you are interested in the conversation, but also tells the other person if you have understood.

In some exams you may have to listen to different people talking, and then match the speakers to specific information or opinions. Some of the speakers may say similar things or use similar words, so listen carefully before you make your final choices.

2 For each example below, say what its function is. Use the information in G1 to help you.

   a Don't touch that! It's boiling hot!

   b Explain why these things interest you.

   c Go onto our website and click the link.

   d Do visit us next time you're in town.

   e Sit down and stop talking!

   f Pass me that book, please.

   g Don't turn right, turn left.

   h Drink plenty of water before you fly.

   i Take as many as you want.

3 Look at the audioscript interview between Pablo and Janine in Appendix 3. Find more examples of the imperative verb form.

4 What would you say in the following situations? Try to use an imperative form.

   a You are watching a film and someone is talking loudly on their phone.

   b Your friend has a bad headache.

   c Your cousin likes the cake you have baked.

   d A family member has just come to visit you.

   e You need to explain to someone how to find your school.

   f Your friend is asking you what to do about a problem he has.

REFLECTION

How well do you think you can do each of these things now?

Give yourself a score from 1: Still need a lot of practice to 5: Feeling very confident about this

In this unit you:	1	2	3	4	5
watched a video of students talking about interviews, and discussed what they said					
listened to a careers adviser giving advice about CVs					
wrote your own CV					
listened to two students being interviewed for a job and answered questions					
listened to six people talking about their interview experiences and matched them to different opinions					

Now set yourself a **personal goal** based on your scores for Unit 9.

Exam focus

Listening, Exercise 4, multiple-choice questions

🔊 **CD1, Track 23** You will hear Joshua, a student, asking Mrs Karima, a head teacher, for advice about finding his first job as part of a school radio programme. Listen to their conversation and look at the questions. For each question, choose the correct answer A, B or C.

You will hear the talk twice.

a Why is finding a first job difficult for teenagers?

    A They don't have the right qualities.

    B They lack the necessary experience.

    C They have too much school work.

b What does Mrs K say must be a priority?

    A Having summer holidays.

    B Studying at school.

    C Getting job experience.

c Getting a summer job is important because …

    A it provides future opportunities

    B it pays good money

    C it includes training.

d What does Mrs K say teenagers should do before their first job interview?

    A Keep in touch with previous employers.

    B Become a member of a club.

    C Write a résumé or CV.

e Which personal skills might help a teenager to get a job?

    A The ability to make money.

    B Having knowledge of computers.

    C Having many strengths.

f Why is it a good idea to sell yourself in an interview?

    A To show you are good with people.

    B It helps you to develop yourself.

    C You have more chance of getting the job.

g How many hours a week can an older teenager work?

    A 16

    B 18

    C 70

h What is the best advice Mrs K has for teenagers?

    A Leave a job on friendly terms.

    B Remember to have a good work history.

    C Understand the requirements of the job.

[Total: 8]

Learning objectives

In this unit you will:

- watch a video of students talking about education, and discuss what they say
- read and talk about the most effective ways to study
- learn and tell each other about the SQ3R study method
- talk about and practise the role-play part of the IGCSE speaking test
- watch and listen to students taking part in a speaking role-play, and assess their performance

A ☺ Watch, listen and talk

1 Watch and listen to some IGCSE students talking about **education**.

   a What do the students think are the best ways to study? Make a note of **three**.

   b In what ways do the students think that studying for an important examination is different from doing homework?

2 Talk to your partner(s) about what **you** think are the best ways to study.

B 🔤 Speaking and vocabulary

1 Look at the pictures which show some students studying in different ways. Name **at least two** things that you can see in each picture.

2 What picture does **not** show you a way to help you study more effectively? What is wrong with it?

3 Which of the following (a–g) do you think could help you to study more effectively? Which do you think would **not** be effective? Why?

   a Break up study time into smaller chunks.

   b Quiz yourself.

   c Study less.

   d Find a dedicated study area.

   e Eat fish, nuts and olive oil.

   f Teach others.

   g Block your social media.

C   Reading and speaking

1 You are going to read an internet article called 'Study Less, Study Smart'. Look quickly at the text and (a) find out which of the study methods in the previous section are mentioned; (b) make a note of **two** further study methods.

Study Less, Study Smart

1 When you're learning new material, it can be completely overwhelming when you consider how much time you need to truly understand it all. The Study Less, Study Smart studying technique can help you stay focused and take on more information with shorter study sessions. Here are some of the best tips.

2 **Study in chunked sessions:** Your ability to retain new information diminishes after about 25-30 minutes, so break it up into multiple, smaller sessions. Reward yourself with fun activities during your breaks.

3 **Have a dedicated study area:** Don't study where you do *anything* else. Don't study in your bed, where you play games (even if it's your computer), or in front of the TV.

4 **Know the difference between recognition and recollection:** Recognition requires a trigger for you to remember something and you may not get that on a test. Study actively with a focus on recollection. Quiz yourself and don't just glance over highlighted notes.

5 **Take good notes:** Find a note–taking method that works for you and expand on them *after* your class lecture to increase retention and understanding.

6 **Be ready to teach what you've learnt:** If you can teach it to someone else you have a solid grasp of the material.

7 **Read textbooks effectively:** Use the SQ3R method (**S**urvey, **Q**uestion, **R**ead, **R**ecite, **R**eview) to actively retain information. Just reading it is not enough.

8 Lastly, divide everything you learn into two categories: facts and concepts. Facts are things that can fall out of your brain, and you may need to come up with a mnemonic device in order to study them. Concepts are the glue that holds the entire big picture together, making them the most important part to study. Concepts are why you're studying something to begin with and, once you learn them, they stick with you. Stop wasting hours studying at only a third of the pace you could be going, and study smart.

From: http://lifehacker.com

2 Decide if the following information is true or false, according to the text. Give reasons.
   a A great deal of time is required to effectively remember large amounts of new information.
   b After about half an hour, we are unable to retain new material.
   c It's a good idea to study in a familiar place, such as in bed or in front of the TV.
   d Tests never supply triggers for recognition.
   e Facts can be easily forgotten.

3 How do you think the SQ3R method (**S**urvey, **Q**uestion, **R**ead, **R**ecite, **R**eview) actually works in practice? What happens during each of the five stages? Discuss with your partner.

4 Read the introductory paragraph below about the SQ3R method. What specific advice does it give you about reading?

SQ3R is a reading comprehension method named for its five steps: **S**urvey, **Q**uestion, **R**ead, **R**ecite and **R**eview. If you follow the steps below, you will learn how to obtain as much information as possible from the text requirements for any class. Remember that the information you gain from reading is important. When you just 'do it' without learning something, you're wasting an enormous amount of your time. Train your mind to learn while reading with SQ3R.

Adapted from: www.ucc.vt.edu

5 Work in groups of four: **A**, **B**, **C** and **D**. Do **one** of **four** things with the text in C4. Your teacher will help you.
   A Think of a question to clarify something you have read.
   B Think of a comprehension question to ask your partners.
   C Summarise the information in the paragraph.
   D Predict what information you will read about in the next section.
   Share with the others in your group.

6 Read the next section. As you read, think about what the underlined words mean. Choose a word or phrase in the box to match each underlined word.

| concentrate   get ready   ignore   support   understand   visuals |

Survey – gather the information necessary to focus and formulate goals

- Read the title and help your mind <u>prepare</u> to receive the information.

- Read the introduction and/or summary in order to help you understand how each chapter fits the author's purposes, and to <u>focus on</u> the most important points.

- Notice each bold-face heading and subheading as this will help to organise your mind before you begin to read, and build a structure for the thoughts and details to come.

- Notice any <u>graphics</u> such as charts, maps, diagrams, and so on because they are there to make a point. Don't <u>overlook</u> them.

- Notice each reading <u>aid</u>, for example italics, bold-face print, chapter objective, and end-of-chapter questions. These are all included to help you sort, <u>comprehend</u> and remember.

Adapted from: www.ucc.vt.edu

7   Work in the same groups of four: **A**, **B**, **C** and **D**, but change your letter. Do **one** of **four** things with the text in C6. Your teacher will help you.

  A   Think of a question to clarify something you have read.

  B   Think of a comprehension question to ask your partners.

  C   Summarise the information in the paragraph.

  D   Predict what information you will read about in the next section.

  Share with the others in your group.

8   Work in the same groups of four: **A**, **B**, **C** and **D**, but change your letter one more time. Each one of you is going to read about one more part of the SQ3R method.

  Student A: read the paragraph on 'SQ3R method (A)' in Appendix 2

  Student B: read the paragraph on 'SQ3R method (B)' in Appendix 2

  Student C: read the paragraph on 'SQ3R method (C)' in Appendix 2

  Student D: read the paragraph on 'SQ3R method (D)' in Appendix 2

  As you read, write 2–3 notes about the content of your paragraph.

9   Now teach the others! Using only your notes (you are not allowed to refer back to your paragraph again), tell your group about what you read.

WORD TIP

engage (verb) = **1 INTEREST**: to interest someone in something and keep them thinking about it; **2 EMPLOY**: to hire someone

concentrate (verb) = to think very carefully about something you are doing and nothing else

Do the exercise in your **Workbook**.

D Language focus: 'alternative' conditional structures

1 Answer the following questions about conditionals.

   a How many conditional structures do you know? Write an example sentence for each one.

     Example: 3rd conditional – *If Abdullah <u>had exercised</u> more carefully, he <u>wouldn't have injured</u> his arm.*

   b For each sentence in D1a, say what the verb structures are.

     Example: *past perfect + would + have + past participle*

   c Now say what the function of each sentence is.

     Example: *to talk about the past, for things which are impossible now*

2 Which of **your** sentences in D1a use the same or similar structures as these sentences from the text at C1?

   a If you follow the steps below, you will learn how to obtain as much information as possible …

   b If you're learning new material at school, it can be completely overwhelming …

   c When you use this technique, reward yourself during your breaks by checking your social media …

   d When you've finished reading the entire chapter using the preceding steps, go back over the questions you created for every heading.

3 Match these structure combinations to the sentences in D2. What do you notice?

   a present continuous + modal + infinitive

   b present perfect + imperative

   c present simple + imperative

   d present simple + *will* + infinitive

4 What is the difference in meaning in the following two sentences?

   a **When** you're learning new material at school or college, it can be completely overwhelming.

   b **If** you're learning new material at school or college, it can be completely overwhelming.

5 Re-read the texts in this unit and find more conditional examples. Which structures are used?

6 Choose **six** different conditional combinations from this unit and write your own sentences.

LANGUAGE TIP

You have probably learnt that there are different types of conditional structures, but quite often conditionals do not 'follow the rules', and use tense combinations that you might not expect. Note that in some cases we can use '*when*' instead of '*if*'.

Complete the exercise in your **Workbook**.

E Speaking

1 Work in small groups. In Unit 5 you learnt about the introductory part of your speaking examination. How much do you know about the second part of your exam? Discuss your ideas and make notes about what you already know.

Examples: *(i) The interviewer chooses the topic card.*
(ii) It's not a good idea to answer a question with just 'yes' or 'no'.

2 Join another group and compare your notes. What can you learn from each other?

3 Which of your ideas could be given as information for someone who is going to take the speaking exam and which are general advice? For instance, example (ii) above is general advice, whereas example (i) is information about the exam. Make a table like the one below in your notebook and list your ideas.

Advice	Information
It's not usually a good idea to answer a question with just 'yes' or 'no'	*The interviewer chooses the topic card*

> **TOP TIP**
>
> You have about 2–3 minutes to study the topic card, but you are not allowed to make any written notes during this time.

4 CD1, Track 24 Listen to twins Fatima and Abdullah discussing their speaking exam, and then answer questions a and b.

   a Who knows more about their speaking exam?

   b Where does Fatima say that they can find plenty of exam topic cards?

5 CD1, Track 24 Listen again. As you listen, add information about the exam to your table. Compare your answers with your partner's.

6 Read the audioscript in Appendix 3 to check that you have all the information.

7 In small groups, look at this speaking exam topic card which contains ideas to help you develop the conversation in an exam situation. Each person in your group should choose one or two of the ideas to prepare alone. Remember – you are not allowed to make any written notes.

Education as a preparation for work

Nearly everyone will one day have to earn a living by getting a job.

Discuss this topic.

Use the following prompts, in the order they are given below, to develop the conversation:

- subjects you are studying that might help you in a job
- whether the study habits you have will be useful later on
- whether some of your subjects seem to have little to do with your intended career
- whether part-time work while you are still at school or college might be a good idea
- aspects of school life, apart from subjects you study, that help you when you work.

You may introduce **related** ideas of your own to expand on these prompts.

Remember, you are not allowed to make any written notes.

---

8 When you are ready, join the other members in your group and talk through your ideas. Other members of the group should ask questions. Try to keep in mind all the advice and information from the previous activities during the discussion.

Example: A: I think that the science subjects I'm studying now might help me to find a job.
B: Why do you think that?
A: Well, I've thought about working in the cosmetics industry.
B: And do you need science for that career?
A: Yes, because I want to work in quality control.

F Watch, listen and talk

1 You are going to watch an IGCSE student talking about **Education**. The student is responding to the same prompts that you have already seen in E7. To what extent does the student follow the advice in E3?

a Use preparation time to think and plan.

b Use expressions like: *In my opinion, On the other hand*, etc.

c Avoid yes/no answers.

d Use 'because' as much as possible.

e Say if the something is not understood.

2 Now watch a second student responding to the same prompts. Do you think they perform better or worse than the first student? Why?

G Listening

1 You are going to hear six people talking about going to Dubai to study. Before you listen, discuss these questions in your group:

a Would you like to study in a different country? Why/not?

b If you could choose, which country would you like to study in? Why? Which country wouldn't you like to study in? Why?

c What do you think are the three greatest challenges in studying abroad? Why?

d If you could study abroad, what would the benefits be? Try to think of at least three.

2 Which of the following words and phrases do you think you will hear when you listen? Why?

40°C air conditioning assignments cosmopolitan desert camping digital age international qualification learn Arabic weather is awful

3 CD1, Track 25 Listen to each of the six people talking about studying in Dubai. As you listen, check your answers from Activity F2.

4 CD1, Track 25 Listen again and decide if the following information is true or false, **according to the speaker**.

Speaker 1: The weather in Nigeria is hotter than in Dubai.

Speaker 2: It is difficult to decide what to do in Dubai.

Speaker 3: Social media helps to reduce the feeling of loneliness.

Speaker 4: Studying so much means there is no time left for relaxing.

Speaker 5: Making journeys to places in Europe from Dubai is full of challenges.

Speaker 6: Finding a good teacher of Arabic in Dubai is not difficult.

5 🔊 Listen again. For each of the speakers 1–6, choose the opinion they express from the list below (a–g). Use each statement only once. There is one extra statement that you do not need to use.

a At first, I was reluctant to study abroad.

b I find the heat difficult to deal with.

c Meeting new people is my aim.

d Making a choice is my biggest challenge.

e I want to see the world.

f Family members told me not to worry.

g I am very busy all the time with my studying.

6 Discuss these questions in your group:

a Did any of the speakers mention the things you discussed in Activity F1?

b Which countries (other than Dubai) were mentioned by the speakers?

c How do you now feel about studying abroad? Has anything you have heard from the six speakers made you change your mind? Why/not?

REFLECTION

How well do you think you can do each of these things now?

Give yourself a score from 1: Still need a lot of practice to 5: Feeling very confident about this

In this unit you:	1	2	3	4	5
watched a video of students talking about education, and discussed what they said					
read and talked about the most effective ways to study					
learnt and told each other about the SQ3R study method					
talked about and practised the role-play part of the IGCSE speaking test					
watched and listened to students taking part in a speaking role-play, and assessed their performance					

Now set yourself a **personal goal** based on your scores for Unit 10.

Exam focus

Speaking, Part 2, topic cards

1 Look at this exam-style topic card. Work with your partner and discuss how you might respond to each of the prompts.

2 In pairs, role-play a speaking exam. Then change roles.

Studying abroad

Nowadays, many young people spend some time studying away from their home country.

Discuss this topic.

Use the following prompts, in the order they are given below, to develop the conversation:

- what you might learn from the experience of a different country
- some of the problems you may have living and learning in a different country
- difficulties of settling down after a period away from home
- how study abroad might be an advantage in finding employment
- some of the problems of studying in a different education system.

You may introduce related ideas of your own to expand on these prompts.

Remember, you are not allowed to make any written notes.

Part 3:
People and achievements

In Part 3: People and achievements, there are five units (11 Achievements, 12 Organisations, 13 Famous people, 14 Medical care, 15 Healthy living). You will:

- watch and listen to some IGCSE students talking about each unit's topic, and speaking in the IGCSE speaking exam;
- think about and discuss what the students said;
- read a variety of texts about Olympic sports, different organisations, famous people, becoming a paramedic, healthy foods;
- listen to someone talking from a worldwide organisation, a report about a famous motorcycle rider, a discussion about Florence Nightingale, a talk about a medical charity;
- practise various exam skills: informal and formal writing, listening, speaking.

Before you start Part 3, look at the picture on these pages:

a   Where do you think the picture was taken? Why do you think this?
b   What do you like and dislike about the picture. Why?
c   What is the man in the picture doing, and what is he about to do?
d   Imagine you are messaging a friend. How would you describe the picture to them?
e   How important do you think it is to win? Why? Are you they type of person who needs to win, or can you accept failure? Under what circumstances?

Learning objectives

In this unit you will:

- watch a video of students talking about achievements and discuss what they say
- speak about world records and achievements
- read articles and answer questions on Olympic sports and the explorer Robert Scott
- improve your understanding of the past perfect tense
- write about your chosen hero

A 😀 Watch, listen and talk

1 Watch and listen to some IGCSE students talking about **achievements**.

   a What do the students think are humankind's greatest achievements? Make a note of **three**.

   b What other achievements do the students think will be accomplished in their lifetime? Make a note of **three**.

2 Talk to your partner/s about what **you** think are humankind's greatest achievements, and what achievements you think will be accomplished in your lifetime.

B 🔤 Speaking and vocabulary

1 *Guinness World Records* is a book that is famous all over the world. What is a 'record'? What are the details of any records that you know? Discuss your ideas with a partner.

2 Look at these pictures. What records do you think are being broken?

3 Discuss the following questions with your partner and be prepared to give feedback to the whole class.

   a What is the difference between *holding* a record and *breaking* a record?

   b Which record would you like to hold? Give reasons.

   c Which record would you like to break? Why?

   d Would you like to hold or break the record for one of those shown in the photos? Why/not?

4 Work with your partner. What do you think is the missing word in the **first gap** in the following records (a–h)? You need a different word in each gap. What do you think is the number missing from the **second gap** in each one?

   a The … professional videogamer, Victor de Leon, was aged … when he set the record in New York, USA.

   b The … collection of Pokémon memorabilia belongs to Lisa Courtney (UK), with … different items, which she has been collecting for over 14 years.

   c The … career as an ice-cream man is … years, achieved by Allan Ganz, in Peabody, Massachusetts, USA.

   d The … BMX time machines (spinning fast on rear bike wheel) in 1 minute is … and was achieved by Takahiro Ikeda (Japan) on the set of 'Lo Show dei Record' in Milan, Italy.

   e The official … recorded temperature is now …, which was measured on 10 July 1913 at Greenland Ranch, Death Valley, California, USA.

   f The … number of decimal places of Pi memorised is …, and was achieved by Rajveer Meena (India) at the VIT University, Vellore, India, on 21 March 2015.

   g The … cabbage weighed … and was presented at the Alaska State Fair by Scott A. Robb (USA) in Palmer, Alaska, USA, on 31 August 2012.

   h The … time to place 24 cans in a fridge is … seconds and was achieved by Silvio Sabba (Italy) in Milan, Italy, on 17 November 2014.

5 Which words in the box go with which record? Are any the same as the ones you chose? There are **three** extra words that you do not need to use.

> brightest   fastest   greatest   heaviest   highest   largest
> longest   most   purest   windiest   youngest

6 Here are four options for each of the missing numbers in the **second gap**. Which set of numbers goes with each record? Which is the correct option in each case?

> **a** 14 410   17 410   20 410   23 410
>
> **b** 3.78 seconds   4.78 secs   5.78 secs   6.78 secs
>
> **c** 36.7 °C   46.7 °C   56.7 °C   66.7 °C
>
> **d** 37   47   57   67
>
> **e** 4   7   10   13
>
> **f** 40 000   50 000   60 000   70 000
>
> **g** 43   83   123   163
>
> **h** 62.71 kg   67.71 kg   72.71 kg   77.71 kg

7 Go to the Guinness World Records website. Search for each of the records and check your answers.

8 How many questions did you get right? Which world record surprised you the most? Why?

9 Should people be encouraged to try to make and break records? Are there any dangers involved? How would you decide whether or not to allow someone to proceed?

> **LANGUAGE TIP**
>
> A *superlative adjective* shows the most or the least of something. You can recognise a superlative by the suffix *-est* (*longest*), or the word most or least (*the most fascinating book, the least attractive building*) in front of the adjective. After a superlative, *in* or *of* + a noun phrase can be used to indicate what is being compared, for example *The fastest tennis server in the world, The longest snake of all time*.
>
> Complete the exercises in your **Workbook**.

C 📖 Reading

1 Look at the five pictures. With a partner, answer the questions.

   a What sports do they show? What equipment are the players using?

   b Which do you think are, or have been in the past, Olympic sports?

   c Which one or ones would you like to participate in? Why?

   d Which sports seem the least and most challenging for you? Why?

2 Which sports from Activity C1 do you think use the following pieces of equipment? Why?

   a A rope.

   b A walking stick.

   c Roller skates.

3 With a partner, choose who is **Student A** and who is **Student B**. Then look at your words in the list below, which come from an article you are going to read about sports. Decide what the words mean and what parts of speech they are (for example *verb* or *noun*). Use different reference sources to help you. Share your ideas with your partner.

Example: *decades = periods of ten years, plural noun*

STUDENT A: braided   debut   ignoble   misleading   precise

STUDENT B: precursor   premise   resemble   sabre   slain

4 Skim the text and complete the gaps (a–j) using the words from Activity C3.

The ten strangest Olympic sports

Basketball, track and swimming have been important events at the Olympics for decades, drawing thousands of spectators. But solo synchronised swimming or live pigeon shooting? They are among the strangest events that have, at one time or another, taken place at the Games. Here are the ten oddest sports that have graced the modern Olympics.

Solo synchronised swimming
This sport features one female swimmer synchronising with herself. The sport made its (a) … in the Los Angeles Games in 1984, with US swimmer Tracie Ruiz winning the gold medal. Similar to the group event, a swimmer performs a kind of water ballet. Despite the seemingly (b) … title, organisers of the sport say the swimmer is actually in sync with the music. The solo event was discontinued after 1992.

Club swinging
Club swinging first appeared in the 1904 Olympics. The athlete stands up straight, holding clubs that (c) … bowling pins in each hand. He then twirls and whirls them around. The more complicated the routine, the more points he wins. Historians say the sport was the (d) … to rhythmic gymnastics events that use ribbons and hoops. Club swinging was only in the Olympics twice, ending in 1932.

Tug-of-war
Once a very competitive Olympic sport, tug-of-war employs teams (originally called 'clubs') that struggle and strain to pull a rope past a certain point. Great Britain actually won the most medals in this event, historians say. A country could enter more than one team, making it possible for one country to win multiple medals. Tug-of-war was an Olympic event from 1900 until 1920.

Live pigeon shooting
The 1900 Olympics in Paris had the great distinction of being the first Games where women competed. It also wore the (e) … badge for the sport of live pigeon shooting, where athletes aimed to bring down as many pigeons as possible. Nearly 300 birds were (f) … , historians say, leaving a bloody, feathery mess. The winner shot down 21 pigeons. The 1900 Games in Paris was the only time live pigeon killing took place in the Olympics.

Swimming obstacle course
As strange as this sport may seem, the obstacles swimmers had to overcome are even more unusual. In the 1900 Games in Paris, swimmers crawled over boats, swam under them and climbed a pole, all the while swimming 200 metres in the River Seine. The sport has not been repeated at subsequent Olympic Games.

Roller hockey
Roller hockey debuted at the 1992 Barcelona Games. The game follows the rules of ice hockey, but with roller skates. Argentina took the gold. The Barcelona Games was the only time that roller hockey was in the Olympics.

La canne
OK, think fencing. Now take away the (g) … and replace it with a cane. You know, the walking stick type of thing? Now you have the French martial art *la canne*, which debuted at the 1924 Olympics, but has never appeared since.

Rope climbing
This activity debuted as an Olympic sport in 1896. Just like in your gym class, the climbers were timed to see how quickly they could reach the top of a (h) … rope. In 1896, the rope was 15 metres long, but was then shortened to 8 metres. After 1932, the Olympics left rope climbing behind.

Trampolining
Despite seeming like an activity you did in your backyard when you were ten, trampolining debuted as an Olympic sport in 2000. Gymnasts take to the trampoline, somersaulting and flipping as stern-faced judges keep score. '(i) … technique and perfect body control are vital for success, with judges delivering marks for difficulty, execution and time of flight, minus penalties' Olympic officials say. Both men and women trampolinists still compete in the Olympics.

Race walking
In this sport, competitors try to outrace one another – without actually running. Even though the (j) … seems a little strange, race walking has actually been an Olympic sport since 1904. To ensure that athletes do not run, race walkers must have one foot on the ground at all times, or risk disqualification. Men compete in 20 kilometre and 50 kilometre races; women only race 20 kilometres.

Adapted from http://edition.cnn.com

113

> **LANGUAGE TIP**
>
> Look again at the final sentence of the text: *Men compete in 20 kilometre and 50 kilometre races; women only race 20 kilometres*. Notice that the word *kilometre* is singular in the first half of the sentence, but plural in the second half. This is because it is being used as an adjective before the word *races* – in other words, it is describing *races*. In the second half of the sentence, the word is being used as a noun, which is why it is plural *kilometres* after the number 20.
>
> Remember that in English, adjectives only have one form; they do not change for singular or plural, or masculine or feminine nouns (for example *Maria is a very interesting woman, James and Davic are very interesting men*).
>
> Complete the exercises in your **Workbook**.

5 Read the text carefully, then complete the table with the necessary information. You may not be able to fill in all the gaps. *Solo synchronised swimming* has been done as an example for you.

Sport	Olympic debut (where + when)	Final Olympic appearance	Equipment	Other information
Solo synchronised swimming	Los Angeles + 1984	1992	None	Swimmer performs 'water ballet'
Live pigeon shooting	...	...	...	...
...	... + 1904	...	...	...
...	...	1932		...
...	...	...	Clubs	...
...	Barcelona + 1992	...	...	...
...	...	...	Boats	...
...	... + 2000	...	...	...
La canne	...	...	...	...
...	...	...	...	Country could win multiple medals

6 For the following questions (a–j) about the text, choose one of the ten sports in the text you read previously.

Which sport...

a allowed a country to be represented by one or more teams?

b both gives and deducts points?

c could be described as a type of fencing?

d could be described as ballet in the water?

e has the same rules as another sport but different equipment?

f ended after its second appearance?

g has been an Olympic event for longer than any of the others?

h involved a race to the top of something?

i involved competitors using a gun?

j used boats, but not for transport?

7 Work alone and choose **six** of the sports from the text. Write **one** question for each sport, similar to the ones in Activity C6. Exchange your questions with your partner's and decide which sport each question refers to.

D Reading and vocabulary

1 Complete the gaps (a–e) in the paragraph about the explorer Robert Scott using words and phrases from the box.

one month   explorer   perished   return journey   South Pole

Robert Scott (1868–1912), a naval officer and an explorer, successfully reached the **(a)** …, only to find that another **(b)** … (Roald Amundsen) had got there **(c)** … before him. Unfortunately, Scott and his team of explorers all **(d)** … on their **(e)** … .

2 You are going to read part of a biography about Robert Scott, describing this tragic event. Before you read, match the following words – which appear in the text – with the definitions. There are two extra definitions that you will not need.

Words	Definitions
stumbled	the action of cutting off a person's arm or leg
blizzard	written clearly enough to be read
dissuade	severe snow storm
amputation	full of liquid or gas
rations	a place where food and other things are stored
depot	try to stop someone from doing something
legible	a situation where something cannot continue
	walked unsteadily and almost fell
	a fixed amount of food or water

3 Quickly look at the Robert Scott text and find the words from Activity D2. Do you think you found the correct definitions?

TOP TIP
Remember to look for key words in the questions to help you find the answers. Key words are the words that will help you to find the place where the answer is in the text. If you do not read the question properly, you may give the wrong answer.

Robert Scott: The return journey

By January 1912, only five remained: Scott, Wilson, Oates, Bowers and Evans. On 17 January, they reached the pole, only to find that a Norwegian party led by Roald Amundsen, had beaten them there. Inside a small tent supported by a single bamboo stick flying a Norwegian flag was a record of the five who had been the first to reach the pole. Scott and his team started the 1 500 km journey back.

The temperature fell to –43 °F. On 16th or 17th March (they lost track of the days), Oates said he couldn't go on and wanted to be left in his bag. The others refused and he struggled on. There was a blizzard blowing in the morning when Oates said, 'I am just going outside and may be some time,' and he stumbled out of the tent. Scott wrote, 'We knew that poor Oates was walking to his death, but though we tried to dissuade him, we knew it was the act of a brave man.' Oates was never to be seen again.

On 20th March, they awoke to a raging blizzard. Scott's right foot became a problem and he knew that 'these are the steps of my downfall'. Amputation was a certainty, 'but will the trouble spread? That is the serious question.' They were only 11 miles from a food camp, but the blizzard stopped them from continuing. They were out of oil and only had two days' rations. 'Have decided it shall be natural – we shall march for the depot and die in our tracks,' wrote Scott. They did not march again and on 29th March, Scott made his last entry: 'It seems a pity, but I do not think that I can write more. R. Scott. For God's sake look after our people.' On another page he scribbled, 'Send this diary to my widow'.

It was not until 12th November that the search party found Scott's tent all but buried in snow. When the tent was opened, the searchers saw three men in their sleeping bags. On the left was Wilson, his hands crossed on his chest; on the right, Bowers, wrapped in his bag. It appeared that both had died peacefully in their sleep. But Scott was lying half out of his bag with one arm stretched out – he had been the last to die.

Remarkably, Scott had been able to find the strength, despite being half-starved and three-quarters frozen, to write 12 complete, legible letters. In one of these he wrote: 'I may not have proved a great explorer, but we have done the greatest march ever made and come very near to great success.'

4 Read the text more carefully, then copy and complete the table.

Date	Event
January 1912	...

5 Read the text more carefully and write short answers to the following questions. Remember that your answers should be brief, but must include all the necessary information. Find the key word/s in each question first.

   a Why did Scott and Bowers have to make camp by themselves?

   b Why are two dates given for the day when Oates began to struggle?

   c What was the weather like when Oates left the tent?

   d Why was Scott worried about his right foot?

   e What prevented Scott and his team from reaching the food camp?

   f What did Scott mean when he wrote, 'Have decided it shall be natural'?

   g What did Scott want to happen to his written notes?

   h In what condition was the tent when the search team found it?

   i How many months after the death of the team were their bodies found?

   j Why was it remarkable that Scott wrote 12 letters?

6 Look at the phrase *and he struggled on* in the middle of paragraph 1 in the text. Focus on the information before and after the word *struggled*, and decide what the phrase means. Choose from these three options:

   a started an argument
            c continued with difficulty

   b managed to survive

7 In what ways do you think Scott's expedition would have been different in the 21st century? What modern equipment could his team have used to help them survive?

E 🔎 Language focus: past perfect simple

1 The past perfect tense shows that something occurred before another action or event in the past. It can also show that something happened before a specific time or period of time in the past. Look at these examples from the texts you have read in this unit:

   a In the 1900 Games in Paris, swimmers climbed a pole, before which they had crawled over boats ...

   b On 17 January, they reached the pole, only to find that a Norwegian party led by Roald Amundsen, had beaten them there.

In each example find (i) the event in the past perfect tense, and (ii) the event or events that happened after it.

2 How is the past perfect formed?

3 Look back at the two texts in this unit and find more examples.

4 Look at the newspaper articles about three different people. For **each** article, combine pieces of information to write **three** sentences which include a verb in the past perfect tense. You can include other words such as *before*, *after*, *previously*, etc, if necessary. Write **nine** sentences in total.

Example (paragraph 1): *Jim had celebrated his nineteenth birthday just one week before the match.*

> ❗ **TOP TIP**
> It is unlikely that you will know what every word means in a reading passage, but don't let that put you off! It is never necessary to understand everything in a text. If there are words you definitely need to check, look them up, or ask for help. You can also look at the context of the word: the words which come before and after it. Furthermore, you can break down a word which are unsure about: look at the prefix, the suffix, the root. All or any of these may help you to understand the word.

117

Heroes:

[1] Heroic goalie saves the day!

Roston village football team was saved from embarrassment by the heroic efforts of Jim Douglas, their second-choice goalkeeper, in a thrilling match last weekend. Jim, a third-year university student who celebrated his nineteenth birthday just one week before the match, is a keen all-round sports player. Apart from football, he also plays tennis every week, and is an enthusiastic member of his university's basketball team which three weeks ago won the local league. The opposing team in last weekend's match, Whitehill Town, managed to fight through brave Roston's defences nine times in total, but on each occasion Jim stopped the ball from going into the net. During the first half of the match, Jim made four amazing saves by diving at full stretch across the goal mouth. In the second half, he saved a penalty, and put two shots over the crossbar. The match finished as a 0-0 draw. Afterwards, Jim said that he does not regard himself as a hero, and that he sees himself as part of the team.

*See the **WORD TIP**

[2] Welcome home for brave Brazilian

Gabriela Rodrigues, from Recife, arrived back in Brazil last night after working for three years as a volunteer doctor in India, her first ever trip abroad. Gabriela, who qualified as a doctor and then immediately signed up as a volunteer, said that while many aspects of the last three years had been terribly **challenging**★ and **difficult**★ for her, the experience was overwhelmingly positive and made her 'a much better person'. Gabriela's parents believe that for her unselfish work and total commitment she is a hero; on the other hand, Gabriela feels differently, and believes that everyone, at some point in their life, should make an effort to involve themselves in volunteer work. While in India, Gabriela made many friends, some of whom are still based there. She promised them that she would return soon but for now she plans to spend some time at home with her family and friends, reflecting on her time and experiences.

[3] Town welcomes local hero

Egyptian businesswoman Maha Fahmy was welcomed by citizens of New Cairo when she opened the new superstore there yesterday. Maha, who won last year's Egyptian Business Award for the second time, grew up in Heliopolis, a suburb of Cairo. After completing her civil engineering degree and then her MBA and PhD at university in Alexandria over a ten-year period, Maha was recruited by a Dubai-based global construction company, which sent her to four different continents for work experience. In 2005 she returned to Egypt and, with the help of her father and sister, established her own business, building low-cost homes for first-time buyers. Such was the success of this venture that in 2012 she became the first woman to receive the African New Business Award, which Maha says helped her company to take on much larger construction projects, such as the superstore in New Cairo. As a result, she has received many other international awards which recognise her skills, the majority for building projects in her home country, but some for work carried out abroad.

All three sections loosely adapted from: http://historysheroes.e2bn.org07/08/16

WORD TIP

challenging = testing one's full abilities or resources, either physical or mental; often enjoyable or interesting

difficult = needing effort or skill to be successful or to complete or understand something

Complete the exercise in the **Workbook**.

F ◎ ◀ ⊜ **Speaking, listening and writing**

1 Read the newspaper articles again. For questions a–h, choose from Jim, Gabriela or Maha. Work alone and answer questions a–h.

Which person …

a did not earn a salary from their first job?

b is still studying?

c has travelled extensively abroad?

d studied for a decade?

e found their work experience very demanding?

f thinks their success results from working in a group?

g believes that we should all offer our skills to those who are less fortunate?

h believes that their success is due to winning a prize?

2 Work in small groups and answer these questions about the previous text.

a What do you think about Jim's, Gabriela's and Maha's achievements? Would you describe them as heroes? Why or why not?

b Do you agree with the following definition of a hero/heroine?

Someone admired for their bravery or abilities, particularly someone who has acted with great courage under difficult or dangerous conditions.

Do you think that Jim, Gabriela or Maha fits this definition? Why or why not?

c Which qualities do you think make someone a hero/heroine? Do they have to be brave? Could a coward be a hero/heroine? Are some heroes/heroines stupid or irresponsible?

d Do you know (or know of) anyone who you regard as a hero/heroine? What did s/he do? Why? What was the outcome? Does the person fit the definition above?

3 ◎ **CD1, Track 26** Listen to two students talking about Maha. The first student thinks that Maha was a hero; the second does not. What do you think? Why?

4 Read the audioscript for Activity F3 in Appendix 3. Notice the way the two speakers give their general opinion about the question at the beginning (*I really do believe that Maha is a special type of hero.* and *I absolutely don't agree with you.*) and then proceed to give specific reasons. How many different reasons does each speaker give to support their opinion? Tell your partner what you think.

5 Choose someone who you consider to be a hero/heroine. Make a list of at least three reasons why you have chosen this person. Rank the reasons in order of importance.

6 Write a paragraph of about 80–100 words in which you give your reasons why you think this person is a hero/heroine. Write your introductory sentence in a similar style to the ones in the audioscript: *I really think XXX was a hero because*, or *For me, XXX was a hero because* …, and then continue your paragraph, giving specific reasons for your opinion.

REFLECTION

How well do you think you can do each of these things now?

Give yourself a score from 1: Still need a lot of practice to 5: Feeling very confident about this

In this unit you:	1	2	3	4	5
watched a video of students talking about achievements and discussed what they said					
spoke about world records and achievements					
read articles and answered questions on Olympic sports and the explorer Robert Scott					
improved your understanding of the past perfect tense					
wrote about your chosen hero					

Now set yourself a **personal goal** based on your scores for Unit 11.

Exam focus

Reading, Exercise 2, multiple matching

1 You are going to read four blogs in which four bloggers comment about people who they admire. For questions a–j, choose from the bloggers A–D. The bloggers may be chosen more than once.

A Sophia Alexandrou

For as long as I can remember I've been fascinated by space travel and exploring the solar system, and my dream has always been to go beyond the Earth's atmosphere and fly to somewhere millions of miles away! I don't have one particular hero, as anyone who has the chance to take off in a spaceship has my vote! Think of the risks they take, and the hardship they have to endure, all in the name of science and trying to make the world a better place for those of us left behind. Anything could go wrong at any time, and remember there's no mechanic down the road who could come and change the battery or bring you a litre of petrol if needed. Astronauts are on their own, physically and mentally, and they have to survive, no matter what happens. My admiration for them and their achievements is enormous.

B Eiji Akiyama

It has to be footballers, definitely footballers. I know all the arguments that modern-day footballers are paid far too much money for what they do, but think about it: they give up their lives and devote themselves entirely to perfecting their bodies so that they can excel on the football field. The risks they take are enormous, and the possibility to be seriously injured in a tackle or a collision with another player or players is frightening. When I watch slow-motion replays of aggressive tackles, I often shudder at the agony a player must be going through, and there's nothing worse than seeing the referee signal for a stretcher to carry off an injured player. So they get paid enormous salaries, but the number of years most players can expect to play regularly is very limited, and they rarely play beyond their 30s. They are my heroes, not least because they give me so much pleasure and enjoyment. Even when my team loses, and I feel unhappy, I still admire the players.

C Maria Gomez

It's an interesting question: *Which person do you most admire?* or *Who is your hero?* But for me I only need one second to give you my answer: my family. Who else could you possibly choose? Ok, so it's not one person, but each and every member of my family is my hero and deserves my admiration, for different reasons. I can think of someone in my family who never fails to make me laugh and smile, even when I feel depressed, and someone else who has always been there to support me when I've needed help with my studies. Other family members deserve my admiration because I can tell them anything I want, all my secrets, all my fears, all my hopes and ambitions, and I know they would never tell anyone else without my permission. For me, a hero is not someone who has done something that nobody else has, but a person who will always be there for me.

D Salim Al Farsi

I'm not sure what the criteria are for someone to be my hero. I suppose that for some people it's based on an achievement, like climbing a mountain or breaking a world record. For others it could be a sportsperson who has won everything there is to win in their particular sport. I think today there are too many people who claim to be, or who are made to feel they are, heroes because of something they have achieved. The world makes many people seem better or more successful than they actually are. We are in an age of hero-worship, where we actively look for people to call our heroes. I'm not saying that some people do not deserve recognition for things they have done, but I really feel that the value of some people's so-called achievements is not as great as we make out.

Which person …

a	admits to feeling fear at the thought of pain?	[1]
b	believes that money is well deserved?	[1]
c	believes that their heroes lead a solitary lifestyle?	[1]
d	explains that their choice of hero is a very personal matter?	[1]
e	has always wanted to get away from home?	[1]
f	has difficulty deciding what a hero is?	[1]
g	says that their heroes only have a short time in which to perform?	[1]
h	thinks their heroes improve life for everyone else?	[1]
i	thinks there are too many heroes in the world?	Extended only [1]
j	describes a group of people as their hero?	Extended only [1]

[Total: 8 Core, 10 Extended]

Learning objectives

In this unit you will:

- watch a video of students talking about organisations, and discuss what they say
- speak and read about organisations that arrange different holidays
- listen to someone from the World Association of Girl Guides and Girl Scouts (WAGGGS)
- read about a youth organisation in Cyprus
- write about WAGGGS

A ☺ Watch, listen and talk

1 Watch and listen to some IGCSE students talking about **organisations**.

  a What do the students think are the benefits of joining a youth organisation? Make a note of **three** things.

  b What activities do youth organisations arrange for their members, according to the students? Make a note of **three**.

2 Talk to your partner/s about your experiences as a member of a youth organisation. If you are not a member, explain why this is the case.

B 🔤 Speaking and vocabulary

1 With a partner, look at the pictures below. Where do you think the people are? What are they doing? Have you ever done this type of thing? If not, would you like to?

2 Look at these icons from a webpage advertising activity holidays for teenagers. What do you think the icons mean? Match each one to a picture in Activity B1.

3 Look at the second set of icons showing the six continents, then answer these questions with your partner.

a Which continent does each icon represent?

b Try to name **at least three** countries in each continent. Which continent is problematic?

c Which continent do you live in? Where exactly? Which countries border your country? If you live on an island, which countries are nearby?

d Have you ever visited any of the other continents? Why did you go there? Who did you go with? What did you do?

e Which continent do you think would be best for the holidays in Activities B1 and B2? Why?

C Reading

1 You are going to read some information about an organisation that arranges summer adventure programmes for teenagers. Before you read the texts, discuss with a partner what you know about these four **destinations***. If you live in one of them, talk about the others! Use different reference sources to find out at least two things about each of the four destinations. Make notes on: ***location****, *size, population, climate, geography, fauna and wildlife*, and so on.

a Galapagos and Ecuador

b Leeward Islands

c British Virgin Islands

d Australia

*See the **WORD TIP.**

> **ABC XYZ**
>
> **WORD TIP**
>
> *location* = a place or position
>
> *destination* = the place where someone is going, or where something is being sent or taken
>
> Complete the exercises in your **Workbook**.

2 Look at the map and identify the location of each of the four destinations in Activity C1. Hint: three are in the western hemisphere and one is in the eastern hemisphere.

3 Read this information and decide which of the four destinations each one refers to.

   a Separated from South America by the Pacific Ocean, this group of islands is an extremely important biological area.

   b Positioned right at the top of the Caribbean island chain, this group of 36 small islands is characterised by steep green hills and white-sand beaches. Around them lie the clear blue waters of the Sir Francis Drake Channel.

   c … the sixth–largest country in the world. Here, you can find the world's biggest coral ecosystem – the Great Barrier Reef.

   d … scattered from the Virgin Islands, southwards to Antigua. The best-known islands of this group include St Kitts, Nevis, St Barts and St Martin.

4 Work in groups of four. See Appendix 2, where you will find a text for Students A, B, C and D. You will each read about **one** of the different holiday destinations. Look quickly at your text, but do not show it to the others in your group. Which information from Activity C3 matches your text?

5 Look at these eight questions. You will find the answers to only **two** of them in **your** text. Read your text again in more detail and decide which **two** questions you can answer. Then write the answers.

   a What is the only living organism visible from outer space?

   b Where can you do a wide range of water sports?

   c Where can you find over 100 islands?

   d Which destination includes a distance of 2,000 kilometres?

   e Which islands display both cultural and geological diversity?

   f Which destination offers both mainland- and island-based activities?

   g Which islands are good for sailing?

   h Which islands are ideal for exploring?

6 In your groups of four, do the following:

   a Tell your group which of the destinations is yours.

   b Find out from the group the answers to the other six questions in Activity C5.

7 In your group, answer these questions.

   a What do you think about organised activity holidays, such as the ones described in this unit? What do you think the advantages and disadvantages might be?

   b Would you like to visit any of the four destinations described? If yes, which one/s? If not, why not?

   c Agree with your partners on one or two more places that would be ideal as activity holiday destinations. How did you decide?

D 🔊 Listening

1 What do you know about the World Association of Girl Guides and Girl Scouts (WAGGGS)? What do you think is the purpose of the organisation? Are you a member or do you know someone who is a member of WAGGGS (or the equivalent for boys) or a similar youth organisation? What do its members do? Discuss with a partner.

2 You are going to listen to someone talking about WAGGGS, but before you listen, match the following five words with the correct definitions. There are two extra definitions that you do not need to use.

fundraising	activity, contribution
	solutions
inspired	collecting money
involvement	evaluate
	concerned
issues	motivated
judge	subjects

3 Check your answers for Activity D2 using different reference sources.

4 Use the words from Activity D2 to complete these phrases from the talk you are going to listen to.

How else can you **(a)** ... the success of ...?

... our members uploaded profile pics during their WTD **(b)** ....

We want people to be **(c)** ... by ...

... and speak out on the **(d)** ... we most care about.

We want to make a global difference by **(e)** ... for projects ...

5 🔊 CD1, Track 27 Listen and find out ...

   a where the conversation takes place

   b how many people are talking

   c what they are talking about.

   and check your answers to Activity D4.

125

6 Listen again to Kigongo Odok interviewing Namono Alupo and complete the notes below. Write one to three words in each gap.

WTD happens annually on …

Main aims: encourage members to consider … and connect with … of GGGS

WTD celebrated in … countries

Number of activity packs downloaded = …, available in four languages: English, …

Best indication of success is use of …

WAGGGS wants members to take … and … out on issues

Also wants members to connect with family, places, or GGGS … internationally

Activity pack contains different activities with different …

Challenge is to complete a … and share connections

More information from website …

Special … version of activity pack available

7 Read the audioscript in Appendix 3 to check your notes in Activity D5.

LANGUAGE TIP

Either is always paired with *or* and *neither* is always paired with *nor*. Both are used to show that two ideas are linked together. Notice these examples of *neither … nor* from the listening activity:

… *neither children nor adults **are** adolescents* …

… *neither a parent nor a school teacher **is** available to help* …

Sometimes there is confusion about whether to have a singular or a plural verb after *either … or* and *neither … nor*, but there is a simple rule: if one or both elements are plural, use a plural verb (***are*** in the first example); if both elements are singular, use a singular verb (***is*** in the second example above).

Complete the exercises in your **Workbook**.

E Reading

1 You are going to read a webpage about a youth organisation in Cyprus, an island in the eastern Mediterranean. The webpage has information about five interest areas:

a nature exploration

b protection of the environment

c civil defence

d quality of life

e general knowledge.

Look at the five pictures (1–5) and with your partner match them to the five interest areas (a–e).

2 In which of the five interest areas would you expect to read the following words and phrases? Why? There are two words or phrases for each area.

> cultures and societies   Cypriot civilisation   emergencies   fire extinguishers
> healthy eating   hiking expeditions   inventors   plastic bags   Save the Planet
> the coast of Cyprus

3 Quickly look at the webpage and check your answers to Activity E2.

4 Read the first paragraph again and make 2–3 written notes about each of the following. Compare notes with your partner.

   a What the group's aims are.

   b How the members are grouped.

   c Who the group's leaders are.

5 Work in groups of **five**. Each person in your group should choose **one** of the five interest areas. As you read your paragraph, write **at least one** clarification question for your group members to answer. For example:

How do you pronounce this word?

What does this word mean?

I'm guessing this word means …. What do you think?

I think the writer is saying …. Do you agree?

Discuss and answer your clarification questions.

Soma Akriton – an independent youth group

At the beginning of 1998, a group of concerned people in Cyprus decided to set up a new organisation appealing to today's youth. The organisation's objective was to be independent, democratic and modern.

On 14th March 1998, in the Kaimakli area of Nicosia, Soma Akriton was established – its main aims being to offer knowledge and new ideas to the youth of Cyprus, to reinforce the ideals of good citizenship and to raise awareness of environmental issues. Now a flourishing organisation, whose activities are run by an elected council, Soma Akriton organises youth groups in the Nicosia area. The groups are divided by age: 6–11 years, 12–15 years, 16–18 years and over 18 years. Currently, there are five groups, with more than 150 children and young people participating in a rich and varied programme of events during the months of September to June, when the members meet every Saturday afternoon. Each group is directed by a leader and two or three assistants, all of whom have considerable experience in working with children of all ages. The leaders are all university or college graduates; they are people with high ideals and a desire to give something back to society.

Nature exploration
This involves the search for new areas of physical beauty in the mountains and along the coast of Cyprus with the aid of maps and compasses. Hiking expeditions and survival excursions take place at different times of the year, with a focus on nature study and observation.

Protection of the environment
Raising awareness and campaigning for the protection of the environment is a top priority for Soma Akriton. In recent years, the European Union has given financial support to Soma Akriton to help with its Save the Planet campaign. Recently, a successful campaign against the use of plastic bags was supported by the European Union and a campaign to encourage a more 'green' approach to consumerism was funded by the United Nations.

Civil defence
Members of Soma Akriton are trained to deal with emergencies, such as fires, accidents and earthquakes. There are special emergency teams made up of leaders and children who are equipped with first-aid kits and fire extinguishers.

Quality of life
The exploration of Cypriot civilisation, with regular visits to archaeological sites, traditional villages and museums, is the focus of 'Quality of life'. Comparisons are made with other cultures and societies to increase and improve members' understanding of how other people live. Trips to Germany and Italy, as well as participation in European Union programmes and events, all add to the aims of the 'Quality of life' activities.

General knowledge
From the Olympic Games to healthy eating, from philosophers to inventors, from sport to medicine, from games to projects, Soma Akriton's members are guaranteed a wide range of interests and activities, all designed to broaden and develop their general knowledge.

F ⊙ Language focus: non-defining relative clauses

1 A non-defining relative clause provides extra information about someone or something. Work with your partner and discuss if the following information (a–f) is true or false.

  a If we remove the non-defining relative clause from a sentence, the sentence will still make sense.

  b Always use a comma before a non-defining relative clause.

  c We can use these relative pronouns *which, who, whose, when, whom, where,* in non-defining relative clauses.

  d The relative pronoun can be omitted in non-defining relative clauses.

  e After words like all, both, many, neither, some, we can use of which or of whom.

  f A non-defining clause always comes at the end of a sentence.

2 Look at the seven examples from this unit in the box. The non-defining relative clause is underlined in each example. Check your answers to Activity F1 and correct any false information.

  a Today I am very happy to welcome to our local studio Namono Alupo, <u>who works for WAGGSS, the World Association of Girl Guides and Girl Scouts.</u>

  b I've heard about something called World Thinking Day, <u>which takes place every year in February,</u> am I right?

  c Well, the activity pack, <u>which I've already mentioned</u>, contains various activities which our members are encouraged to participate in.

  d Now a flourishing organisation, <u>whose activities are run by an elected council</u>, Soma Akriton organises youth groups in the Nicosia area, <u>where the group has a club house</u>.

  e … programme of events during the months of September to June, <u>when the members meet every Saturday afternoon.</u>

  f Each group is directed by a leader and two or three assistants, <u>all of whom have considerable experience in working with children of all ages.</u>

  g The exploration of Cypriot civilisation, <u> which includes regular visits to archaeological sites, traditional villages and museums</u>, is the focus of 'Quality of life'.

3 Write seven sentences, one about each of the following subjects from Unit 11. Use the examples A–G to guide you, and refer back to Unit 11 for more information about each subject.

  a Victor de Leon

  b superlative adjectives

  c trampolining

  d 17 January

  e the South Pole

  f Roston, Derbyshire

  g footballers

G Writing

1 These three key words have been removed from the exam-style question in Activity F3: *explain*, *describe*, *suggest*. The words ask you to do different things, but what exactly? Match each verb with the information (a–c) given:

   a express an idea or plan for someone to consider

   b make something clear or easy to understand by giving reasons for it or details about it

   c give information to show what someone, somewhere or something is like.

2 Which of the following phrases (a–l) could you use to *explain*, *describe*, *suggest*? Can any of the phrases be used for more than one function?

   a I think we should …

   b If we did this …

   c My school is located …

   d Our school would benefit by …

   e She was born in the early 1940s …

   f The building is more than 30 storeys tall …

   g The country is planning to …

   h The Head Teacher has told us that …

   i The organisation was established …

   j The project is attempting to …

   k There are several reasons for this situation …

   l There is no reason not to …

3 Read the exam-style question and discuss it with a partner. Decide what you have to do to answer the question successfully, and then make five written notes. Example: write an article for school magazine, so not very informal.

You have just spent a day with one of the girls involved in the WTD project. Write an article for your school magazine in which you describe your experience. Here are some comments from other project members that you met:

'World Thinking Day gets people thinking about important international issues'

'WTD involves not only fun activities but also raising awareness using social media'

Write your article

The comments above may give you some ideas and you should try to use some ideas of your own

Your article should be 150–200 words long [Extended].

You will receive up to 8 marks for the content of your article and up to 8 marks for the style and accuracy of your language.

4 Read this answer written by a student in response to the question in Activity F3.

The girl I met was named Kayla Kalanga from Botswana and she was born 17 years ago. She came here last week to explain me about WTD and how to connect with people around the world. She was her third year doing WTD.

I learnt that she has been doing WAGGGS for five years now and has learnt many different things. She has connected with girls the same age as she is, but there are different ages groups as well. The idea is to connect with friends everywhere and to try to get money to help people. When she completes the puzzle Kayla will go to see her friends and explain to them about the connections she made. She will take her activity pack with her and explain them how they can connect around the world.

TOP TIP

When writing in English, you may be asked to write an article or narrative, or to give a simple description, or to write something persuasive. It is important that you read the question very carefully and that you express yourself effectively. You should also show that you can vary the style of your writing, depending on the topic. Remember to use formal and less formal styles, as appropriate to the task.

TOP TIP

In some writing tasks, you may be given a stimulus or prompts to help you. These could be pictures or comments, often written as speech bubbles.

I suggest at our school we look at www.wagggs.com and find out more. We can also download the activity pack to try some of the connection activities for ourselves. [180 words]

5 The writer of the article has made some mistakes. With a partner, identify the mistakes, but do not rewrite the article. Don't just think about spelling and grammar mistakes – also consider whether or not the writer has answered the question.

   a Is anything missing from the answer?

   b Is the layout correct?

   c What about the length?

   d Is there repetition?

   e Does the writer use a range of vocabulary?

6 Use the notes below to write your own answer to the question in Activity F3. You may add ideas of your own, but try to include all the information the question asks for.

   Remember: the limit is 150–200 words for Extended (100–150 for the Core curriculum). Also try to use some of the phrases from Activity F2.

   a Kayla Kalanga, 17, tall, from small village in Botswana, three brothers, two sisters, both parents work as farmers.

   b Member of WAGGGS – learns about important international issues.

   c Started five years ago; been taking part in three WTDs.

   d Connects with network of girl guides and girl scouts.

   e Wants to raise money for projects around the world.

   f Uses activity pack for ideas about fundraising.

   g Challenged to make four special global connections.

   h School can find out more www.wagggs.com and download activity pack.

   i Check where local WAGGGS group meets.

7 Exchange your writing with a partner. Use the checklist in Activity F5 to check their work.

REFLECTION

How well do you think you can do each of these things now?

Give yourself a score from 1: Still need a lot of practice to 5: Feeling very confident about this

In this unit you:	1	2	3	4	5
watched a video of students talking about organisations, and discussed what they said					
spoke and read about organisations that arrange different holidays					
listened to someone from the World Association of Girl Guides and Girl Scouts (WAGGGS)					
read about a youth organisation in Cyprus					
wrote about WAGGGS					

Now set yourself a **personal goal** based on your scores for Unit 12.

Exam focus

Writing, Exercise 6

1   A youth group you volunteer with has been raising funds for charity. Your teacher has suggested you write a report describing your activities. In your report explain why the group wanted to raise funds for charity and describe what the funds will be used for.

Here are two comments from other volunteers:

> We know that the funds we raise can be used for many different projects

> It would be good if more people would volunteer in their free time

Write the report

The comments above may give you some ideas and you should try to use some ideas of your own.

Your report should be 150–200 words long [Extended]

You will receive up to 8 marks for the content of your report and up to 8 marks for the style and accuracy of your language.

2   The tourist organisation in your country is trying to encourage people not to take their holidays abroad. Here are some comments that have been made in letters to an online newspaper.

Write an article for your school magazine, giving your views.

> If more of us took our holidays here, it would create more jobs and improve the local economy.

> Staying here does nothing to improve our awareness of the rest of the world.

Your article should be 150–200 words long [Extended].

The comments above may give you some ideas and you should try to use some ideas of your own.

You will receive up to 8 marks for the content of your article and up to 8 marks for the style and accuracy of your language.

Learning objectives

In this unit you will:

- watch a video of students talking about famous people, and discuss what they say
- speak and read about famous people and their achievements, and make notes
- listen to and answer questions about someone describing his motorcycling adventures
- practise using vocabulary for descriptions
- write a blog about a famous person - Optional

A 😊 Watch, listen and talk

1 Watch and listen to some IGCSE students talking about **famous people**.

 a What do the students think people need in order to become successful or famous? Make a note of **three** things.

 b How important do the students think ambition is? Do they all agree?

2 a Tell your partner/s what **you** think people need in order to become successful or famous, and give reasons.

 b Discuss with your partner/s which successful or famous person or people **you** most admire, and why.

B 🔤 Speaking and vocabulary

1 Who are the people in the pictures? What do you know about them? What made them successful and famous? Discuss with a partner.

2 Match the name and two pieces of information to each of the pictures. If you know any more information about any of the people, tell your partner.

Names	Information
Sarah Attar	Iraqi-British architect
	competed in 2012 Olympics
Zaha Hadid	co-founder of Facebook
	film actor
Mark Zuckerberg	Saudi Arabian
	studied at American University Beirut
Bruce Lee	died 1973
	born 1984

3 With your partner, decide which of the following words you think are connected with being successful and famous. Give reasons.

> confidence   dedication   determination   fearlessness   independence
> selfishness   skill   strength

4 Which of the qualities in Activity B3 would you say Sarah Attar, Zaha Hadid, Mark Zuckerberg and Bruce Lee have or had? Why?

5 Think of a famous person. How would you describe them? Are the words in Activity B3 sufficient, or do you need to use other words? Why?

C 🌐 📄 Reading and writing: Making notes

1 You are going to read about the famous Portuguese footballer Eusébio. Before you read, look at these words and phrases from the text and make sure you have a general idea of what they mean. Discuss the list with your partner and use different reference sources to help you.

> a stinging shot   bewildering   ferocious   homages   humility   intimidated
> prolific   renowned   runner-up

2 Look at these phrases. Which ones do you think you will read in the text? Why?

a A Mozambican-born Portuguese footballer.

b One of the greatest footballers of all time.

c More goals than any other player.

d He could run 100 metres in 11 seconds.

e He played for Benfica for 15 out of his 22 years.

f Nicknamed the Black Panther, the Black Pearl or *o Rei* (the King).

g Could use both left and right feet, as well as his head.

h He is considered Benfica's and Portugal's most renowned player.

i Eusébio was an ambassador of football.

3 Skim the text and check your answers to Activities C1 and C2.

Eusébio da Silva Ferreira

Eusébio da Silva Ferreira (1942–2014) was a Mozambican-born Portuguese footballer. Although born in Mozambique and with an Angolan father, Eusébio could only play for the Portuguese team, since both Mozambique and Angola were overseas territories and their inhabitants were considered to have Portuguese nationality. He is regarded as one of the greatest footballers of all time. During his professional career, he scored 733 goals in 745 matches. He was capable of bewildering skill, possessed a stinging shot and it was said he could run 100 metres in 11 seconds. He also had the physical and mental strength not to be intimidated by anyone.

Eusébio helped the Portuguese national team reach third place at the 1966 World Cup, being the top goal scorer of the tournament, with nine goals (including four in one match against North Korea) for which he received the Bronze Ball award. He won the Ballon d'Or award in 1965 and was runner-up in 1962 and 1966. He played for Benfica for 15 out of his 22 years as a footballer, thus being mainly associated with the Portuguese club, and is the team's all-time top scorer with 638 goals scored in 614 official games. At Benefica, he won 11 Primeira Liga titles, five Taça de Portugal titles, a European Cup (1961–62) and helped them reach three additional European Cup finals. He was the European Cup top scorer in 1965, 1966 and 1968. He also won the Bola de Prata (Primeira Liga top scorer award) a record seven times. He was the first ever player to win the European Golden Boot, in 1968 – a feat he repeated in 1973.

Nicknamed the Black Panther, the Black Pearl or *o Rei* (the King), he was known for his speed, technique, athleticism and his ferocious, accurate right-footed shot, making him an outstandingly prolific goal scorer and one of the greatest free-kick-takers in history. He is considered Benfica's and Portugal's most renowned player and one of the first world-class African strikers.

From his retirement until his death in January 2014, Eusébio was an ambassador of football and was one of the most recognisable faces of the sport. He was often praised for his fair play and humility, even by opponents. Homages by FIFA, UEFA, the Portuguese Football Federation and Benfica have been held in his honour. Former Benfica and Portugal teammate and friend António Simoes acknowledges his influence on Benfica and said: 'With Eusébio maybe we could be European Champions, without him maybe we could win the League.'

135

4 Read the text again and answer these questions.

a What was Eusébio's nationality?

b Why was Eusébio not permitted to play for Mozambique or Angola?

c Why was Eusébio not afraid of other footballers?

d In which tournament did Eusébio score four times in one game?

e What did Eusébio win before anyone else?

f What particular skills helped Eusébio to score so many goals?

g What caused Eusébio's opponents to praise him?

5 You have decided to tell your school sports club about Eusébio, but first you need to make some notes in order to prepare your talk. Which three of the following headings do you think would be suitable to help you make your notes? Why?

| Home and education   Nationality and family   Physical skills |
| Achievements in football   Hobbies and interests |

6 Make three notes under the three best headings.

TOP TIP

You only need to make **brief** notes for each heading. Your notes must be related to the text you have read. In the text about Eusébio, for example, under the heading *Nationality and family*, you could make the note: *born in Mozambique, Angolan father.*

D 📖 🔤 Reading and vocabulary

1 You are going to read another text, about a different type of person. Look at this list of eight phrases taken from the text and try to guess what type of person you are going to read about. Work with your partner and give reasons for your answers.

a dual disability

b bachelor's degree

c childhood illness

d badly behaved

e system of hand signals

f practise lip-reading

g raising funds

h numerous awards

2 Which of the following people do you think the text is **not** about? Discuss with a partner and give reasons for your choice.

> F1 racing driver   footballer   musician   politician   zookeeper   author

3 Quickly scan the text about Helen Keller and check your answers to Activities D1 and D2. Do not worry yet about the gaps at the start of each paragraph.

> **TOP TIP**
>
> Remember that there might be more than three pieces of information in the text for a particular heading, but you only need to make notes for each bullet point. If you write four pieces of information when there are only three bullets (and three marks), you can still only receive three marks!

Helen Keller: survivor

1 ... was an American author and campaigner for deaf and blind charities who became deaf and blind as a young child and had to struggle to overcome her dual disability. Despite this, she became the first deaf-blind person to attain a bachelor's degree and became an influential campaigner for social and disability issues. Her public profile helped de-stigmatise blindness and deafness, and she was seen as a powerful example of someone overcoming difficult circumstances.

2 ... in Tusculum, Alabama, Helen Keller was only 19 months old when she experienced a severe childhood illness which left her deaf and almost completely blind. For the first few years of her life, she was only able to communicate with her family through a rudimentary number of signs. However, she had a little more success communicating with the six-year-old daughter of the family cook, with whom she had become friendly. Nevertheless, being unable to communicate properly, she was considered to be badly behaved and a '**problem**'*.

3 ..., Helen was sent to see an eye, ear and nose specialist in Baltimore. The specialist put them in touch with Alexander Graham Bell, who was currently investigating issues of deafness and sound. Bell would later also develop the first telephone. Bell helped Keller to visit the Perkins Institute for the Blind, and this led to a long relationship with Anne Sullivan, who was a former student herself. In spite of being visually impaired, quite young (she was only 20 when they met) and with no prior experience, Sullivan set about teaching Helen how to communicate. The two maintained a long relationship for nearly 50 years.

136

Learning to communicate

4   …, Keller was frustrated by her inability to pick up the hand signals that Sullivan was giving. Nonetheless, after a frustrating month, Keller picked up on Sullivan's system of hand signals through understanding the word water. Sullivan poured water over Keller's left hand and wrote out on her right hand the word water. This helped Helen to fully understand the system, and she was soon able to identify a variety of household objects.

5   … made rapid progress and quickly overcame many **obstacles**★. She became proficient in Braille, and was able to begin a fruitful education, even though her disability held her back. Keller made more progress than anyone had previously expected. She would later learn to write with a Braille typewriter.

6   … into contact with the American, Mark Twain, the author of *The Adventures of Tom Sawyer*. Twain admired the perseverance of Keller so much that he helped persuade Henry Rogers, an oil businessman, to fund her education. Although she faced great difficulties, Keller was able to study at Radcliffe College, where in 1904, at the age of 24, she was able to graduate with a Bachelor of Arts degree. During her education, she also learnt to speak and practise lip-reading, with her sense of touch becoming extremely subtle. Keller became a proficient writer and speaker, and in 1903 she published her autobiography *The Story of My Life*, which recounted her struggles to overcome her disabilities.

Charity work

7   …, she devoted much of her time to raising funds for and increasing awareness of blind charities. She worked hard to raise money and also improve the living conditions of the blind, who at the time were often badly educated and living in rather unfriendly accommodation. Her public profile helped to de-stigmatise blindness and deafness. Sadly, towards the end of her life, she suffered a stroke and died in her sleep on 1 June 1968. She was given numerous awards during her lifetime, including in 1964 the Presidential Medal of Freedom, by President Lyndon B. Johnson.

Adapted from: www.biographyonline.net

★See the **WORD TIP**.

4   The opening words from each paragraph have been removed. Scan the text again and decide which of the phrases from the list below fit the paragraphs. Give reasons for your choices. Be careful, there are two extra phrases that you do not need to use.

a   At the turn of the century

b   Born on 27 June 1880

c   From 1918

d   Helen Keller (1880–1968)

e   In 1886

f   In the beginning

g   Keller came

h   Keller never

i   Keller then

5   Work with a partner and answer the following questions. Use different reference sources to help you as well as the strategies in Unit 11 for understanding words you don't know.

a   Look at paragraphs 1 and 2. What do the following words mean?

   i   campaigner [paragraph 1]

   ii   influential [1]

   iii de-stigmatise [1]

   iv   rudimentary [2]

b Look at paragraphs 3 and 4. Find words or phrases that have a similar meaning to the following:

   i someone with a lot of knowledge and skills in a particular subject (3)

   ii at the present time (3)

   iii unable to do (3)

   iv started doing something (3)

   v continued (3)

   vi annoyed at not being able to do something (4)

   vii learnt (4)

c Look at these words from paragraphs 5 and 6. What are the missing words? Can you supply a word for every gap?

Adjective	Noun	Adverb	Verb
rapid	...	...	...
...	...	quickly	...
proficient	...	...	...
...	disability	...	...
...	...	previously	...
...	...	...	persuade
...	difficulty	...	...
...	...	...	fund

d Look at the whole text.

   i Find all the *-ly* adverbs. What do they mean?

   ii Do the words have adjective and noun forms? If so, what are they? Write a list.

6 Work in small groups and complete the following.

a Do you know anyone who has overcome difficult circumstances, like Helen Keller? Tell each other.

b Try the method that Anne Sullivan used with Helen, and teach each other a word. Your teacher will help you.

c Go onto the internet and find images of the following:

   i a Braille typewriter

   ii a Braille computer

   iii all the people mentioned in the text

   iv lip reading.

LANGUAGE TIP

In English, words ending in *-ly* are usually adverbs (for example *quickly* and *previously*), but there are also *-ly* words that are not adverbs – for example *lovely* and *friendly*, which are both adjectives. Other examples are *family* and *apply*, which are a noun and a verb respectively.

Complete the exercise in your **Workbook**

WORD TIP

problem = a situation, person or thing that causes difficulties and needs to be dealt with

obstacle = something that makes it difficult or impossible for you to move, go somewhere or to succeed at something

Complete the exercises in your **Workbook**.

138

E ⊘ Language focus: discourse markers showing contrast

1 Discourse markers are words or short phrases that give us clues to help us understand a text or to understand how the speaker or writer is feeling about something. Look at these examples. Which **three** show contrast?

Additionally   As a result   Finally   For example   Generally speaking Even though   In spite of   On the other hand   Similarly

2 Which other discourse markers do you know which show contrast? Write a list.

3 Go back to the text about Helen Keller and find **seven** different examples of discourse markers showing contrast. Do any appear in the list in Activity E1 or your list in Activity E2?

4 Complete the gaps (a–f) in the table using the discourse markers from Activity E3.

Despite	her problems,	
(a) …	having problems,	
(b) …	she had problems,	
(c) …		
She had problems.	**(d)** …,	
	(e) …,	
	(f) …,	she became famous.

5 Complete the rules for the discourse markers above.

   a   Despite/In spite of + …

   b   Although/Even though + …

   c   However/Nonetheless/Nevertheless + …

6 Combine the following phrases (a–c) in two different ways, using the different discourse markers in brackets. For phrases d and e, choose your own discourse markers to combine the phrases.

   a   She had to struggle to overcome many obstacles. She obtained a university degree. (However/In spite of)

   b   She could only communicate using signs. Her young friend helped her to be more successful. (Although/Nevertheless)

   c   Sullivan was also visually impaired. She taught Keller how to communicate. (In spite of/Even though)

   d   Keller was frustrated at her lack of progress. Sullivan helped her to start understanding.

   e   Keller then progressed very quickly. She had to overcome a great many obstacles.

F 🔊 Listening

1 You are going to listen to someone talking about Nelson Suresh Kumar, who was famous
   for riding his motorcycle on the world's highest motorable (for motor vehicles) road – the
   Khardung La. Before you listen, work with a partner and answer the following questions.

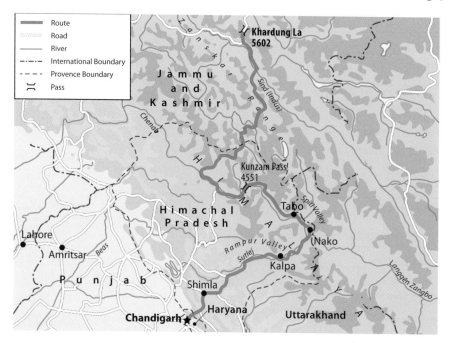

a Look at the map and find Chandigarh (Kumar's starting point) and the Khardung La.

b Describe Kumar's route. Which places did he travel through? Use the information on
   the map.

c How far do you think Kumar travelled? Chandigarh to Shimla is about 120 kilometres.
   Use this information to roughly calculate the distances between these places:

   Shimla to Kalpa

   Kalpa to Nako

   Nako to Tabo

   Tabo to Leh

   Leh to Khardung La.

   What is the approximate total distance?

d Match the pictures to **seven** of the 13 geographical features in the box. Then use different
   reference sources to check the meaning of any of the other six you are unsure about.

> deserts glaciers gorges gravel lakes mountains mud plains
> rivers sand dunes slush snow valleys

e Many geographical features are mentioned. Decide which ones from the list above you
   think you will hear. Give reasons for your choices.

f Only **one** animal is mentioned. Do you think this will be: donkey, bird, snake, camel, lizard or catfish? Give reasons for your choice.

g The speaker talks about **one** other interesting feature. Choose which **one** you think it will be. Give reasons for your choice.

the world's highest battlefield   bright orange sand   a cave village in the mountains   a telecommunications radar

2 You will hear the following words and phrases. Use different reference sources to make sure you understand what they mean.

Accessible   biodiversity   en route   entire   feat   fuelled my passion resembles

3 🔊 **CD1, Track 28** Listen and check your answers to Activities F1e, F1f and F1g.

4 🔊 **CD1, Track 28** Listen again and answer the following questions.

a Where was Kumar born?

b How long did the solo ride take?

c When did Kumar decide to start his tour company?

d What happened on the world's second longest glacier?

e Give **four** geographical features of the Himalayan Moto Adventure.

f Apart from geographical features, what other things can be seen on the Himalayan Moto Adventure? Name **three**.

g Why is the Himalayan Moto Adventure only possible during four months?

h What is unusual about the animal in danger of extinction?

G 💬 Writing - Optional

1 Look back at the two reading texts in this unit about Eusébio and Keller. In which text is the content organised like this?

a Dates, birthplace, famous for.

b Achievements, awards.

c Other information.

d Later life, recognition.

2 How is the other text organised?

3 You are going to update your personal blog with a description of a person who you think deserves to be called 'famous', or someone who you particularly admire and look up to. Firstly, choose a person to write about. It could be someone you have come across in this or a previous unit, or someone else, even a family member. Make a list of things you could include in your description, for example:

a background information (when/where born, family, early life/education) and appearance/features

b work and achievements, honours/awards received, ambitions

c reasons for choosing this person, how the person impresses you.

> **TOP TIP**
> Remember that you need to be able to show that you can write using the appropriate style and level of formality for different audiences (readers) and purposes (reasons for writing). In Unit 12 you practised writing more formally, while this unit provides less-formal practice.

141

4   As with most things you write, your blog will need an introductory paragraph and a concluding paragraph. What information can you put in these two paragraphs?

5   Make notes for your blog, using the headings you have chosen, including the introduction and conclusion.

Example:

My great-grandfather: *Gregoris Gregorou*

Introduction: *Gregoris Gregorou, Nicosia, Cyprus, born 1938, married Christina in 1955, 3 sons, 4 daughters*

Background information: *lives with wife, same house as where he grew up, never went to secondary school, still does carpentry as hobby, tall and broad, full head of hair*

Work and achievements: *started carpentry work with his father in 1948, never done any other job, always worked in same workshop in Nicosia until retirement in 2008, daughter and son now run business, received Cyprus 'master carpenter' award in 2000*

Reasons for choosing this person: *a role model for me, hard-working, family-loving, extremely skilled in his profession, also intelligent and wise, makes me feel proud*

Conclusion: *admire his never-ending ability to make people laugh and smile, tolerance of others, can't imagine life without him*

---

6   Write your blog, using all the information from your notes in Activity G5. Remember to use discourse markers and the unit vocabulary, where appropriate.

REFLECTION

How well do you think you can do each of these things now?

Give yourself a score from 1: Still need a lot of practice to 5: Feeling very confident about this

In this unit you:	1	2	3	4	5
watched a video of students talking about famous people, and discussed what they said					
spoke and read about famous people and their achievements, and made notes					
listened to and answered questions about someone describing his motorcycling adventures					
practised using vocabulary for descriptions					
wrote a blog about a famous person					

Now set yourself a **personal goal** based on your scores for Unit 13.

Exam focus

Reading and writing, Exercise 3 note-making

1   Read the following article about the famous violinist, David Garrett, and then complete the notes about him.

The beauty of the violin

1   David Garrett was born in 1980 in Aachen, Germany, close to the borders with Belgium and the Netherlands. The son of an internationally famous ballerina, he had a childhood that allowed him to practise and improve his natural talents as a musician. Growing up, he had the chance to hear the wonderful music of classical composers as background music all over the family home. His father, Georg, was an antiques dealer, specialising in violins and other stringed instruments, and when Garrett was four years old, his father brought home a violin for his older brother, Alex. Nevertheless, it was the younger Garrett who took a great interest and soon learnt to play.

2   And so David began the long, hard crawl to excellence. At the age of five he was being driven to Holland each weekend to study. Only two years later, when he was seven, he was travelling six hours every week to the Lübeck Conservatoire in the north, to study with a different teacher. He was home-schooled by a private tutor until the age of 17, and gave his first performance with the Hamburg Philharmonic Orchestra aged ten. By the age of 12, Garrett began working with the distinguished Polish violinist Ida Haendel, often travelling to London and other European cities to meet her. After leaving home at 17, he enrolled at the Royal College of Music in London, leaving after the first semester. In 1999 he moved to New York to attend the Juilliard School, and four years later he won the School's Composition Competition with a piece composed in the style of Johann Sebastian Bach. While at Juilliard he studied under Itzhak Perlman, one of the first people to do so, and graduated in 2004.

3   Unlike the multitude of mediocre violinists marketed as geniuses, David Garrett is a true prodigy. He's also a superstar with hordes of fans and someone who has a talent that goes beyond what we would normally expect. He breathes a different type of life into classical music. Thanks to his skill and technique, you will find it impossible not to listen, no matter what your thoughts are on classical music. It does not matter what he plays, or whether or not you are familiar with the piece. Everything Garrett plays he does so with confidence, and the music takes on a different feel and shape in his hands, whether it's a classical or modern piece, and whether he plays alone or with a classical orchestra or rock band accompanying him.

4   However, life is not easy. David Garrett spends up to 340 days a year living out of a suitcase, eating hotel room-service food, his 300-year-old Stradivarius violin strapped to his back, probably the most precious rucksack in the world (it's worth £3.6 million). Garrett says that he tries to do breathing meditation for sleep and relaxation, but also spends time in the gym. However, he only allows himself to do this once he has completed his compulsory daily four hours of violin practice.

5   In 2008, Garrett held the Guinness World Record for the World's Fastest Violinist when he played Flight of the Bumblebee in 1 minute and 5.26 seconds, and in May 2012, he joined the great opera tenor Jonas Kaufmann in a special performance at the final of the UEFA Champions League between Chelsea and Bayern Munich. Although he is still young, Garrett's long crawl to excellence has been more than successful.

You are going to give a talk about David Garrett to your Music Studies group at school. Prepare some notes to use as a basis for your talk. Make short notes under each heading.

Where Garrett was educated

- *age 5 went to Holland every weekend to study*
- … [1]
- … [1]

Garrett's skills as a musician

- … [1]
- … [1]
- … [extended only] [1]

Challenges in Garett's life

- … [1]
- … [1]
- … [1]
- … [extended only] [1]

[Total: 7 Core, 9 Extended]

Writing, Exercise 5

You were recently at a performance given by a famous actor or musician.

Write an email about the experience.

In your email you should:

- explain where you saw the performance and why
- describe what happened
- say how you felt about the performance.

The pictures above may give you some ideas, and you should try to use some ideas of your own. Your email should be 100–150 words long [Core] or 150–200 words long [Extended]. You will receive up to 6/8 marks for the content of your email, and up to 6/8 marks for the style and accuracy of your language.

Learning objectives

In this unit you will:

- watch a video of students talking about medical care, and discuss what they say
- listen to a discussion and answer multiple–choice questions about Florence Nightingale
- read about how to become a paramedic
- listen to a talk about the ICRC – the International Committee of the Red Cross/Crescent – and write notes
- talk about the ICRC

A 😃 Watch, listen and talk

1 Watch and listen to some IGCSE students talking about **medical care**.

  a What do the students say the work of a nurse involves? Make a note of **three** things.

  b Would the students consider nursing as a job for themselves? What **reasons** do they give?

2 Talk to your partner/s about other medical care jobs that **you** know about.

B 🔤 Speaking and vocabulary

1 This unit focuses on people who work in medical care, especially nurses and nursing: the job, the history of the profession, and so on. Look at the pictures and, with a partner, make a list of as many words and phrases as possible connected with the topic.

Examples: *injection, looking after people*

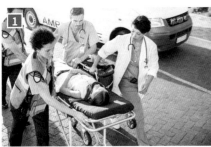

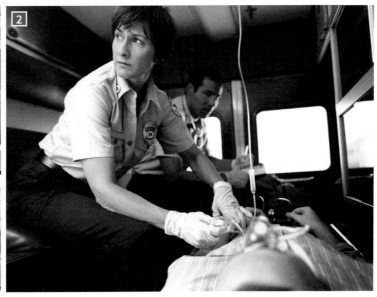

2 Work with your partner. Look at the verbs in column **A** and make sure you understand what they all mean.

A	B
alleviate, diagnose and treat, perform, prescribe and dispense, prevent, promote, provide, restore	care, health (×2), illnesses (×2), medications, suffering, surgery

3 Match the verbs in column **A** with the nouns in column **B** to make common phrases to do with health care and the work that nurses do. Some verbs may match with more than one noun.

4 Quickly read the paragraph about nurses. Find the phrases from Activity B3 and check that you have understood them correctly.

> Nurses care for the sick and injured in hospitals, where they work to restore health and alleviate suffering. Many people are sent home from the hospital when they still need nursing care, so nurses often provide care in the home that is very similar to the care they give to patients in the hospital. In clinics and health centres in communities that have few doctors, nurses diagnose and treat common illnesses, prescribe and dispense medications and even perform minor surgery. Nurses are also increasingly working to promote people's health and to prevent illness in all communities.

5 You are going to hear about the work of a paramedic. What exactly does a paramedic do? How does their job differ from what nurses do?

6 Look at the words in the box. Work with a partner and make sure you understand what they mean.

> accidents   ambulance   care   casualties   emergency   incidents   injuries   patient   treatment

7 You are going to hear a brief talk about the work of a paramedic. Before you listen, which words from Activity B6 do you think best complete the notes below?
- Paramedics respond to **(a)** ... medical calls.
- Assess condition of **(b)** ... and give **(c)** ... and **(d)** ... before hospital admission.
- Unexpected situations may include **(e)** ... and sudden illness, as well as road **(f)** ... and other **(g)** ....
- Some paramedics work alone.

8 CD2, Track 2 Listen and check your answers.

9 Using words and phrases from the previous activities, talk to your partner about the differences between the job of a nurse and the job of a paramedic.

C 🔊 Listening: multiple-choice questions

1 Florence Nightingale is one of the most famous nurses in history. Work with a partner and write down at least three things that you know, or can guess, about her. Use the picture to help you.

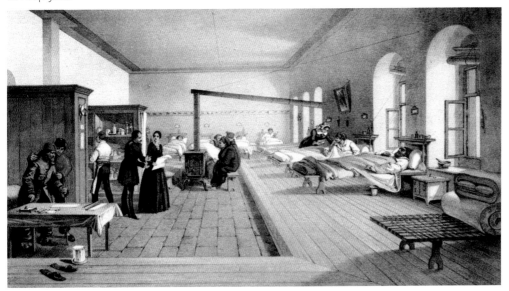

2 Look at the following information about Florence Nightingale. With your partner, decide if the information is true or false. Give reasons.

147

   a Florence Nightingale was born in Florence, Italy.

   b Her parents refused to allow her to become a nurse.

   c She completed a three-month nurse training course in England.

   d The British government asked her to work in British military hospitals in Turkey.

   e Florence Nightingale received several medals for her nursing work.

   f When she died, Florence had been blind for 15 years.

3 🔊 **CD2, Track 3** You will hear John, a nursing student, asking Dr Mary Winterson, a specialist in nursing, some questions about Florence Nightingale. Listen to John and Dr Winterson and check your answers. Correct the false information.

4 Before you listen again, look at the multiple-choice questions below. How much can you remember? With your partner, guess which of the three answers is correct: A, B or C.

   a Florence Nightingale was born in …

      A 1812.   **B** 1820.   **C** 1822.

   b At school, Florence performed …

      A well.   **B** below average.   **C** very poorly.

   c Why was Florence not allowed to become a nurse?

      A There were no training courses available.

      B She wanted to get married first.

      C It was not considered appropriate for her.

   d Why did Florence travel to Europe with friends?

      A Because Florence needed looking after.

      B Because of an argument with her parents.

      C She wanted to find a job helping sick people.

e How many countries did she travel to in 1850?

    A 3   **B** 4   **C** 5

f What caused the British Government to send Florence to Turkey?

    A Inadequate medical facilities for soldiers.

    B The number of wounded soldiers.

    C To train nurses.

g What did the doctors think about the arrival of nurses in military hospitals?

    A They showed their gratitude.   **C** They were unsure.

    B They thought the nurses were heroines.

h What did Florence Nightingale do after she received her medal?

    A She retired.   **B** She wrote books.   **C** She carried on with her work.

i 🔊 **CD2, Track 3** Now listen again and check your answers.

5 How much can you remember? Work with a partner and complete the notes.

6 🔊 **CD2, Track 3** Listen again and check your answers.

Florence Nightingale

Born: Florence, Italy

School studies: (a) …

Teenage years: visited sick people and investigated (b) …

Nursing in 19th century not (c) …

In 1850, travelled with friends to Italy, (d) … , (e) … and (f) …

Started work in a clinic in London in (g) …

Went to Turkey in 1854 with (h) …

Nurses eventually accepted by Scutari doctors because of (i) …

In 1907, awarded a (j) …

Became (k) … in 1895

D 🔘 Language focus: future in the past

1 Look at this phrase from the talk about Florence Nightingale:

… the expectation was that she would marry and start a family.

Which part of the phrase is about past events? Which part moves forward in time?

2 Complete the gaps (a–e) using words from the box.

> correct   future   past   past continuous   will

This use of *would* (as the past tense of **(a) …**) is often referred to as 'future in the past'. It is used to express the idea that in the **(b) …** you (or someone else) thought that something else would happen in the **(c) …**. It does not matter if you are **(d) …** or not. Both *was/were going to* and the **(e) …** can also be used to express the future in the past.

TOP TIP

In multiple-choice questions, there is only one correct answer! Usually, one of the other choices is completely wrong and the other choice is there to distract you – it seems as if it could be right, but it isn't! It is a good strategy to guess possible answers to the question in your head and then look at the choices.

WORD TIP

wound (noun) = a damaged area of the body, such as a cut or hole in the skin or flesh made by a weapon

injury (noun) = physical harm or damage to someone's body caused by an accident or an attack

Complete the exercise in your **Workbook**.

See Appendix 3, CD 2, Track 3

3 Use the notes in the box to write **three** complete sentences, with each one using a different verb form for the 'future in the past'.

> when doctors hear / Florence Nightingale / work with them / feel threatened

4 Make complete sentences using these notes. Use all the different forms for the future in the past.

a My parents / move to Australia / but / decide / stay / Bahrain.

b My sister / think / be / doctor / but / change her mind.

c I think / we / eat / out tonight.

d He believe / he / pass / all his exams.

e I know / you not help / him / with his homework.

f Ali say / Hamed / come with him / but / he come alone.

g She promise / text / her parents / as soon as / she arrive.

h I already tell Sami / when / he arrive / we go / to the cinema.

E 📖 Reading

1 How much can you remember about the work of a paramedic? Match the sentence halves.

Example: *3 + e Paramedics provide an immediate response to emergency medical calls.*

1	A paramedic will attend emergencies, including minor injuries, sudden illness,	**a**	with the other crew member being an ambulance technician or emergency care assistant who helps them.
2	They are usually in a two-person ambulance crew,	**b**	using an emergency response car, motorbike or bicycle to get to a patient.
3	Paramedics provide an immediate response	**c**	and they are responsible for assessing the condition of a patient and providing treatment and care prior to hospital admission.
4	Some will work alone however,	**d**	and casualties arising from road and rail accidents, criminal violence, fires and other incidents.
5	They are usually the first senior health–care professional on the scene,	**e**	to emergency medical calls.

2 Put the five sentences into the same order as the paragraph in Activity A6. The first sentence is *Paramedics provide an immediate response to emergency medical calls.* Compare your order with your partner's, then look again at the audioscript in Appendix 3 to see if you are right.

3 You are going to read an internet article about the entry requirements and training for young people who want to become paramedics. What would you like to find out? Write **three** questions.

Example: *What subjects do I need to study to become a paramedic?*

4 Quickly read the text '*A career as a paramedic*'. Were your questions answered?

A career as a
paramedic

Entry requirements and training

This page outlines the entry requirements and training to become a paramedic. Anyone wishing to work as a paramedic needs to either secure a student paramedic position with an ambulance service trust, or attend an approved full-time course in paramedic science at a university.

Traditionally, staff joining the ambulance service could work their way up, with experience and additional training from care assistant, through ambulance technician to paramedic. However, this route is no longer open to new entrants.

A Entry requirements

Entry requirements for student paramedic positions will vary, depending upon the employer. The range of paramedic science courses at university varies in terms of entry requirements, but a minimum of five GCSEs (including English, Mathematics and/or a science) plus at least two A Levels or equivalent qualifications is typically needed. However, it is essential that you contact each university directly for information on its admissions policy and entry requirements. You can use our course finder to find courses.

You'll also need a full, manual driving licence. Ambulance services use vehicles of different gross weights and staff will be required to hold a driving licence with the appropriate classifications.

B Training

To practise as a paramedic, you must be registered with the Health and Care Professions Council (HCPC). In order to register with the HCPC, you must successfully complete an HCPC-approved programme in paramedic science.

Courses tend to be modular, with flexible entry and exit points, depending upon your academic qualifications and any relevant experience. They last from two to five years, depending on whether you study full or part time. It's important to check entry requirements with the university concerned and with the ambulance service trust/s in the areas where you want to work.

C Applying for paramedic training

Students applying for full-time university courses usually need to apply through the Universities and Colleges Admissions Service (UCAS). Those already working as student paramedics (or qualified ambulance technicians where these posts still exist) should speak to their employing ambulance service about applications for part-time courses.

D Funding for paramedic training

Students on full-time courses in paramedic science are not eligible for financial support through the National Health Service (NHS) Bursary Scheme. However, in some cases there may be local funding arrangements between the NHS and some universities, so you are advised to contact universities directly to enquire about these. In many ambulance trusts, student paramedics receive a salary whilst training on the job. For further information on the funding available, please contact the individual ambulance service trust within your region.

Adapted from www.nhscareers.nhs.uk

5 Read the article again, then write the answers to these questions. Compare your answers with your partner's.

a What does someone who wants to work as a paramedic need to do?

b Which route to becoming a paramedic is no longer available?

c Which subjects are essential qualifications? Name **two**.

d Apart from academic qualifications, what is also essential?

e How can you register with the HCPC?

f How long does a paramedic science course last?

g Who is not eligible to receive financial assistance from the NHS?

> **LANGUAGE TIP**
>
> Look at these two sentences from the text you have just read:
>
> *This page outlines the entry require<u>ment</u>s and train<u>ing</u> to become a paramed<u>ic</u>. Anyone wishing to work as a paramed<u>ic</u> needs to either secure a stud<u>ent</u> paramed<u>ic</u> posit<u>ion</u> with an ambulance service trust, or attend an approved full-time course in paramed<u>ic</u> scien<u>ce</u> at a univers<u>ity</u>.*
>
> The underlined letters are all noun suffixes: for example: *-ment, -ing, -ic, -ent, -ion, -ance, -ce, -ity*. These suffixes appear frequently in English, and knowing that they indicate that a word is a noun can help you in understanding what the word means.
>
> Re-read the text and see how many examples of these suffixes you can find. How many other noun suffixes can you identify?
>
> Complete the exercise in your **Workbook**.

F 💬 🔊 Speaking and listening: completing notes

1 Look the picture. What do the letters ICRC stand for?

2 What types of assistance do you think the ICRC provides? To whom? Where in the world would you expect the organisation to operate?

3 You are going to listen to someone who works for the ICRC being interviewed. Before you listen, look at these words and phrases taken from the interview. What do they mean? Discuss them with a partner. Use different reference sources to help you.

a relief workers

b victims of famine and drought

c instability

d insecure

e ethnic

f foundations

g hygiene

h veterinary care

i priorities

j waterborne.

4 Here are three of the questions the interviewer asks. What do you think the interviewee's answers might be? Discuss your ideas with a partner.

  a Can you tell us about how the ICRC assists victims of famine and drought, and other natural disasters?

  b Does the ICRC only assist when there is a crisis?

  c Is it dangerous working for the ICRC?

5 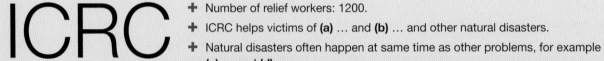 CD2, Track 4 Listen to the interview and check your answers to the questions in Activity F4.

6 CD2, Track 4 Listen to the interview again and complete the notes below. Write one or two words in each gap.

ICRC

+ Number of relief workers: 1200.
+ ICRC helps victims of **(a)** … and **(b)** … and other natural disasters.
+ Natural disasters often happen at same time as other problems, for example **(c)** … and **(d)** … .
+ ICRC help adapts to different contexts: geographic, **(e)** … , **(f)** … and **(g)** … .
+ In the 'Assistance Pyramid', preference is given to **(h)** … , **(i)** … and **(j)** … first.
+ Second place **(k)** … .
+ Third place **(l)** … .
+ ICRC also gives assistance to both **(m)** … and **(n)** … a disaster.
+ This is done by distributing **(o)** … and **(p)** … and providing medical help with animals.
+ Water is often unhealthy and carries diseases, such as **(q)** … and **(r)** … .
+ ICRC programme of assistance includes **(s)** … and **(t)** … , as well as access to water and hygiene, and environmental protection.
+ ICRC workers have these qualities: motivated by **(u)** … and can cope with **(v)** … .

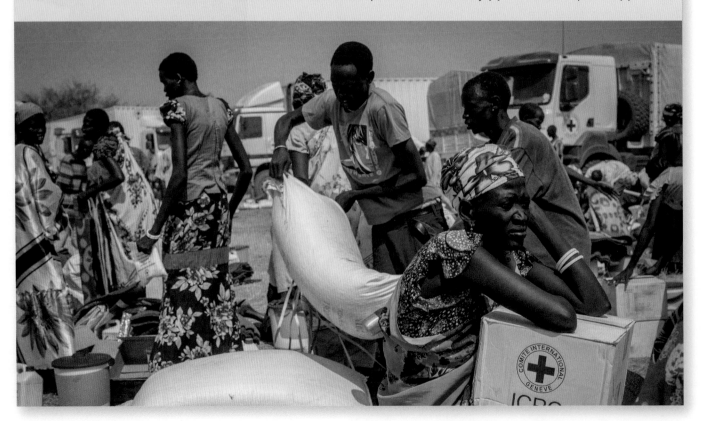

7 Check your answers with a partner. If you are unsure, read the audioscript in Appendix 3.

G Speaking

1 What do you now know about the ICRC? Without looking at your notes, tell your partner about the organisation.

2 Answer these questions in pairs.

a People who work for the ICRC need to be prepared to leave for any destination in the world at a moment's notice. How would you feel about being in that position? Would you find it exciting or frightening? Why?

b Do you think you could work for an organisation like the ICRC? Why, or why not?

c What might be some of the advantages and disadvantages of that kind of life?

d The ICRC employs people who are mentally mature, motivated and who have potential for personal development. Does that description fit you or anybody you know? Why, or why not?

e What other care organisations do you know about? Which ones exist in your country?

> **TOP TIP**
>
> Make sure you check how many words you are required to write in each gap. Some questions ask you to write one or two words; other questions may ask you to write only one single word. Remember also that you must use the correct part of speech in the gap.
>
> **Example:** *Natural disasters often happen at same time as other problems, for example (c) … and (d) …. (c) economic crisis, (d) political instability are correct, but (c) economy crisis, (d) political instable would be wrong.*

REFLECTION

How well do you think you can do each of these things now?

Give yourself a score from 1: Still need a lot of practice to 5: Feeling very confident about this

In this unit you:	1	2	3	4	5
watched a video of students talking about medical care, and discussed what they said					
listened to a discussion and answered multiple–choice questions about Florence Nightingale					
read about how to become a paramedic					
listened to a talk about the ICRC – the International Committee of the Red Cross/Crescent – and wrote notes					
talked about the ICRC					

Now set yourself a **personal goal** based on your scores for Unit 14.

Exam focus

Listening, Exercise 5, completing notes (Extended only)

1 You will hear an expert giving a talk about problems with traffic.

🔊 CD2, Track 5 Listen to the talk and complete the notes in Part A. Write only one or two words in each gap. You will hear the talk twice.

Part A

The cause

Road-traffic accidents are just one problem; the other is … from traffic.

The problem is greatest in … countries.

1.5 billion people suffer from excess levels of pollution daily.

The damage

Young people's health and also … potential affected.

Cars increase problems for poor people, as deaths and injuries occur mainly to pedestrians, cyclists, bus users and children.

Their levels of education, health, water and … , as cars take economic priority over people.

The solution

Reallocation of … in South America has improved lives of poorer people.

Solution should be repeated all over the world.

[5]

2 🔊 CD2, Track 6 Now listen to two students discussing a talk they heard from a medical care professional about road traffic problems and complete the sentences in Part B. Write only one or two words in each gap. You will hear the talk twice.

Part B

Information about problems with traffic

In the UK, death from road accidents has fallen by nearly … since 2000.

For every 100 000 people in some … , more than 40 people die on the roads.

Deaths involve … , cyclists and motorcyclists.

These are the … road users who are more at risk.

More emphasis needed on bicycle- and people-only paths and roads.

In many places, banning cars has resulted in more people going … .

[5]

[Total: 10]

Learning objectives

In this unit you will:

- watch a video of students talking about healthy living, and discuss what they say
- talk about different activities and healthy living
- read about two different healthy foods and discuss them
- watch and listen to students taking part in a speaking role-play, and assess their performance
- read about gardening and make notes and write a summary

A 😃 Watch, listen and talk

1 Watch and listen to some IGCSE students talking about **healthy living**.

   a What do the students say are the reasons for taking care of our health? Make a note of **three**.

   b What do the students do to have a healthy lifestyle? Could they improve it? How?

2 Talk to your partner/s about how the lifestyles of other people influence your own.

B 🔤 Speaking and vocabulary

1 Look at the pictures (1–7). What can you see in each one?

2 Match the following information with the pictures in B1. You can use a phrase for more than one picture. Then discuss with your partner and add **one** more piece of information of your own to each picture.

> couch potatoes   eat what you grow   high in fat and calories
> intense aromatic flavours   no pain no gain   reduces stress and high blood pressure

3 Which activities in B1 would you associate with healthy living? Why? What are their benefits? What impact might they have on someone's health and lifestyle?

4 Which activities shown in B1 do you do? Why do you do them? What other activities do you do that you associate with healthy living?

C ◉ ◉ Reading and speaking

1 Work with your partner and answer these questions about ginger and honey, two of nature's most amazing and healthiest foods.

   a Have you ever eaten either of them? If yes, how often do you eat them? If not, why not?

   b Which one do you like most? Why? If you do not like them, explain why.

   c How do you eat them? As an ingredient in a dish, or as an addition to something?

2 Which of the following pieces of information do you think relates to ginger and which to honey? Why? Give reasons for your choices.

   a … has an interesting history …

   b … produces clusters of white and pink flower buds which bloom into yellow flowers …

   c A great natural source of carbohydrates which provide strength and energy to our bodies …

   d A thick, golden liquid produced by …

   e Furthermore, high blood pressure and severe headaches can also be alleviated …

   f By the 17th century, sugar was being used regularly as a sweetener …

   g Cave paintings in Spain from 7000 BCE show the earliest records …

   h It can also be brewed in boiling water to make … tea …

   i It's definitely not pretty to look at …

   j Each flower has a varied vitamin and mineral content …

3 Find a partner, work as **Student A** and **Student B**, and do the following **on your own**.

   a **Student A:** Find the text: 'Ginger – part of nature's pharmacy' in Appendix 2.

   Student B: Find the text: 'Honey – nature's oldest food' in Appendix 2.

   b Quickly read your text and check your answers to Activity C2. Do not say anything to your partner yet.

   c Read your text again. Find and write notes about the following:

   i at least **three** pieces of information about the history of either ginger or honey

   ii at least **four** geographical locations

   iii the production process of either ginger or honey

   iv at least **four** different uses of ginger or honey

   v at least **one** thing that particularly surprised/interested you.

4 Work with your partner and tell each other what you found out.

5 Discuss the following:

   a Which of the two foods do you think is the most amazing? Do you agree with each other? Why/not?

   b How popular are ginger or honey in your country? Why do you think this is so? What kind of dishes do people use them in?

   c Do people in your country use ginger or honey for medicinal purposes or remedies? How?

   d Do people in your country generally have a healthy lifestyle? Give examples to support your opinion.

D 🔍 Language focus: quantifying phrases

1 We can use certain expressions before nouns to express something about **quantity**. These expressions are known as quantifying phrases:

   Example: *a number of honey bee fossils date back to ….*

   a What do you notice about the noun that follows the phrase *a number of*?

   b What do you notice about the verb that follows the noun *honey bee fossils*?

2 Which quantifying phrases precede these plural nouns in the two texts you have just read?

   Example: *a number of + (honey bee) fossils*

a countries	**e** sweetmeats and cakes
b (other) luxuries	**f** areas
c (different) uses	**g** vitamins and minerals.
d studies	

3 Some plural-only nouns can be quantified by: *a pair of.*

   Example: *a pair of scissors*

   Think of **at least three** other plural-nouns which can be quantified by *a pair of.*

4 Which other phrases do you know which can be used to indicate quantity? Write a list.

   Examples: *a bottle of, a slice of, …*

5 Complete the gaps in this paragraph from a magazine article about high intensity exercise using four suitable quantifying phrases from the box. Could any of the quantifying phrases be used to complete more than one gap?

---

a majority of   a large number of   a mix of   a few minutes of   the minority of
one of the   a variety of   twenty hours of

High intensity exercise: Can less really be more?

Could just … exercise a week be good for your health? Apparently it can. According to … studies (as well as … fitness fanatics who can't stop talking about it), short and intense 'High Intensity Training' (HIT) workouts are the way to go. Of course, not every exercise is perfect, and … drawbacks of HIT is that if participants increase the level of intensity of each workout too quickly, they run the risk of incurring an injury.

Adapted from: 'High Intensity Exercise: Can less really be more?' in *Wings of Oman* (Oman Air in-flight magazine) May 2016

E 🔊 💬 Listening and speaking

1 Look at this example role-play card from a speaking examination. Work with your partner and remind yourselves of what you need to do in the role-play.

Healthy living

More and more people are concerned about having a healthy lifestyle.
Discuss this topic.

Use the following prompts, in the order given below, to develop the conversation:

- what you do to have a healthy lifestyle
- some people you know who try to have a healthy lifestyle and the reasons for this
- the advantages and disadvantages of a healthy lifestyle
- the stresses and dangers of being obsessed with health and fitness
- the suggestion that the people who profit from the health and fitness industry are not motivated by the right reasons.

You may introduce related ideas of your own to expand on these prompts.

Remember, you are not allowed to make any written notes.

---

2 Look at each of the five prompts more carefully. Which ones do you think are the least and most challenging to answer? Why?

3 🔊 CD2, Track 6 Listen to six different students responding to the five prompts but in the wrong order. Match each student's response to the correct prompt. One response doesn't fit – put an X.

Adam _____

Hana _____

Mustafa _____

Sara _____

Miska _____

Layla _____

4 🔊 CD2, Track 7 Now listen to the five students who responded to the prompts. Which of the following **six** phrases could be added to what each student says? Which one does **not** fit? Match each phrase to the correct student.

a But I know that I should do more. The longer you wait, the more difficult it gets to change.

b They all say how much they enjoy it, and they never seem to be bored with nothing to do.

c I think the key is moderation. If you do the right amount, it is obviously very beneficial, but too much could cause an injury.

d This type of lifestyle can take over everything you do, and I think that can be risky and cause you to worry.

e I think that when you pay for something, it's up to you to make sure you are getting good value for money.

f There aren't enough opportunities for healthy living where I live.

LANGUAGE TIP:

FILLERS

Notice how the speakers use different *fillers* in their connected speech. These make what they say sound more natural and fluent.

To be honest … , I guess that …

Look again at the audioscript and find more examples of fillers used by the other four speakers. Complete the exercise in your **Workbook**.

5 ◉ Listen to the **five** students again, this time responding to the prompts in the correct order. You will also hear each student saying something **extra** about their prompt. As you listen, decide which student:

a believes that a healthy lifestyle involves exercising the brain as well as the body

b is not convinced about the benefits of healthy living

c says that making money is part of life

d thinks that they eat well and exercise enough

e worries about being embarrassed.

6 Read the audioscript in Appendix 3 to check your answers.

7 Look at these exam-style follow-up questions to the five responses. Discuss each question with your partner and give suitable responses. Try to use some of the fillers from the **Language Tip** in this and other units.

a Tell me what you consider to be a healthy diet.

b What do you think you are missing out on by not joining in?

c How can mental activities lead to healthier living?

d Why do you think that living in a healthy way is not enjoyable?

e What motivation, apart from financial profit, might someone have for being in the health and fitness business?

F 💬 Speaking

1 In many speaking examinations, students are assessed in several broad areas. What do you think these might be?

Example: *vocabulary*

2 In the Cambridge IGCSE speaking exam, the following three areas are assessed: *Structure, Vocabulary,* and *Development and Fluency*. In which of the three areas do you think you would find each of the following nine criteria (a-i)? Why?

a Errors will occur when attempting to use more complex structures

b Is confidently in control of the structures used

c Makes an attempt to respond to questions and prompts

d Pronunciation and intonation are generally clear.

e Shades of meaning are achieved

f Shows sustained ability to maintain a conversation

g There is likely to be hesitation, repetition and searching for words

h Uses a range of structures accurately

i Uses a sufficient range of vocabulary

TOP TIP

In speaking exams, you are not being assessed on your knowledge of the topic itself, but on your ability to communicate effectively in English.

159

G 🕐 Watch, listen and talk

1 🕐 You are going to watch an IGCSE student talking about **Healthy Living**. The student is responding to the same prompts that you have already seen in **Section D**. Which, if any, of the criteria from Activity E2 could apply to the student? Why?

2 🕐 Now watch a second student responding to the same prompts. Do you think they perform better or worse than the first student? Why? Which, if any, of the criteria from Activity E2 could apply to the student? Why?

H 📖 📝 Reading and writing

1 You are going to read a magazine article about gardening to keep fit. The article contains three paragraphs with the answers to these three questions:

a Is gardening good exercise?

b What makes gardening good exercise?

c How can I get the most exercise out of gardening?

Before you read, what do you think the answers to the questions are?

2 Make six complete sentences by matching the phrases in **A** and **B**. All the information comes from the article.

A		B	
a	Besides the exertion involved, gardening	1	provide resistance training similar to weight lifting.
b	Gardening definitely	2	can burn 150 to 300 calories.
c	Gardening for 30 to 45 minutes a day	3	has other pluses that make it a good form of exercise and calorie burning.
d	Gardening isn't usually enough exercise to	4	replace your daily walk or swim.
e	It takes at least 30 minutes of exercise several days a week, to really	5	has many health and therapeutic benefits.
f	Lifting bags, pushing wheelbarrows and shovelling all	6	receive any health benefits from gardening.

3 In which of the three paragraphs do you think you will find the sentences from Activity H2? There are two sentences from each paragraph.

4 Read the text and fill the gaps using the six sentences from Activity H2.

Dig and get fit

Is gardening good exercise?

People certainly feel like they have put in a good day's work after gardening for hours on end. But is gardening really considered good exercise? Well, for the most part, yes, it is. **(a)** This is especially true with 'eat-what-you-grow' or 'edible' gardening, and is just as effective as other moderate to strenuous forms of exercise, like walking and bicycling. It all depends on what gardening task you are doing and for how long. However, as with any other form of exercise, you have to be active for at least 30 minutes for there to be a benefit. **(b)** Be aware that this is not just standing there watering the flowers, but weeding, digging, hoeing, raking and planting.

What makes gardening good exercise?

While enjoying yourself in the garden, you are also working the full range of major muscle groups: legs, buttocks, arms, shoulders, neck, back and abdomen. Gardening tasks that use these muscles build strength and burn calories. **(c)** There can be a great deal of stretching involved with gardening, like reaching for weeds or tall branches, bending to plant and extending a rake. **(d)** This which leads to healthier bones and joints. Yet while doing all this, there is minimal jarring and stress on the body, unlike aerobics or jogging.

How can I get the most exercise out of gardening?

(e) However, researchers are now saying that you can break that 30 minutes up into shorter active periods throughout the day. As long as each activity lasts at least 8 minutes and is of moderate **intensity★**, when you total them up to 30 minutes per day, you'll receive the same benefits as if you had been gardening for 30 minutes non-stop. So you can do a little weeding in the cool of the morning and go back out to the garden

in the evening to do the shovelling. **(f)** However, it is good to know those tired muscles you feel after turning the compost are actually something good you did for your body and your health. As with any other form of exercise, check with your doctor first, if you are not used to strenuous exercise. Make sure you incorporate a little stretching before and after gardening and take things slowly in extreme heat. We garden for the pleasure, after all. Getting in shape, building up body **strength★** and losing weight are just the icing on the cake.

★See the **WORD TIP.**

Adapted from: http://gardening.about.com

5 **Work alone.** Read the text in more detail and find **one** piece of information in each paragraph that particularly surprises or interests you. Tell your partner – do you agree or disagree with each other's choices? Why?

161

6 Read the text again and complete the notes. Write three pieces of information under each heading.

Is gardening good exercise?
Has many healthy and therapeutic benefits

–

–

–

What makes gardening good exercise?

–

–

–

How can I get the most out of gardening?

–

–

WORD TIP

intensity (noun) =
the quality of being
felt strongly or
having a very strong
effect

strength (noun) =
the ability to do
things that need a
lot of physical or
mental effort

Complete the
exercise in your
Workbook.

7 Use your notes in Activity H6 to help you write a summary of the health benefits of gardening.

8 Do you have a garden, or access to one? If yes, how likely are you to think about doing some gardening as a form of exercise? Why? If you don't have a garden, would you like to have one and do some gardening as a form of exercise? Why/not?

REFLECTION

How well do you think you can do each of these things now?

Give yourself a score from 1: Still need a lot of practice to 5: Feeling very confident about this

In this unit you:	1	2	3	4	5
watched a video of students talking about healthy living, and discussed what they said					
talked about different activities and healthy living					
read about two different healthy foods and discussed them					
watched and listened to students taking part in a speaking role-play, and assessed their performance					
read about gardening and made notes and wrote a summary					

Now set yourself a **personal goal** based on your scores for Unit 15.

Exam focus

Speaking, Part 2, topic cards

1   Look at this exam-style role-play card. Work with your partner and discuss how you might respond to each of the prompts.

2   In pairs, role-play a speaking exam. Then change roles.

Lifestyle changes

There have been many changes in the way people live in the past one hundred years.
Discuss this topic.

Use the following prompts, in the order given below, to develop the conversation:

*   things that you have today that people one hundred years ago had no idea about
*   your idea of a healthy lifestyle compared to your grandparents' lifestyles
*   standards of living and differences in income and possessions
*   opportunities to know more about healthy living and different lifestyles
*   the idea that people in the past had a much better understanding of a healthy lifestyle than we do today.

You may introduce related ideas of your own to expand on these prompts.

Remember, you are not allowed to make any written notes.

Part 4:
Ideas and the modern world

In Part 4: Ideas and the modern world, there are five units (16 Social media, 17 The environment, 18 Hunger, 19 Fashions, 20 Technology). You will:

■ watch and listen to some IGCSE students talking about each unit's topic, and doing an IGCSE speaking exam roleplay;

■ think about and discuss what the students said;

■ read a variety of texts about spending time online, recycling and climate change, biotechnology, ethical fashion;

■ listen to someone talking mobile phone risks, an interview about chewing gum, people talking about fashion;

■ practise various exam skills: note-making, summary writing, writing for purpose, listening, speaking.

Before you start Part 4, look at the picture on these pages:

   a   What do you think the picture shows? Why?

   b   Would you like to have a picture like this on a wall in your home? Why?

   c   What connection does this picture have with the theme for Part 4: Ideas and the modern world?

   d   Imagine you are messaging a friend. How would you describe the picture to them?

   e   How important is the study of science and technology to you? Why?

Learning objectives

In this unit you will:

- watch a video of students talking about social media, and discuss what they say
- discuss information about social media presented in a graphic
- read and talk about the negative impacts of spending too much time online
- listen to someone talking about the physical risks involved in over-using mobile phones
- read about people's favourite social media and their reasons

A 😀 Watch, listen and talk

1 Watch and listen to some IGCSE students talking about **social media**.

   a What do the students understand by the term 'social media'? What examples of social media do they give? Make a note of **three**.

   b Which social media do the students use most, and with whom? What **reasons** do they give?

2 Talk to your partner/s about the social media **you** use, and why you choose not to use others.

B 🔤 Speaking and vocabulary

1 You are going to look at some statistics about the global digital age. Before you study the graphics decide with your partner what the following three words and phrases mean.

> active social media users   unique mobile users   urbanisation

2 Look at these five icons. What information do you think each icon is showing? Match these headings to the icons:

> Active mobile social users   Active social media users   Internet users
> Total population   Unique mobile users

3 Look at the following two graphics. What **general information** does each one give? Match these headings (i) *Annual Growth*, (ii) *Global Digital Snapshot*, to the graphics.

4 Work in pairs: Student A and Student B. Look carefully at your graphic (A or B) and **in one sentence** tell your partner what it shows. Do **not** give any **specific** information from the graphic. You could begin like this: *My graphic shows/gives information about …*

Total population: 7.395 billion

Internet users: 3.417 billion

Active social media users: 2.307 billion

Unique mobile users: 3.790 billion

Active mobile social users: 1.968 billion

Growth in the number of active internet users: +332 billion (since Jan 2015) +10%

Growth in the number of active social media users: +219 billion (since Jan 2015) +10%

Growth in the numbers of unique mobile users: +141 billion (since Jan 2015) +10%

Growth in the number of active mobile social users: +283 billion (since Jan 2015) +10%

5 Now find the answers to these questions.
There are **three** questions for each graphic.

According to the graphic:

a How many more people are now active internet users than in January 2015?

b How many people live in the world?

c What does the number 1.968 billion refer to?

d What does the number 219 billion refer to?

e What has increased by 10% since January 2015?

f What percentage of 7.395 billion is 2.307 billion?

6 Tell your partner the answers to your three questions and together decide which information is the most interesting or surprising.

7 Design a graph or chart showing some or all of the information in your graphic. Prepare to present the information to your class.

C Reading

1 Doing things online can take up a lot of your time. In groups, discuss and answer these questions.

a How much time do you think you spend online each day? Is this a problem?

b How often do use social media or watch TV while doing homework? Does it affect your school performance?

c Are you someone who texts all the time? Do you find it difficult to stop texting? What do you think might be the result of too much texting?

d Do you think that using your phone before you go to sleep could have an impact on the quality of your sleep? Why/not?

2 You are going to read a web article about how much time teenagers spend online, and the effects that this has on them. Before you read, work with your partner and check the meaning of the following:

> abstained   avid multitaskers   compulsively   mind-boggling
> self-esteem   suppressed   traits   tweens

> **TOP TIP**
> When answering questions that refer to a chart or a table, or some other graphic, make sure that you look carefully at all the information, as well as any text and the title. Look for questions that start with the words *According to the diagram/graph/ etc …*

167

3 Read the text and complete the gaps a–h using the words and phrases from Activity C2.

Teens spend a (a) ... nine hours a day using media, report says

1 The fact that teenagers spend a lot of time using different media probably comes as no surprise to anyone. What is shocking, however, is just *how much* time they are actually spending doing this. Teens spend about *nine hours* daily using media, and this only includes media used for enjoyment purposes. Media used at school or for homework purposes is not even included. The nine-hour figure includes media of all types. When just media on screens (laptops, smartphones and tablets) is counted, teens spent more than 6.5 hours daily, while **(b)** ... spent more than 4.5 hours.

2 Indeed, today's young people have become **(c)** ..., often using media while engaged in other activities. Half of them reported that they 'often' or 'sometimes' use social media or watch TV while doing homework, while 60% say they text, and 75% listen to music **while★** doing so. Two-thirds of the kids believed TV or texting had no influence on the quality of their schoolwork, **while★** 50% believed social media usage made no difference. However, research (and experience) will tell you otherwise. A study by researchers found, for instance, that 'media multitaskers' performed worse in tests.

3 A study of more than 400 teens revealed that teens who text **(d)** ... are more likely to have trouble sleeping and achieve lower academic performance. Compulsive texters are not only defined by the number of texts they send, but they also have

(e) ... such as lying about the amount of time they spend texting, difficulty in stopping the behaviour, and losing sleep to text. Girls in the study were much more likely to text compulsively than boys. Past studies have also linked excessive texting to lower grades. In one study, students who **(f)** ... from texting during a lecture wrote down 62% more information in their notes and recalled more detailed information from the lecture than those who were texting. The non-texters also scored a full letter-grade-and-a-half higher on a multiple choice test. A separate study similarly revealed that students who texted or used Facebook while doing schoolwork had lower overall grades.

4 Overall social media use, and especially night-time use, was associated with poorer sleep quality, lower **(g)** ..., and higher levels of anxiety and depression among 12- to 18-year-olds, according to research. On the one hand, teens are staying up late to respond to messages and monitor what is happening so they do not miss out. Teens may also be woken up by text messages they receive. On the other hand, even the light from a smartphone, computer, or tablet could be interfering with teens' sleep. Melatonin is a regulator of your sleep cycle, and when it is **(h)** ... there is less stimulation to promote sleepiness at a healthy bedtime. Computer screens and most light bulbs emit blue light, to which your eyes are particularly sensitive simply because it is the type of light most common outdoors during daytime hours. As a result, they can easily disrupt your melatonin production and keep you awake. Research shows, for instance, that children who use electronic media at night go to bed later, get fewer hours of sleep per week, and report more daytime sleepiness. Also, adolescents with a television in their bedroom go to bed later, have more difficulty falling asleep, and have a shorter total sleep time. Furthermore, sending texts or e-mails after initially going to bed increases daytime sleepiness among teens (even if it is done only once a week).

★See the **WORD TIP.**
Adapted from: http://articles.mercola.com

4 Read the text again and think back to your discussion in Activity C1. How much of what you and your partners talked about was confirmed (or not) in the text?

> **WORD TIP**
>
> *while* (conjunction) = **1 DURING**: during the time that; **2 COMPARING**: used to compare two different facts
>
> Complete the exercise in your **Workbook**.

5 There are a lot of numbers in paragraphs 1–3. Look back at the text and say what the following refer to.

Example: *nine hours = the amount of time teenagers spend each day using social media*

a 6.5 hours and 4.5 hours

b 60% and 75%

c 50%

d 400 teens

e 62%

> **LANGUAGE TIP**
>
> Some English words have an *–ia* ending in the plural, and *–ium* in the singular, for example: *many social media, one social medium*. These words often (but not always) come from Latin.

6 Read the text again and answer these questions.

a How long do teenagers spend using different media each day?

b Which use of media is not counted in this number?

c How many young people admit to using social media while doing their homework?

d What do studies show us about people who multitask?

e What are the likely results for teenagers who are unable to stop texting? Give **two** details.

f What reasons are given for teenagers not going to sleep early? Give **two** details.

g Apart from the noise from a smartphone, what other factor might affect someone's sleep?

h What does melatonin do?

i Why are our eyes sensitive to the light from a phone or tablet?

D 🔊 Listening

1 You are going to listen to an extract from a radio talk in which the speaker continues on the subject of social media usage. Before you listen, match the words in column A with a suitable meaning from column B.

A	B
sedentary	assess
detrimental	strong material between bones
arteries	extremely significant
profound	blood-carrying tubes
gauge	indications
precursors	harmful
disc	inactive

2 Work with your partner. Match the phrases in columns A and B to make complete sentences.

A	B
a Children spend more than 60% of their waking day sitting down …	**1** but texting may also play a significant role.
b However, after sitting for three hours, playing on tablets or watching movies …	**2** so it is best to encourage kids to stay active.
c The girls' artery function had returned to normal a few days later …	**3** there was a '**profound**' negative change in functioning arteries by up to 33% in the girls.
d Still, no one knows what effect sitting for hours, day after day, has on kids' health …	**4** when they returned to the laboratory for tests.
e Not surprisingly, researchers have found that higher cellphone use …	**5** was linked to reduced physical activity and fitness.
f The researcher connected this to carrying heavy school books, watching TV, and playing video games …	**6** and by some estimates children sit for an average of 8.5 hours a day.

3 🔊 CD2, Track 8 Listen and check your answers to Activity D2.

4 🔊 CD2, Track 8 Listen again and answer the questions. For each question choose the correct answer A, B or C.

a Why did researchers choose to focus their study on young girls?

    A Evidence shows that their activity levels decrease from the age of eight.

    B Young girls sit on average for 8.5 hours per day.

    C Because sitting down has a high risk factor.

b What was noticed after three hours of sedentary activity?

    A The girls were completely healthy.

    B One-third of girls displayed problems.

    C 13% had increased heart disease.

c What was the positive outcome from the research?

    A There was a 1% decline in heart problems.

    B The girls' medical condition went back to the usual level.

    C More girls started to do cycling.

d According to the writers of the research, using cellphones …

    A causes health problems in 10% of young people.

    B creates problems when carrying heavy books.

    C may create back problems in children aged ten.

LANGUAGE TIP

In the listening text, you heard these two expressions: *According to (the authors)* … and *Depending on (the research you read)* …. Both can have several meanings, depending on their context.

In *According to (the authors)* …, we are being told where the information or ideas have come from *(the authors)*. In *Depending on (the research you read)* …, we understand that one thing (in this case which research you read) is changed or affected by something else *(the possibility of having back problems)*.

Complete the exercise in your **Workbook**.

E 🌐 Language focus: -ing forms

1 Words ending in –ing can be used in many different ways. Look at these examples:

a	as a verb after a preposition:	Before <u>going</u> to sleep, switch off your mobile phone.
b	as sentence subject:	<u>Using</u> your phone in bed can affect your sleep pattern.
c	to list activities:	<u>Texting</u>, <u>taking</u> photos, <u>making</u> videos, recording …
d	to add information in a clause:	He walked down the street <u>texting</u>.
e	in continuous tenses:	She was <u>falling</u> asleep when her phone rang.
f	after certain verbs:	They enjoy <u>chatting</u> online with their friends overseas.
g	as an adjective:	It's <u>surprising</u> that teens perform so poorly in tests.

2 In the reading text earlier in this unit there are many examples of words ending in –ing. For each example from the text, say in which way the **–ing** word is being used. How many different ways can you identify?

   a What is **shocking**, however, is just *how much* time they are actually **spending** doing this.

   b … such as **lying** about the amount of time they spend **texting**, difficulty in **stopping** the behaviour, and **losing** sleep to text.

   c students who abstained from **texting** during a lecture

   d students who texted or used Facebook while **doing** schoolwork

   e teens are **staying** up late to respond to messages and monitor what is **happening**

3 Look at the first paragraph only of the listening audioscript in Appendix 3. Find at least three examples of words ending in –ing, and say how they are being used.

F 📖 Reading: multiple matching

1 What do you know about Instagram, Facebook, Pinterest and Snapchat? Work in small groups and tell each other which, if any, of these social media you use. What are the advantages and disadvantages of each one?

2 You are going to read a magazine article about four people who use the different social media from Activity F1. What do you think each person might say about how, why and when they use their chosen social medium?

   A Ada Fischer – a travel journalist – Instagram

   B Pavlos Theodolou – a university student – Facebook

   C Renata Fierro – a stay-at-home mother – Pinterest

   D Adrian Larsen – a school-age student – Snapchat

3 Here are some of the things the four people said. Match each comment (a–h) to Ada, Pavlos, Renata or Adrian, and give reasons for your choices. Could any of the comments apply to more than one person? There are two comments for each.

a … at the same time, I get to call them, chat with them and even video chat with them without paying …

b I get to play around with my friends …

c I had lots of people, from all over the world, following me …

d I'm very proud when I see food that I made …

e … keep in touch with all my friends and family back home …

f … now they've grown up a bit …

g … requires me to constantly visit new places around the world …

h … the photo or the video only lasts up to 10 seconds and then disappears forever …

4 Work in pairs: **Student A** and **Student B**. Student A quickly look at what Ada and Renata wrote, Student B quickly look at what Pavlos and Adrian wrote. Check and share your answers to F2.

Ada Fischer

My job as a travel journalist requires me to constantly visit new places around the world, and I use Instagram to post all my wonderful experiences. When I started travelling for work four years ago, I wanted to find a way that I could share my unique experiences with others. I tried a few other forms of social media, but none of them were really what I was looking for. My friend suggested Instagram to me and I loved it immediately! I could post countless photos and very soon I had lots of people, from all over the world, following me and liking my photographs. It was great that I was finally able to share my travel experiences with so many people, and by posting all my photographs on Instagram, I preserved all my memories of my travels.

Pavlos Theodolou

I'm currently studying at Nottingham University in the UK, although I'm originally from Cyprus. I've been using Facebook for years, but lately, ever since I've moved to the UK, it's been the perfect way for me to keep in touch with all my friends and family back home. It's great because I can post photos of my time here at Nottingham University so they see how I'm getting on, but at the same time I get to call them, chat with them and even video chat without paying, which is important for a student. It's also great, because while they can see what I'm doing here in the UK, I can see what they're getting up to back in Cyprus. It makes me feel homesick sometimes, but the fact that I can speak with them so easily makes being away from home for such long periods a lot easier for me, and the distance seems less.

172

Renata Fierro

When I gave birth to my second child I decided to become a stay-at-home mum, but now they've grown up a bit I want to be able to do some work from home. I've always been a very keen baker and cook, so my sister suggested to me that I should start posting my recipes on social media. I found Pinterest was the best way to do this, as I could create different boards on my profile for different categories of recipes. My creations have been well-received and lots of people have been pinning my recipes and photographs onto their profiles! I'm very proud when I see food that I made appear on Pinterest. It gives me a sense of purpose and I have definitely become more self-assured, and my creations have become much more adventurous.

Adrian Larsen

A lot of school-age teenagers, like me in Norway, are really into social media, and recently Snapchat has come onto the scene. I know a lot of people aren't too sure about its suitability, but I think it's brilliant! I get to play around with my friends taking ridiculous photographs with them, adding silly effects and sending them to people I know. It's a great laugh for when you're out and about with people, or you just want to document what you're doing at that specific point in time. The most important thing is that the photo or the video only lasts up to 10 seconds and then it disappears forever, along with any embarrassment, thank goodness! You can also add a video or photo to your story which lasts for 24 hours and all your friends on Snapchat can see it. It's good fun and always makes you laugh.

5 Read all four paragraphs. For questions a–j, choose from the people A–D. The people may be chosen more than once.

Which person (A, B, C or D) …

a decided not to go out to work because of a new baby?

b does not stay at home for their work?

c feels more confident now?

d has a family member who gave them encouragement to do something?

e is able to look back and remember places?

f is aware of feeling some discomfort because of photos and videos?

g knows that not everyone thinks their choice of social media is appropriate?

h needs to consider the cost of social media?

i thinks that their choice makes home and family seem closer?

j uses their social medium to have a lot of fun?

6 What is your favourite social medium? Why? Write a paragraph of about 150 words in the same style as the ones you have just read.

REFLECTION

How well do you think you can do each of these things now?

Give yourself a score from 1: Still need a lot of practice to 5: Feeling very confident about this

In this unit you:	1	2	3	4	5
watched a video of students talking about social media, and discussed what they said					
discussed information about social media presented in a graphic					
read and talked about the negative impacts of spending too much time online					
listened to someone talking about the physical risks involved in over-using mobile phones					
read about peoples' favourite social media and their reasons					

Now set yourself a **personal goal** based on your scores for Unit 16.

Exam focus

Reading, Exercise 2, multiple matching

1 You are going to read a magazine article about four people and their opinions about social media. For exercises a–j, choose from the people A–D. The people may be chosen more than once.

A Ethan Atwood

I've grown up in an age where social media is getting bigger every day and it's pretty hard to avoid it even if you wanted to. On my part, I think it's a great thing and I'm proud to have grown up in a time when technology has made such giant advances. It's easier to keep in touch with people, you can find out what's going on in the world and you're constantly reading articles or watching videos posted on social media platforms that teach you something new. The only bad thing is that it takes up so much time, making it sometimes easy to forget what's going on around you, because you're so focused on the screen in front of you.

B Areya Atitarn

These days in Thailand, wherever you go, you see young people carrying tablets, or those smartphones. When teenagers are walking in the street they hardly look up from their screens to take in their surroundings and they are constantly taking photos and posting them on social media. I on the other hand have no use for social media, and neither do I like the idea of it. It concerns me that people have become too interested in the lives of celebrities and trying to copy what they wear and how they look, that they have begun to forget the traditions of their own country. Teenagers don't want to make conversation any more, they prefer to talk to their friends on these phones, something that would never have been allowed when I was a child.

C Kweben Dumashie

When I moved to the USA from Ghana five years ago, I had no idea what social media was. It was a very strange thing for me, seeing so many people holding mobile phones, typing on laptops and using social media. I began using social media soon as well, and now the best thing is the fact that I can get in contact with my friends and family who also live abroad, and meet new people. Although at the beginning I thought it would be difficult to become accustomed to this way of life, I now see that it is much easier than I thought; I have even started writing a blog about my experiences here in the USA. The only thing I dislike about social media is how we think it is more important to post what we are doing and where we are, rather than enjoying ourselves.

D Samirah al Nejem

I don't use social media very much, though my friends do and they always rave about how much fun it is. They convinced me to get started on one of the social media platforms so I could advertise the clothes I make. I am an aspiring fashion designer and yesterday, thanks to social media, I made my second sale online. I'm not a fan of using it constantly and nor is it my idea of fun, but I do like the fact that it can eventually help me establish my business and get my hard work recognised. I come from a very small community, and I don't believe I would ever be able to get my fashion designing started if I didn't have the help of social media to get me the attention that I so desperately need.

Which person …

a	believes that social media helps us to improve our understanding?	[1]
b	feels it is difficult to escape from different types of social media?	[1]
c	has started to make money through social media?	[1]
d	is not interested in using a phone or tablet?	[1]
e	learnt about social media when they moved to a different country?	[1]
f	publishes online information about their life?	[1]
g	says that young people no longer want to talk to each other?	[1]
h	sees social media as a way of communicating with people in a similar situation?	[1]
i	uses social media to advertise themselves and their work?	[1]
j	worries that people are no longer individuals?	[1]

[Total: 10 Extended]

Learning objectives

In this unit you will:

- watch a video of students talking about pollution and the environment, and discuss what they say
- discuss information about pollution and its impact on our lives
- read and talk about a recycling system in Indonesia
- read and talk about climate change in Europe
- write notes and summaries using notes

A 🙂 Watch, listen and talk

1 Watch and listen to some IGCSE students talking about **pollution** and the **environment**.
   a What do the students think are the main causes of pollution? Make a note of three things.
   b What do the students say about the measures being taken in their own countries to reduce or control pollution and to protect the environment? How successful are they?

2 Talk to your partner/s about pollution in your country, what is being done to reduce or control it, and how successful these measures are.

B Speaking and vocabulary

1 Work with a partner. Look at the five pictures and answer the questions.

   a Make a list of **at least two** nouns or adjectives for each picture. You do **not** need to describe the pictures in detail.

   b In which parts of the world do you think the photographs were taken? Why do you think this?

   c What has caused the situation in each picture?

   d What is the likely impact on humans, animals and vegetation?

   e What can be done to stop or reduce these types of situations from becoming worse?

LANGUAGE TIP

Look at these commonly confused introductory phrases that we often use when describing things. Complete the exercise in your **Workbook**.

Introductory phrase	+ verb (phrase)	+ noun (phrase)	+ adjective (phrase)
It looks/seems like … (+ verb OR + noun)	we have destroyed the planet. the bears won't survive. it's too late.	a desert. complete destruction.	
It looks/seems as if/though … (+ verb)			
It looks/seems … (+ adjective)			disgusting. totally untouched.

   f Describe in more detail what each of the five pictures shows. Use your words from Activity B1a and the introductory phrases in the **Language Tip**.

2 Answer the questions about the following places.

> the Arctic   the Atlantic Ocean   the Pacific Ocean   Europe   Canada
> Russia   Asia   North America

   a Is it a continent, a country or region, or something else?

   b Where would you find it on a map?

   c Do you think any could be the places shown in the pictures from Activity B1?

   d Which place is nearest to where you live?

   e If you could choose to live in one of the places from the list, which one would it be? Why?

   f Which place or places would you **not** like to live in? Why?

C 📖 ✍ **Reading and writing**

1 You are going to read a newspaper article about a system used in Indonesia for recycling waste. Before you read, work with your partner and check the meaning of the following words and phrases from the article.

> shape the mindset   beverage   biodegradable   consensus   a cooperative
> discarded   brooches   fertiliser and compost   gather   inorganic   a glimpse of

2 What do you now think you are likely to read about in the article? Make a list of **two** or **three** things.

3 Here are five newspaper headlines. Take a few minutes to look quickly at the article and choose the best one. Do not worry about the gaps a–k and the words in boxes at the moment.

a 70 categories for inorganic waste

b Earning money from waste

c Citizens' handicrafts for sale

d Differences between organic and inorganic waste,

e Trash, garbage, rubbish, waste – it's all the same to us

A trash bank in East Java helps create economic and environmental benefits as citizens make and sell products from recycled materials

1   As heat from the morning sun rises, a number of women and elders are packing used articles and trash into plastic bags and sacks in their house yard. These early risers take the packs by motorcycle and pushcart to a local resident's house to be weighed. This is just **(a)** … the waste handling activities in a trash bank community unit in Malang, East Java, Indonesia. The Bank Sampah Malang (BSM) is **(b)** … set up in 2011, which also serves as the centre of trash collection and management, receiving three tonnes of dry or **(c)** … rubbish daily.

2   The members of the BSM cooperative are from community units and school groups, as well as individuals, who **(d)** … and sort trash from their homes and workplaces, separating organic and inorganic rubbish. The former is **(e)** … and can be processed in the presence of oxygen, and can be recycled as **(f)** … later on, while the latter is any waste of non-biological origin, of industrial origin or some other non-natural process, for example: plastics and synthetic fabrics. Group members take their separated trash for weighing to a local leader, while individual members send their trash directly to the central BSM location. Trash delivery time is based on a **(g)** ... for groups, and once a month for individuals. The trash is collected by dump trucks and taken for further sorting, packing and weighing by warehouse workers, and information is then sent to the trash bank where calculations are made about its value, and payments are made to individuals' or groups' bank accounts. Members who strictly sort their rubbish according to the 70 categories for inorganic trash can earn a lot more money, and information is readily available for them on how to do this.

3 Used plastic **(h)** ... bottles are directly processed into plastic chips after being separated from their labels and caps and grouped by colour. **(i)** ... plastic bags, paper, iron and bottle caps are packed and sent to factories in Malang and Subabaya, where some of what was once seen as trash will return to the central BSM in the form of plastic sheets for making handicrafts. Plastic packaging for food, soap, detergent, shampoo and coffee, among others, is also recycled into various everyday products,

including umbrellas, handbags, hats, tissue holders and jewellery such as **(j)** ...

4 As a BSM member, each person receives training and learns skills in how to make handicrafts using recycled materials. They are also advised about how to sell their products online. Not all of the money earned through the trash bank can be distributed freely, especially for group members, as some of the earnings are spent on environmental development, such as a park construction or tree planting. Additionally, BSM assists members with their savings which can be exchanged for basic necessities, electricity bill payments and health insurance.

5 So far, only inorganic waste is handled by the BSM, leaving wet garbage to the Supit Urang landfill as the trash bank's land area is too small for a worm-breeding and compost-making site. However, BSM feels it has provided a solution for the problem of inorganic waste, and believes that its efforts will gradually **(k)** ... of locals so that they avoid carelessly and unnecessarily dumping waste.

Adapted from: 'Earning from Waste' in *Muscat Daily* newspaper 17 February 2016

179

4 Read the text more slowly and decide which words and phrases from Exercise C1 can complete the gaps a–k.

5 Look at this exam-style question. With a partner, decide exactly what you have to do. What information is asked for? How many notes do you need to write in total? Do **not** write an answer yet.

You have been asked by your teacher to make a presentation to students about the BSM system and you need to make notes in order to prepare. Make short notes under each heading.

What happens after trash collection

- trash taken for sorting and packing
- ... [1]
- ... [1]
- ... [extended only] [1]

How BSM helps its members

- ... [1]
- ... [1]
- ... [extended only] [1]

Products made from recycled trash

- ... [1]
- ... [1]
- ... [1]

[Total: 7 Core, 9 Extended]

6 Work with your partner. For each paragraph 1–5, decide which of the following topics a–f is the best match. There is one extra topic which you do not need.

   a Changing attitudes

   b Handicraft products

   c How the BSM operates

   d Paying bills

   e Sorting, collection and delivery of waste

   f Selling products online

7 Go back to the text and for each paragraph write 2–3 notes about each topic.

   Examples: *Paragraph 1 How the BSM operates*: *(i) people take waste to be weighed, (ii) BSM started in 2011, (iii) collects three tonnes of waste daily*

8 Which if any of your notes could you use to answer the exam-style question in Exercise C5?

9 Look at this answer to the question in Activity C5. The student has mixed up some of their notes. Look at the text again and decide with a partner under which heading each of the notes should appear. Be prepared to say why.

> **TOP TIP**
>
> When you are taking notes, you may be given bullet points to respond to. In these cases, make sure you look carefully at the number of bullet points. This will tell you how many notes you are expected to write.

What happens after trash collection

- *trash taken for sorting and packing*
- *plastic sheets for making handicrafts*
- *assists with savings*
- *everyday products such as umbrellas and hats*

Products made from recycled trash

- *information sent to trash bank*
- *jewellery: brooches*
- *gives training*

How BSM helps its members

- *payments made*
- *advice on how to sell products*
- *trash weighed*

D Language focus: referring words

1 We often need to refer back to something in a text, and to avoid repeating particular words we may choose to use *referring words*. Look at these examples from the first paragraph of the text about the BSM system:

As heat from the morning sun rises, a number of women and elders are packing used articles and trash into plastic bags and sacks in their house yard. These early risers take the packs by motorcycle and pushcart to a local resident's house to be weighed.

2 Look at the remaining paragraphs. For each boxed word or words, say which word or words it is referring back to.

E Speaking and vocabulary

1 The following phrases appear in the next text you are going to read. What do you think the text is about?

   a Forest fires, heavy flooding and confused Lithuanian birds …

   b Extreme weather events are no longer restricted to far-off, exotic places …

   c Surveys reveals that half of Danes are worried about their homes flooding …

   d The EU has released its package of climate measures for 2030 …

2 With a partner, make a list of ten more words or phrases that you think might appear in the text. Give reasons for your choices. You will find out later if the words you think of are actually used.

3 Look at these ten words and phrases taken from the text. Discuss each one in small groups and try to agree on its meaning.

> ambitious   bloc   curtail   ecology   exotic   vulnerable
> future prosperity   impacts   mild winters   storm surges

TOP TIP

When you are making notes about a text, remember that they should be brief and must relate to the text you have read. You cannot include information that does not appear in the text.

F 🌐 📖 Reading and writing

1 Look quickly at the text below. Were your predictions in Activities E1 and E2 correct? Do not worry about the gaps in the text at the moment.

REPORT

Europe already feeling climate change impacts

Extreme weather is becoming the new normal across Europe, according to a report from the Climate Action Network By Sophie Yeo

[1] Forest fires, heavy flooding and confused Lithuanian birds – these are some of the effects that climate change is already having in Europe, according to a new report. The study, assembled by the Climate Action Network (CAN) campaign group, examines how climate change is already affecting Europe, from the points of view of (a) … , health and food security. It reveals that countries across Europe are already suffering from the (b) … of climate change, which is putting their environments and economies at risk.

[2] 'Europe and the rest of the developed world can no longer ignore the impacts of climate change,' writes Wendel Trio, director of CAN Europe, in the report. 'Extreme weather events are no longer restricted to far-off, (c) … places. They are also happening on the doorsteps of the richest, most powerful countries, here in Europe, in our communities, affecting our daily lives.'

Regional impacts

[3] A region-by-region analysis highlights the impacts on different countries across the continent. In Lithuania, for instance, birds are dying because the unseasonably (d) … means many decide not to migrate in the winter, leaving them to face the cold when it finally hits.

[4] Low-lying coastal areas across the Nordic region of Europe are already at a high risk of flooding, with sea-level rise leading to stronger and more frequent (e) … . North Sea countries, such as Denmark, are especially vulnerable, with its coastal capital of Copenhagen at particular risk. Surveys reveal that half of Danes are worried about their homes flooding.

[5] France's €30 million a year tourism industry, central to its economy, will be increasingly depressed as the temperatures warm. In the Alps and the Pyrenees, significant snow loss and a greater chance of avalanches threatens to (f) … the ski season and shut some resorts down altogether.

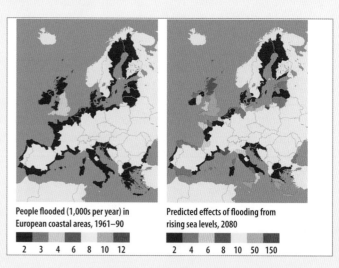

People flooded (1,000s per year) in European coastal areas, 1961–90

2 3 4 6 8 10 12

Predicted effects of flooding from rising sea levels, 2080

2 4 6 8 10 50 150

[6] While a combination of geographical and economic factors mean that the developing world remains the most (g) … to climate change, the report hopes to highlight the fact that Europe needs to play a part in the discussion on the impacts of climate change that are already here. By focusing on the impacts of climate change across Europe, Trio hopes that the European Union (EU) can be encouraged to adopt (h) … targets for reducing emissions. The (i) … is close to meeting its 2020 target of a 20% cut in greenhouse gases, and there is a call for politicians to go beyond this before the end of the decade.

[7] The EU has released its package of climate measures for 2030, which recommend a 45% emissions reduction target. 'Climate change is causing damage to our societies, our environment and to our current and **(j)** … This damage is only going to get worse, unless we take action at the global level, but also at the European level,' says Trio. 'Europe can do much more to take effective action on climate change. Europe can lead by example and adopt more ambitious greenhouse gas emissions reduction targets for 2020.'

Adapted from www.rtcc.org

2 Look at the text more carefully and identify which of these words is needed to complete each gap a–e. Check your answers with your partner's.

| it   its   many   their   they |

WORD TIP

effect (noun) = a change or reaction or result that is caused by something

affect (verb, often *passive*) = **1 CAUSE CHANGE**: to influence someone or something or cause them to change; **2 CAUSE EMOTION**: to cause a strong emotion, especially sadness

Complete the exercise in your **Workbook**.

3 Look at gaps f–j. Think of a suitable referring word for each one. Check your answers with a partner's.

4 Answer the following questions. Then give your answers to your partner to check.

a What does the report say about countries across Europe?

b Why can Europe no longer ignore climate change?

c Does climate change affect European countries in the same way? How do you know?

d What reason is given for birds dying in Lithuania?

e Why are coastal areas in Nordic Europe at a high risk of flooding?

f Why will France's skiing season be at risk? Give **two** reasons.

g According to the second map, what do the red areas indicate?

h Why is the developing world still more at risk than Europe?

i What does Wendel Trio hope will be the effect of focusing on European climate change?

j According to Trio, what things is climate change damaging? Give **three** details.

5 Read the following exam-style question. Decide with your partner exactly what you have to do. Do not write anything yet.

> Read the article about climate change in Section F1.
>
> **Write a summary about the impact of climate change in Europe.**
>
> **Your summary should be about 100 words long. You should use your own words as far as possible.**
>
> You will receive up to 8 marks for the content of your summary and up to 8 marks for the style and accuracy of your language.

183

6 Re-read the text and note the points that relate directly to the summary question in Activity F5. Then make brief notes. Compare your notes with a partner's. Have you chosen the same information? Has your partner included anything that you have not?

7 Write your answer to the summary question in Activity F5, paying particular attention to the advice given in this unit. When you have written your paragraph, exchange it with your partner's and check each other's writing. What exactly should you be looking for? Think about the information given in the exam-style question in Activity F5.

TOP TIP
Summary questions will usually direct you to a specific topic in the text, so it is very important that you underline the key points and make brief notes before you write your answer.

G ⊜ Speaking

1 Work in small groups and answer these questions.

   a What do you use water for? On your own, make two lists: four things you use water for inside your home and four things for outside your home. Compare answers as a group.

   b Imagine that you could only have water for half of the things in your lists in the activity above. Which four would you choose? Why? What if you could only have a quarter – which two would you choose? Why?

   c Does your country have enough water? Where does its water come from? How?

   d How might a flood affect your daily life?

   e Think about the water you drink. Where does it come from?

   f Are there any restrictions on how much water you can have? If not, why not? If there are restrictions, why do they exist?

REFLECTION

How well do you think you can do each of these things now?

Give yourself a score from 1: Still need a lot of practice to 5: Feeling very confident about this

In this unit you:	1	2	3	4	5
watched a video of students talking about pollution, and discussed what they said					
discussed information about pollution and its impact on our lives					
read and talked about a recycling system in Indonesia					
read and talked about climate change in Europe					
wrote notes and summaries using notes					

Now set yourself a **personal goal** based on your scores for Unit 17.

Exam focus

Reading and Writing, Exercise 3, note-making and Exercise 4, summary writing

1 Read the article about drinking water, and then complete the notes.

A dangerous thirst

We are told that we should drink at least 2 litres of water a day, and more if we are exercising, but what many people do not realise is that too much water can be fatal.

The result is hyponatraemia (literally 'low salt'), a condition also known as 'water intoxication'. When we sweat, we lose vital salts that the body needs to maintain its equilibrium. Excessive sweating combined with drinking dilutes the concentration of salts in the body to a dangerous level. The result is nausea, apathy, lethargy, dizziness and mental confusion; sufferers can lapse into a coma and die.

Hyponatraemia was first noticed in 1981 by a doctor in South Africa, when he treated a woman running a marathon. However, anyone is susceptible if they drink water for a prolonged period without ingesting salts.

There are four main factors that could predispose someone to suffer from hyponatraemia. Those most at risk are the very young and the very old because they are less able to regulate their thirst, and their water and salt levels, by themselves. Secondly, anyone who exercises for a prolonged period is at risk; this includes marathon and triathlon competitors. However, it is not the elite athletes who are in danger, but those who run marathons for charity, or as an occasional hobby. You do not have to be especially fit to suffer from hyponatraemia.

Thirdly, heat and humidity increase susceptibility as sweat loss rises

to a litre an hour. The kind of heat at which hyponatraemia can set in is not particularly hot: 20°C. The highest number of incidents recorded at one time was when 24 runners were hospitalised during a marathon in California when the temperature was only 23°C. As it gets hotter, runners slow down, but drink more and do not replace any lost salts. Drinking more than a litre an hour for five or more hours can lead to hyponatraemia.

Lastly, people in nightclubs are also at risk because the atmosphere is hot and humid, and they tend to stay there for a long time without eating anything, but drinking excessive quantities of water. A young woman was recently admitted to hospital after drinking 10 litres of water while exercising in a gym. It took the hospital staff about two hours to diagnose her condition, by which time the young woman was unconscious. Her salt levels were found to be dangerously low and she spent four days in hospital recovering.

Of course, we should all drink water, and we need more during hot and humid conditions, but it is best to have drinks with carbohydrates in them, such as squash, and to take sports drinks when exercising.

Adapted from *The Times*.

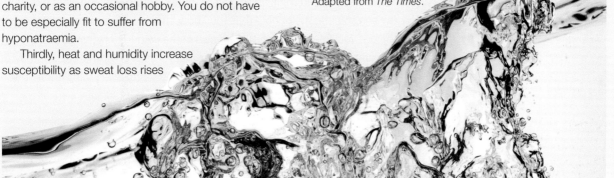

185

You are going to give a talk about drinking water to your class. Prepare some notes to use as a basis for your talk. Make short notes under each heading.

Results of hyponatraemia

- apathy and lethargy
- … [1]
- … [1]
- … [1]

Advice about drinking water

- … [1]
- … [1]
- … [extended only] [1]

People at risk

- … [1]
- … [1]
- … [extended only] [1]

[Total: Core 7, Extended 9]

2   Read the article about the environment and write a summary of what the environment is **and** how important it is. Your summary should be about 100 words long. You should use your own words as far as possible. You will receive up to 8 marks for the content of your summary and up to 8 marks for the style and accuracy of your language.

[Total: 16 Extended]

The Environment

[1] Take a second and think about all the things around you: the wind blowing, the sun shining, the people that you know, the vegetables in your kitchen, the bus you ride to school, the animals in the fields. Everything you encounter every minute of every day is part of your environment. We may think of the environment as just the sky, the sea and everything green, but it is much more than that.

[2] Bacteria and insects break down organic materials to produce soil and nutrients to allow plants to grow. Birds and bees pollinate these plants so that they can continue to serve us in different ways. All plants take in carbon dioxide and release oxygen, creating the clean air that we all breathe. But not only do we need plants for clean air, we also need them for our own nutritional and health needs.

[3] However, the importance of nature does not stop there. The gifts from our environment have provided humans with raw materials to create shelter for ourselves as well as tools and medicine. The medicine nature provides us with has helped cure many diseases, including certain cancers. Around 40 per cent of all medical prescriptions are created from natural compounds found in plants, microorganisms, and animals.

[4] But how much do we actually know about the importance of our environment? Most of us spend numerous hours sitting in an office or a classroom, or in a virtual world. With this indoor lifestyle, we do not expose ourselves to the wonders of nature and do not always understand how the environment impacts our lives every day. Our relationship with the environment is a two-way street. If you want the environment to take care of you and keep you healthy, you have to take care of it. A healthy environment leads to a healthier population and a better quality of life.

[5] By taking part in actions that are good for the environment, we are helping ourselves to cleaner water, cleaner air, and chemical-free food. Learning about the world around us and about how we impact on it every day will help us become more thoughtful and helpful citizens of the world. Taking care of the environment is important for our health both now and in the future.

[6] A helpful way to think about taking care of our environment is to think of it as the 3 Rs: Reduce, Reuse, Recycle. These three words encapsulate the ways that we can help conserve and protect our environment for future generations to benefit from and enjoy. At school, there are many things we can do to implement the 3 Rs. For example, if you bring a packed lunch to school every day, how much packaging do you throw in the dustbin? You can create as much as 50 kg of waste every year, so only bring a no-waste lunch to school. How? Use a lunch box, not a plastic bag, and utensils that you can take home, wash and reuse, and reduce food which is pre-packed. At home, switching off the power overnight for your phone, TV, laptop and other things requiring electricity is a great way to reduce consumption, and drinking from reusable water bottles is an effective way to recycle.

Adapted from www.pamf.org

Please see the Exam Focus section at the end of Unit 7 for a **Core** Exercise 4, summary writing exercise.

Learning objectives

In this unit you will:

- watch a video of students talking about hunger, and discuss what they say
- discuss information about chewing gum, food and hunger and their impact on our lives
- listen to a doctor being interviewed about chewing gum and make notes
- read and talk about biotechnology and food production and write an article
- read about harmful foods and write a report on a visit to a laboratory

A 😬 Watch, listen and talk

1 Watch and listen to some IGCSE students talking about **hunger**.

   a What do the students think are the main causes of global hunger? Make a note of **three** things.

   b What opinions do the students have about global hunger?

2 **a** Do you agree with the students? Why/not?

   b Discuss with your partner/s about what could help to stop the world's food problems.

B 🔤 Speaking and vocabulary

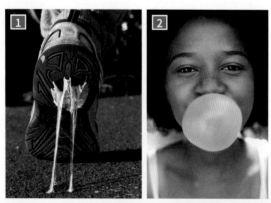

1 Work in small groups and answer these questions.

a What can you see in the pictures?

b Do you chew gum? If yes, when and why do you do it? If not, why not?

c Do you think chewing gum is good for you? Why/not?

d What do you think happens if you swallow a piece of gum?

e What is chewing gum made from?

f What do people do when they have finished chewing a piece of gum? What do they do with it?

g What impact does discarded gum have on the environment?

2 Look at the following information about chewing gum. Which information do you already know? Which information do you find particularly surprising? Why?

a The ancient Greeks chewed a type of gum more than 2,000 years ago.

b The first manufactured chewing gum was available in 1870.

c Bubble gum became available in 1928.

d In the 1950s, the first sugarless gum was produced.

e Powdered sugar is used to stop pieces of gum from sticking to machinery and packaging.

f In the USA, 180 sticks of gum is the average consumption per person, per year.

g It is illegal to manufacture, import or sell gum in Singapore, unless it is for medicinal purposes.

h Turkey is the country with the most gum-manufacturing companies.

i The Portuguese for chewing gum is *pastilka elastika*.

j The main ingredients in chewing gum are sugar, gum base, corn syrup, softeners, flavouring and colouring.

k When you swallow gum, it won't be digested, so it comes out in one piece. It will, however, stay inside you for a few days.

3 Answer these questions in your group.

a Why do you think that Singapore has such strict laws about chewing gum?

b What do you think is the average consumption of chewing gum per person per year in your country? If you do not know, how can you find out?

c How do people dispose of their chewed gum in your country? How much of a problem does this create? What can be done to reduce the problem?

d What do you think the two individual Portuguese words *pastilka* and *elastika* mean? Why do you think this? If you know Portuguese, find out how to say *chewing gum* in another language that you do not know. How do you say *chewing gum* in your language?

4 Do you think that chewing gum can be classified as food? Why/not?

5   Which do you think is more popular: gum, sweets or chocolate? Why? Look at the graph below, which shows the daily percentage confectionery intake of teenagers in Asia. Which do you prefer? Why? - Optional

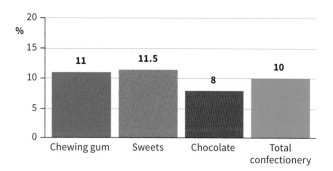

Daily percentage confectionery intake of teenagers in Asia

6   Work on your own. Use the information in this unit so far to write a 'fact file' about chewing gum. Do not try to include all the information, only that which you consider to be the most important or interesting. Do not write more than 100 words. Remember to use your own words as far as possible.

7   Look at your partner's fact file. How similar or different is it to yours? Why do you think that is?

C 🔊 Listening

1   You are going to listen to a dental expert being interviewed about chewing gum. Before you listen, work with your partner and decide on the meaning of the six following words and phrases. Copy them onto a piece of paper.

> the bark from mastic trees   a nicotine hit   saliva   stave off hunger
> weight gain   cognitive function

2   🔊 CD2, Track 9 Listen and …

   a   tick the six items from Activity C1 as you hear them

   b   make a note of the advice that Dr Bealing gives to Thomas.

3   🔊 CD2, Track 9 Listen again and complete the notes. Write one or two words only in each gap.

   a   Ancient Greeks chewed bark as …

   b   Someone trying to give up smoking may need a … hit

   c   Chewing gum alerts the brain that digestive process is …

   d   In cephalic stage the body gets ready for arrival of …

   e   Brain uses senses to see, smell or … food

   f   … to prepare mouth for chewing and … also prepare to receive food

   g   No proof that gum-chewing helps to …

   h   One benefit: chewing can increase …, the ability to concentrate during a …

4   Compare your answers with your partner's. Then read the audioscript in Appendix 3 to check whether your answers are correct.

5   Look back at the question you answered in Activity B1c. Is your answer still the same, or do you think differently now?

WORD TIP

breath (noun) = the air that goes into or out of your lungs

breathe (verb) = to move air into and out of the lungs

Complete the exercise in your **Workbook**.

See Appendix 3, CD2, Track 9

D 📖 Reading

1 Dr Bealing said that *'scientific studies haven't successfully proven that gum can stave off hunger'*. What do **you** do when you feel hungry? Do you try to stave off your hunger, or do you simply eat something?

2 Look at this introduction from a magazine article you are going to read. Work with your partner and match each underlined word in the text with its correct meaning (a–g).

Saving through science

Biotechnology is one of today's most dynamic fields, offering innovative ways to increase crop productivity in the hope of alleviating world hunger. Is it possible we could invent our way out of starvation?

a a plant grown in large quantities by farmers

b full of ideas, enthusiasm and energy

c making problems or suffering less extreme

d severe hunger causing illness or even death

e using living cells in chemical food processes

f using new methods and ideas

g create or design.

3 Complete the gaps in the table.

Noun	Verb	Adjective
...	alleviate	...
...	...	innovative
...	invent	...
starvation	...	...

4 What do you and your partner think is the answer to the question in the introduction: *Is it possible we could invent our way out of starvation?* Why do you think this?

5 Which **six** of the following **eight** ideas do you think appear in the rest of the text? Why?

   a Agricultural science has been a victim of its own success.

   b Agricultural science has been responsible for saving huge numbers of lives.

   c Biotechnology will not save the world from starvation.

   d Food technology works at a molecular level to biologically affect crops.

   e Nature has always been manipulated for agricultural (and therefore human) needs.

   f Farmers growing crops are able to help the environment.

   g Science fiction television has done a lot to shape how we view the meals of the future.

   h There are many complexities when dealing with food.

6 The **six** ideas from Activity D5 have been removed from the six paragraphs in the text below. Look quickly at the text and decide where each one fits.

1 **(a)** … , from an evening dinner in pill form to replicator machines giving us any meal we desire, on demand. Nobody would ever starve if food were this easy to obtain. However, while these ideas for food creation are more than fifty years old, the way we produce and consume food has not changed very much. Even though there is enough food available today to feed the world, more than 870 million people do not have enough to eat, and, incredibly, hunger kills more people than disease does. With the global population expected to grow to more than nine billion by 2050, demand for food will only increase, with more people and fewer croplands, along with additional problems created by climate change. No pills or machines have solved our food problems yet.

2 However, **(b)** … , because without science and technology, we would not exist today. Science helped us out of starvation during the 1960s and 70s when the world's population exploded and scientists were genuinely worried that we would run out of food, and mass starvation was predicted by some experts. The result of this panic was the 'green revolution', which saw the introduction to farming of high-yielding cereal grains, improved irrigation systems, hybrid seeds, and synthetic fertilisers and pesticides, saving over one billion people from starvation.

3 With these advances in food production, people assumed that starvation had been conquered, but in fact **(c)** … . The green revolution led to several decades of relatively plentiful food at low prices and as a result people stopped investing in agricultural development aid for countries in need. In 2008 there was a spike in food prices, and with it the realisation that the world cannot expect that food will always be plentiful. Scientists now predict that by 2050 we will need 60% more food resources.

4 **(d)** … . Having enough food is only the first step, as complications with natural disasters, conflict, poverty, infrastructure and environmental exploitation can all mean that the food supply is put at risk. Then there are the issues we face when it comes to food experimentation, with many people concerned about 'playing around with nature', modifying how food looks and tastes and smells, and the overuse of pesticides and other human interferences, all of which are widespread.

5 Of course, to some extent, **(e)** … . For thousands of years, humans have worked to improve our ability to grow stronger and more productive crops to help feed a continually expanding population. Using scientific methods to develop new technologies has always played a key role in improving the quality and quantity of food. Plant biotechnology is just another step in this ever-evolving process to improve farmers' abilities to create a food-secure world.

6 Ultimately, **(f)** … , but it shows us the path for getting there. Biotechnology has brought about some stunning advances, not only in improving the lands, livelihoods and communities of the farmers, but also in helping us to produce vast quantities of biotech seeds in thirty countries during the past twenty years. Now seeds can be produced which are tolerant to drought, allowing them to survive with little water. Also, seeds which require less care and attention have an impact on the amount of fuel needed for farming machines (such as tractors), as well as how much the soil is polluted by machine oils.

Adapted from: 'Saving Through Science', in Etihad in–flight magazine, September 2013

7 Read the text in more detail and answer these questions about the content of each paragraph.

   a Find words which have a similar meaning to the following:

     i get

     ii production

     iii eat

     iv world. [Paragraph 1]

   b Apart from the word *starvation*, there are five other nouns ending in *–ion*. Create a table like the one in Activity D5 and fill in as many gaps as possible. Which of the five *–ion* words has only one possible form? [2]

   c Think of a synonym for the following:

     i assumed

     ii conquered

     iii aid

     iv spike. [3]

   d Choose **three** words or phrases you are unsure about and find out what they mean. [4]

   e Write **three** questions for your partner to answer, based on the content of this paragraph. [5]

   f

     i Apart from assisting farmers, what is the other benefit of biotechnology?

     ii What is the effect of seeds needing less care? Give **two** details. (6)

E Writing

1 Work with a partner and answer these questions.

   a Look at this exam-style question. Decide exactly what you have to do. Do **not** write anything yet.

> Your class recently visited a biotechnology laboratory. Your teacher has asked you to write an article on what you saw. In your article say what you learnt from the visit and give your opinion about using science to help us to produce more food.
>
> Here are two comments from other students in your class. (EXTENDED)
>
> Here are some comments from other students in your class. (CORE)
>
> - *We should be thankful for biotechnology as it makes sure we produce enough food to eat.* (Extended and Core)
>
> - *I won't touch food that is full of chemicals – it's the same as poisoning myself.* (Extended and Core)
>
> - *There is nothing anyone can do to stop science interfering with farming.* (Core only)
>
> - *There is already enough food on the planet, and we don't need science to help us to produce even more.* (Core only)

TOP TIP

Sometimes, you may be asked to write your opinion about something in the form of a newspaper article, or perhaps for your school newsletter or magazine. You will usually be given help, perhaps in the form of a list of ideas or other people's opinions, or sometimes pictures, but you do not have to use them in your answer. You should try to use some of your own ideas – but make sure you stick to the topic. You must show that you can use the English language for a specific purpose and that you can organise your ideas in a logical way.

> **Write the article for your teacher.**
>
> The comments above may give you some ideas, and you should try to use some ideas of your own.
>
> **Your article should be between 100–150 words long [Core] or 150–200 words long [Extended].**
>
> You will receive up to 6/8 marks for the content of your article and up to 6/8 marks for the style and accuracy of your language.

b What do you think the layout of your answer should be? How many paragraphs should it include? Do you need an introduction and a conclusion? Why/not?

c How should you organise the content of your article? What exactly should each paragraph include? Make notes about what is needed.

2 Look at these three introductory sentences in response to the question in Activity E1. Work with a partner and decide which you think are the most and least effective. Give reasons for your choices.

   a Personally I think governments should spend more money on biotechnology research so that the world will always have enough food.

   b The visit to the biotechnology laboratory provided us with an enormous amount of information about scientific food production.

   c There is nothing we can do about the global food shortage but science can help.

3 Add **at least two** ideas to follow on from the sentence you have chosen, in order to create an introductory paragraph. Use your notes and ideas from the previous activities. Remember that in this paragraph you need to introduce the topic and give your opinion about it.

4 Look at these three concluding sentences in response to the question in Activity E1. Work with a partner and decide which you think are the most and least effective. Give reasons for your choices.

   a In conclusion, and taking into consideration all the different arguments, my firm belief is that we should thank science.

   b On the other hand, there is already enough food so we should share it out more equally.

   c Another point is that food and science do not mix, so let's eat natural food.

5 Add **at least two** ideas to follow on from the sentence you have chosen, in order to create a concluding paragraph. Use your notes and ideas from the previous activities. Remember that in this paragraph you need to restate your opinion about the topic, and bring the article to a natural close.

6 Read someone else's two paragraphs. What do you think? Have they given a reason for writing and restated their main opinion in the conclusion?

7 Now write the 'body' of the article. Think carefully about how many paragraphs you need in order to express your opinions, and remember the word limit. You can use the comments from other students but also try to use some comments of your own.

TOP TIP

Make sure that your introduction is brief and to the point. It needs to state clearly your own opinion and should attempt to capture the reader's attention, to encourage them to continue reading.

TOP TIP

The conclusion needs to be a brief summary of the main arguments or points from your writing. It is also useful to restate your opinion from the introduction.

195

> **LANGUAGE TIP**
>
> Your writing will feel more natural and fluent if you use sequence markers (e.g., *However, Furthermore, Finally, Besides*, etc) to introduce and reinforce your ideas.

8 Read as many answers from other students as possible. How are they similar or different to your answer? Why is this?

F 📖 💬 Reading and speaking

1 Work with a partner and answer these questions.

  a What foods are bad for your health? How do you know?

  b There are many foods that are bad for the Earth's health, as well as your own health. What do you think they are? Why do you think this?

  c Think about your daily diet: what does it consist of? Do you think you have a healthy diet? Why or why not?

  d How does what you eat impact the Earth?

2 Look at this list of food types.

fast food   genetically modified (GM) foods   non-organic foods   meat
non-local food   packaged and processed food   rice   seafood   sugar
white bread

  a Which do you think are bad for the future of Earth's health? Why do you think this? Consider not only what the food contains, but also how and where it is produced.

  b What impact do you think food production has on our planet?

3 Match the text (a–f) below with **three** of the food types from Activity F2. There are **two** phrases for each of the three food types. Give reasons for your choices.

  a … annual consumption is expanding each year by about two million tonnes

  b … is an important food staple for more than half the world's population

  c … is present in many products we consume every day

  d … most, if not all, of this is produced in factory farms

  e … uses up a lot of water, and as fresh water supplies are growing scarce, this can be a problem

  f … wasteful use of wrappers, straws, bags, boxes, tomato sauce packets and plastic is the biggest source of urban litter in many countries.

4 As you read the text below, fill in the gaps (a–f) with the text from Activity F3. Which piece of information about the three foods do you find the most surprising? Why?

Satisfying our hunger is bad for planet Earth

Nowadays, everyone has a pretty good idea about which foods are good for us and, of course, which foods are not OK to eat. And the old saying, 'Everything in moderation, nothing in excess' holds true today just as much as it did when Socrates (supposedly) said those words more than 2500 years ago. But something we need to remember is that there are many foods that are bad for Earth's health, let alone our own – mainly due to the processes used in producing them and getting them into our shops and kitchens. Some of these foods that are bad for the planet are: fast food, genetically modified (GM) foods, non-organic foods, meat, non-local food, packaged and processed food, rice, seafood, sugar, white bread.

Read about three of the main culprits.

Sugar

Sugar **(a)** … , yet we rarely give a second thought to how and where it is produced, nor to what toll it may take on the environment. More than 145 million tonnes of sugar (sucrose) is produced per year in about 120 countries and

(b) … . Sugar production does indeed have a negative impact on soil, water and the air, especially in threatened tropical ecosystems near the equator. Sugar production destroys the natural habitats of many living creatures, to make way for new plantations. Furthermore, it uses water intensively for irrigation and pollutes the environment through excessive use of agricultural chemicals. As if those were not bad enough, the sugar-production process also discharges huge quantities of polluted waste water. Not so sweet after all, is it?

Fast food

It is not just the chemicals in fast food that affect the environment, but the whole production chain itself. One of the most common ingredients in fast food is meat, and **(c)** … . It is an unfortunate fact that factory farms contribute more to global warming than all of our cars put together. Consider also that many fast-food products have to be transported long distances, further increasing their impact on air quality. But it does not end there. Fast-food products also have a negative impact on local water quality, due to the hormones, drugs and fertilisers that are used in their production. These enter groundwater, potentially causing illness to humans as well as to fish. And of course fast-food outlets also use a lot of packaging. This **(d)** … . Now, do you want extra fries with your burger?

Rice

Rice **(e)** … . However, the use of chemicals, in the form of pesticides and other chemicals to treat the rice or the soil it is growing in, damages not just the pests, but it also affects the entire ecosystem in the area. It reduces the quality of the soil and harms animals and plant life in the process. Rice farming typically requires intensive irrigation. This **(f)** … . Rice farming can be made less wasteful by switching to more efficient means of irrigation, such as drip-feed irrigation. So, did you order plain or fried rice with your meal?

5 Work in groups of three for the following activity.

  a Allocate between you the three food types from the text: sugar, fast food, rice.

  b On your own, find out as much **new** information as you can about your food type.

  c Report back to your group. Agree between you who has discovered the most interesting facts.

6 How many of the foods and food types you have read about and researched in Activities F4 and F5 do you eat regularly? Are you likely to change your eating habits as a result of what you have read? Why or why not?

G ⊙ Language focus: word building

1 In Activities D3 and D7 you looked at the noun, verb and adjective form of certain words. Here are four more –*ion* words from this unit: *production, exploitation, realisation, creation.* Make a list of other forms for each of the four words, and say what part of speech each one is.

Example: *production (noun–thing): produce (verb), producer (noun – person)*

2 Compare your lists.

a Look at the words in the box. What part of speech is each one? What other forms for each word can you think of?

Example: *exceed = verb, excessive = adjective, excess = noun, excessively = adverb*

> exceed growth requirement ill negation plentiful wasteful entirety

b Use the correct forms of the words in the box to complete the sentences (i–viii) from the texts in this unit. The part of speech you need is given in brackets at the end of each sentence.

   i With the global population expected to … to more than nine billion by 2050, demand for food will only increase … (verb)

   ii The green revolution led to several decades of relatively … food at low prices … (adjective)

   iii Everything in moderation, nothing in … (noun)

   iv Sugar production does indeed have a … impact on soil, (adjective)

   v The sugar-production process also discharges huge quantities of polluted … water. (adjective)

   vi These enter groundwater, potentially causing … to humans as well as to fish. (noun)

   vii It also affects the … ecosystem in the area. (adjective)

   viii Rice farming typically … intensive irrigation. (verb)

3 Use each of the following words from the texts in **two** sentences of your own. For the second sentence, make sure you change the form of the word.

a growth

b length

c process

d enter

e package.

H ⊙ Writing

1 Look at this exam-style question. Do not write anything yet.

> You have just finished researching how the production of food impacts on the environment.
>
> **Write a report to your teacher telling them about your findings.**
>
> In your report you should:
>
> • explain to your teacher why you conducted the research
>
> • describe the most interesting information you found
>
> • say what you are going to do as a result of your research.
>
> Your report should be between 100–150 and 150–200 words long. The pictures above may give you some ideas, and you should try to use some ideas of your own.
>
> You will receive up to 6/8 marks for the content of your report and up to 6/8 marks for the style and accuracy of your language.

2 Consider exactly what you have to do and plan your answer accordingly. What are three important instructions that you must follow? How is this writing question different from the previous one?

3 There are no set rules or format for writing a report. However, there are some general sections that should be included:

• Title/heading of report

• Short introduction to purpose of report

• Main section with subsections and subheadings

• Conclusion and recommendations

For the exam-style question above:

    a think of a suitable title for your report

    b think of a short introduction which states the purpose of the report

    c decide how many subsections you need

    d write a subheading for each one.

4 Write your introduction. Begin like this: *The purpose of this report is to* …. Use the information in the question to help you complete the sentence.

5 For each of your subsections, decide on **one** key phrase that you could include. Then add more information to make complete sentences.

    Example: *The main reason I conducted this research was … in order to investigate how food production affects our environment.*

6 Now add one further piece of information to each sentence.

    Example: *In addition, I wanted to try to find out what we can do to protect the countryside without having a negative impact on farming.*

7 You now have an introduction and three paragraphs. How many words have you written so far? How many words do you have left for the final part of your report?

8 For the conclusion and recommendations, decide on **two** key phrases that you could include. Then add more information to make complete sentences.

    Example: *In conclusion, my research showed me that … modern food production definitely has a negative impact on our environment. As a result, I recommend that we carefully investigate different ways to produce food.*

TOP TIP
Whenever you do a writing task, planning is very important: you should underline the key word/s in the question to make sure you do exactly what is asked. Write very brief notes, putting your ideas into a logical order. Check for repetition in your notes, then write your answer. When you have finished, check your spelling, grammar and punctuation.

How well do you think you can do each of these things now?

Give yourself a score from 1: Still need a lot of practice to 5: Feeling very confident about this

In this unit you:	1	2	3	4	5
watched a video of students talking about hunger, and discussed what they said					
discussed information about chewing gum, food and hunger and their impact on our lives					
listened to a doctor being interviewed about chewing gum and made notes					
read and talked about biotechnology and food production and wrote an article					
read about harmful foods and wrote a report on a visit to a laboratory					

Now set yourself a **personal goal** based on your scores for Unit 18.

Exam focus

Writing, Exercise 6

Scientific research plays an important part in making sure we have enough food to eat.

Here are some comments that you have heard on the subject:

> We must use science to help us to produce more food. [Extended and Core]

> If I'm hungry, I'll buy and eat anything I want. [Extended and Core]

> Fewer chemicals, more flavour = what's wrong with that? [Core only]

> I only eat organic, locally grown produce. [Core only]

Write an article for your school website, giving your views.

The comments above may give you some ideas and you should try to use some ideas of your own.

Your article should be 100–150 words long [Core]. You will receive up to 6 marks for the content of your article, and up to 6 marks for the style and accuracy of your language.

Learning objectives

In this unit you will:

- watch a video of students talking about fashions, and discuss what they say
- talk about what fashion means to you
- read a newspaper article about 'ethical fashion' and answer questions about it
- listen to different people talking about fashion and understand what their opinions are
- listen to a talk about school uniforms, and to two students talking about school uniforms, and answer questions

A ☺ Watch, listen and talk

1 Watch and listen to some IGCSE students talking about **fashions**.

    a What do the students think 'fashion' means? Make a note of **three** ideas

    b Does fashion affect the students in a positive or negative way? What examples and reasons do they give?

2 **a** What does the word 'fashion' mean to you? Is it only clothes that are fashionable? What about furniture? Food? Mobile phones? Cafés? Opinions? Holidays? Pets?

    b What or who do you and your partner/s consider to be fashionable nowadays? What makes it or them fashionable?

B ABC XYZ Speaking and vocabulary

1 Work with your partner. Look at the pictures and statements, then answer the questions.

i 'People in the future will laugh at today's fashions'

ii 'Fashion is a personal statement'

iii 'Fashion doesn't always mean comfortable'

iv 'There are no rules in fashion'

a Does fashion affect you in a positive or negative way? How?

b What do you consider to be fashionable nowadays? Why?

c Do you follow fashion? If not, why not? Are you a fashionable person? Why, or why not?

d Is fashion only for people who can afford it? Why, or why not?

e Which of the picture statements above do you agree and disagree with most? Why?

f Write your own statement about fashion. Do not use more than ten words.

2 Work in small groups and discuss these questions.

a What was fashionable when your parents and grandparents were young?

b Is there anything from those days that you consider fashionable today? Why/not?

c What types of things tend to remain in fashion? Give reasons.

d Fashions and being fashionable can have an impact on the environment. How?

C 📖 Reading

1 Here is the headline from a newspaper article you are going to read:

> **From fast fashion to ethical fashion**

Work with your partner and discuss what information you think you might find in the text. Try to list **at least three** things. Give reasons for your answers.

2 Work in groups of three: A, B and C, and check the meaning of the following phrases from the first two paragraphs. Student A look at phrases a–c, Student B look at d–f, and Student C look at g–i.

a a new crop of designers

b rich ethnic heritage

c remote hills

d hand-spun cotton

e fermented indigo leaves

f tapping into this growing global trend

g ethnic minority groups

h drawn inspiration

i weave on hand looms.

3 Quickly read the first two paragraphs.

a Check that the phrases from Activity C2 make sense in context.

b Check your predictions from Activity C1.

c Choose the best headings for the two paragraphs.

> Carving shoes   Changing skills   Fashion capitals   It's all about colour
> Made in Vietnam   Natural is best   Tradition, tradition

From fast fashion to ethical fashion

[1] ...

<u>A new crop of designers</u> are trying to transform the Made in Vietnam label and save the country's <u>rich ethnic heritage</u> at the same time. In the <u>remote hills</u> of Cao Banh, some 300 kilometres north of the capital Hanoi, Vietnamese designer Thao Vu is happily dropping strips of <u>hand-spun</u> <u>cotton</u> into a large bucket of <u>fermented indigo leaves</u>. Her label, Kilomet 109, is at the forefront of Vietnam's new 'ethical fashion' movement, an approach to design that seeks to maximise the benefit to communities while minimising environmental harm.

[2] ...

The 38-year-old designer has been <u>tapping into this growing</u> **global★** <u>trend</u> by working with some of

Vietnam's 54 <u>ethnic</u> <u>minority groups</u>, each of which have their own unique textiles and traditional clothing designs. Thao says that she learns the techniques from them, and explains how she has <u>drawn</u> <u>inspiration</u> from Nung women in Phuc Sec village, who use natural dyes and <u>weave on hand looms</u>. She then adds a more contemporary touch to style garments that will appeal to clients in fashion capitals like Berlin and New York.

4 Now you have read the first two paragraphs, which of the following things do you think you will read about in the rest of the newspaper article? Why?

> harsh chemicals   international design awards   London and Paris   multi-billion-dollar global fashion business   natural dyes and textiles   platform shoes   roots and leaves   shirts and dresses   teaching traditional woodworkers

5 These words and phrases appear in the rest of the article. Work in pairs to find out what they mean. First, Student A look at the words in column A, and Student B look at column B. Then share what you have found out.

A	B
bridging this divide	attracted accolades
manufactured from scratch	ancient artisan techniques
a range of hues	ornate pillars
inherently eco-friendly	pagodas

6 Quickly read the text and ...

a check your predictions in Activity C4

b make sure the meanings you found for the words and phrases in C5 are correct.

[3] ...

But bridging this divide is not always easy. Thao says that the Nung women were shocked when she suggested experimenting with colours outside of their traditional dark indigo shade. After much persistence, she now uses local roots and leaves to colour organic silk, cotton and hemp, which are also manufactured from scratch, in a range of hues from deep indigo to pale grey, and earthy oranges and browns.

[4] …

In recent decades, Vietnam has benefited enormously from the multi-billion-dollar global fashion business, but has drawn some criticism for poor environmental and labour regulations. However, products made by the country's traditional fabric spinners are inherently eco-friendly, as they are made with natural dyes and textiles, not harsh chemicals or synthetic fibres. Thao says that at first she just wanted to keep the traditional techniques alive but then realised the need to be concerned about the environmental and ethical side of fashion, before it is too late. She has already attracted accolades, winning international design awards and selling her products to high-fashion buyers. The local women who work with Thao say they have benefited financially from the collaboration, and see the things they weave going to different countries.

[5] …

In central Hue, the former capital of Vietnam, another label, Fashion4Freedom, is also helping local artisans market their skills to the global fashion industry. The founder of the company, Lan Vy Nguyen, used her business skills to save ancient artisan techniques. She knew that local people had generations of skills, but there was a need to unlock the skills so that the global market could appreciate them. Fashion4Freedom helps by teaching traditional woodworkers, who carve ornate pillars in pagodas or local houses, to learn how to make platform shoes that can cost up to US$600 a pair. Do Quang Thanh, a carpenter, said the idea of making shoes initially struck him as strange, but now he is glad he gave it a try. In the past he carved traditional wooden houses, but now he carves shoes in a modern style for people all over the **world**★.

Adapted from: 'From fast fashion to ethical couture', in *Oman Daily Observer*, 7 April 2016

★See the **WORD TIP**.

WORD TIP

global (adjective) = relating to the whole world, or to all parts of a subject or situation

world (noun) = the Earth and all the people, places and things on it, or a planet of other part of the universe where life might exist

Do the exercise in your **Workbook**.

203

7 Choose appropriate headings for paragraphs 3, 4 and 5 from the list in Activity C3c.

8 Read the whole text more carefully and answer these questions.

  a What are designers trying to achieve with the Made in Vietnam label?

  b What is the 'ethical fashion' movement's methodology? Give **two** details.

  c How does Thao benefit from working with ethnic minority groups?

  d What equipment do the Nung women use to make textiles?

  e Where are Thao's garments likely to sell?

  f How did the Nung women react to using non-traditional colours?

  g Why are Vietnam's traditional products eco-friendly?

  h What have local women received as a result of their cooperation with Thao?

  i How is Fashion4Freedom supporting local crafts people?

  j What might Lan Vy Nguyen's business skills be?

D 💬 🔊 Speaking and listening

1 Which of the following words and phrases do you think you are likely to hear when people are talking about fashion? Work with your partner and give reasons for your choices.

  a alternative styles

  b being 'in'

  c current fashion trends

  d design and engineering

  e Ferrari or Lamborghini

  f pair of trainers

  g sunglasses

  h the latest gear

TOP TIP

Some questions may ask you to identify people's feelings and attitudes, or to 'read between the lines' (to *infer*). Try to recognise these questions because you will not find specific details in the text. You need to use the information given to guide you in writing your answer.

2 Look at the pictures of the six people and try to match them with the words and phrases above. Give reasons for your choices.

3 Now match the pictures 1–6 with the comments A–G below. Work with a partner and give reasons for your choices. There is one extra comment that you do not need to use.

a I think we should wear what we can afford and what we feel comfortable in.

b I will do anything to have the latest gear.

c Fashion is art, design and architecture all combined.

d It's crazy how much we parents have to spend, just because of so-called fashion!

e I'm going to have to keep dreaming for a few more years yet!

f To be honest, I hate fashion and all that it represents: money, beauty, and so on.

g I don't understand the fashion for pets and food – how can they be fashionable?

4 Do the following:

a Work in A/B pairs. Each of you should choose three different people from the six in Activities D2 and D3. On your own, think about words and phrases that each person might think or say. Write down two words or phrases for each person, making a total of six.

b With a partner, take turns to read out things from your lists. Your partner guesses the person and gives a reason.

5 Look at this exam-style question and answer the questions with your partner.

You will hear six people talking about fashion. For each of the speakers 1–6, choose from the list, a–g, which opinion each speaker expresses.

Write the letter in the box. Use each letter only once. There is one extra letter that you do not need to use.

Speaker 1 ☐   Speaker 4 ☐

Speaker 2 ☐   Speaker 5 ☐

Speaker 3 ☐   Speaker 6 ☐

a   I think we should wear what we can afford and what we feel comfortable in.

b   I will do anything to have the latest gear.

c   Fashion is art, design and architecture all combined.

d   It's crazy how much we parents have to spend, just because of so-called fashion!

e   I'm going to have to keep dreaming for a few more years yet!

f   To be honest, I hate fashion and all that it represents: money, beauty, and so on.

g   I don't understand the fashion for pets and food – how can they be fashionable?

[Total: 6]

TOP TIP

In some listening exercises, you have to listen to a number of short extracts and match each speaker to appropriate content. There is usually one extra piece of content that you do not need to use. Remember:

- It is important to read the question carefully and make sure you understand the topic that the speakers are going to talk about before you do anything else.

- Then read the options that you are going to match to each speaker.

- You will hear everything twice, so try to make all the matches during the first listening.

- Then check them during the second listening.

a   How many people will you hear?   **e**   How many times can you use each letter?

b   What will they be talking about?   **f**   What do you have to do with the extra letter?

c   How many options are there?   **g**   How many marks are there for this exercise?

d   Where do you put your answers?

6   🔊 **CD2, Track 10** Listen and complete the exam-style question in Activity D5.

E 🔊 Listening

1   Work with your partner and discuss these questions.

     a   Think of **at least five** jobs where a person has to wear a uniform. Why is a uniform required in these jobs: safety, cleanliness, something else? Is it always for the same reason?

     b   Do you have to wear a uniform at school? How do feel about this?

     c   What are the advantages and disadvantages of wearing a uniform at school?

2 Look at these words and phrases taken from a talk you are going to listen to and check their meanings.

> avoid ridicule, embarrassment or abuse   an atmosphere of pride, loyalty and equality   confrontation   distractions   erase their individuality   mandatory   merchandise   sweeping the nation   the latest peer-pleasing designs

3 Complete these phrases from the talk with the words and phrases from Activity E2.

  a Schools have a long history of using school uniforms to create **(i)** ...

  b It provides for a more business-like approach to learning, removing some of the **(ii)** ... normally encountered when children feel they should possess the latest designer fashions, or follow the latest trend **(iii)** ... at any given time.

  c This is not so as to **(iv)** ... , but to include everyone on the same level, as far as image and dress are concerned.

  d With fashions constantly changing from year to year, and even from season to season, parents have always felt the pressure from their children to provide them with **(v)** ... .

  e And their cost, in relation to fashion **(vi)** ... is very appealing over the long term.

  f Wearing a uniform at school, as opposed to wearing the latest fashions, may also help the child **(vii)** ... from others that can be caused when the 'have-nots' are compared with the 'haves'.

  g Uniforms assist in avoiding such conflicts by removing the chance for **(viii)** ... over clothing, at least during the child's time at school.

  h But more and more people in education – students, parents, teachers and administrators – are convinced that **(ix)** ... school uniforms lead to success.

4 🔊 CD2, Track 11 Listen to the talk about school uniforms and check your answers.

5 🔊 CD2, Track 11 Listen and again and make a list of the reasons given **for** wearing school uniforms.

6 🔊 CD2, Track 12 Now listen to a conversation between two students about wearing school uniforms and complete the sentences. Write only one or two words in each gap. You will hear the conversation twice.

> # Discussion about school uniforms
>
> 'Uniform' means the same so nobody worries about their **(a)** ....
>
> Giving students **(b)** ... would be better than forcing them to wear uniforms.
>
> Problem for teachers checking what is **(c)** ... and what isn't.
>
> Bullying, fights and **(d)** ... may occur over fashion clothes.
>
> Being in uniform makes people part of school community and increases pride in school and **(e)** ... .
>
> School uniforms can improve academic results.

7 Read the audioscript in Appendix 3 to check your answers.

F Language development: position of adjectives

1 Look at these two phrases from the texts in this unit and do the tasks a–c that follow.

- … nobody has to worry if they look different.
- Thao Vu is happily dropping strips of hand-spun cotton …

a Identify the adjectives in each phrase.

b Which sentence has an adjective before a noun?

c Which sentence has an adjective after a verb?

> **LANGUAGE TIP**
>
> Adjectives usually appear before a noun, and in some cases after certain verbs: be, seem, look, become, appear, sound, taste, feel, get.

2 Phrases with adjectives before nouns can be rewritten with the adjective after a verb. Look at these phrases from the texts. Firstly, identify the adjective in each phrase. Next, change each phrase so that the adjective appears after the verb, and then use it in a sentence of your own. Use a different verb from the list above in each example.

Example: *hand-spun cotton = The cotton in the market looked hand-spun*

a fermented indigo leaves

b contemporary touch

c traditional wooden houses

d complex subject

e alternative styles of clothes

f business-like approach

g mandatory school uniforms

h fashionable clothes.

G Speaking

1 Work in small groups and discuss the following questions. Use your own ideas and the ideas presented in the unit.

a What image is connected with students in uniform?

b Is it possible to have a fashionable school uniform? Why/not?

c How do school uniforms include everyone on the same level?

d How does wearing a school uniform help parents to save money?

e What do many people believe about the compulsory wearing of school uniform?

f Which of the six people in Section D is most like you? In what way/s?

g Tell your group your own opinion about ethical fashion. Make some written notes first.

How well do you think you can do each of these things now?

Give yourself a score from 1: Still need a lot of practice to 5: Feeling very confident about this

In this unit you:	1	2	3	4	5
watched a video of students talking about fashions, and discussed what they said					
talked about what fashion means to you					
read a newspaper article about 'ethical fashion' and answered questions about it					
listened to different people talking about fashion and understood what their opinions are					
listened to a talk about school uniforms, and to two students talking about school uniforms, and answered questions					

Now set yourself a **personal goal** based on your scores for Unit 19.

Exam focus

🔊 CD2, Track 13 **Listening, Exercise 1, short extracts**

You will hear four short recordings. Answer each question on the line provided. Write no more than three **words** for each detail. You will hear each recording twice.

1 **a** What lesson is the book for? [1]
   b What TWO things does the woman take from the shop? [1]

2 **a** Who is the man going to meet? [1]
   b Which two floors does he need to go to? [1]

3 **a** How is the coffee different in 'Coffee Cup'? [1]
   b Where can you sit with your friends at 'Coffee Cup'? [1]

4 **a** Where will the children go after one hour? [1]
   b What are the children not permitted to do? [1]

[Total: 8]

🔊 CD2, Track 14 **Listening, Exercise 2, note-making**

You will hear a talk given by a woman about the role that cats have played in the history of humans. Listen to the talk and complete the details below. Write one or two words only in each gap. You will hear the talk twice.

1 The role of cats in the history of humans.

  a Talk about cats and how they became part of our lives. First domesticated cat found by archeologists about … years ago. Lived on Mediterranean island of Cyprus. **[1]**

  b Cat buried next to its … in an area now known as the Near East although … named Mesopotamia. **[1/2 + 1/2]**

  c Studies show domesticated cats … from African wildcat. Ancestors were lions and tigers from about 10–15 million years ago. Originally from … Asia. **[1/2 + 1/2]**

  d Domesticated cats settled down, around 10 000 years ago, when humans built … settlements, storing crops, for example: … and barley. **[1/2 + 1/2]**

  e … attracted to these crops, so cats became important … to humans. **[1/2 + 1/2]**

  f Domestic cat only in Egyptian culture and … for around 4,000 years. The word 'cat' originally from North African word 'quattah'. … by European countries, so 'katze' in German, 'gatto' in Spanish and 'cat' in English. **[1/2 + 1/2]**

  g Cat most … pet in world with men and women. In the United States about 90 million domesticated cats and the … is more than 500 million. **[1/2 + 1/2]**

  h Not all cats have … lives as pets. **[1]**

                                      [Total: 8]

🔊 CD2, Track 15 **Listening, Exercise 4, multiple-choice questions**

1 You will hear Alfonso Fiore, a fashion magazine journalist, asking Valentina Santinia, fashion expert, some questions about what fashion is. Listen to their conversation and look at the questions. For each question choose the correct answer, A, B or C and put a tick in the appropriate box. You will hear the talk twice.

  a How many homes does Valentina have in Europe?

    A 1

    B 3

    C 4

  b Alfonso thinks that Valentina

    A only knows about shoes and clothes fashion

    B is knowledgeable about everything in fashion

    C cannot define what fashion is

  c What does Valentina compare fashion to?

    A the sea

    B a pond

    C food

  d The biggest part of the fashion industry is

    A furniture

    B makeup

    C clothing

e According to Valentina, how many furniture fashion styles are there?

    A ten

    B hundreds

    C thousands

f Valentina says fashion changes because of

    A fashion houses

    B celebrities

    C everyone

g What makes something fashionable nowadays?

    A it has to be expensive

    B it has to follow the guidelines

    C it has to be new

h What advice does Valentina give to people who love fashion?

    A it should control them

    B it should define them

    C it should guide them

[Total: 8]

Learning objectives

In this unit you will:

- watch a video of students talking about technology, and discuss what they say
- talk about different technologies
- read about the latest technologies and discuss with your partner
- watch and listen to students taking part in a speaking role-play, and assess their performance
- read about ten great technologies and write a summary

A 🙂 Watch, listen and talk

1 Watch and listen to some IGCSE students talking about **technology**.

   a What do the students say about how technology has changed and developed? Make a note of **three** examples they give.

   b What technology could the students never give up? What reasons do they give?

2 Discuss with your partner/s the technology that you would like to see and use in the future. Do you agree with the students?

B 🔤 Speaking and vocabulary

1 Work in small groups and look at the pictures (1–4). Tell each other what technology each picture shows.

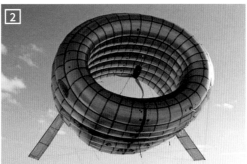

2 Match the following information with the pictures in B1. There are two pieces of information for each picture. Give reasons for your choices.

  a every single movement of its fleet

  b sharpening their wearer's concentration

  c from the supermarket aisle

  d a 747 Jumbo jet's 60 m wingspan

  e the best possible repair solution

  f the future is beyond the horizon

  g thousands of recipes

  h automatically tightens the shoe.

3 You are going to read about each of the technologies in the pictures. Before you read, think of **at least three** more words or phrases that you think might appear in each of the texts. Give reasons for your choices.

4 Which of the technologies shown in the pictures do you think are the least and most interesting? Why? Which one would you like to know more about? Why?

5 Work in groups of four: **A**, **B**, **C** and **D**. Each one of you is going to read something about one of the four technologies. First, decide which of the headings below could fit with each technology. Give reasons for your choices. There are two extra headings that you do not need to use.

  a The problem solvers

  b Hot new tech

  c Smart kitchen knows what's in the fridge

  d A clean solution to energy needs

  e The perfect thing for anyone going at a rate of knots

  f Oceans on distant planets

C 📖💬 Reading and speaking

1 In your groups of four: **A**, **B**, **C** and **D**, do the following:

  a Find your texts:

    Student A: The perfect thing for anyone going at a rate of knots in Appendix 2

    Student B: A clean solution to energy needs in Appendix 2

    Student C: Smart kitchen knows what's in the fridge in Appendix 2

    Student D: The problem solvers in Appendix 2

  b Quickly read your text and check your answers to Activities B2 and B3. Do not say anything to your partners yet.

  c Take it in turns to tell your partners which of the words and phrases from Activity B2 appeared in your text, and whether or not any of your guesses for Activity B3 were correct.

2 Look at the 12 questions below and decide which **three** you can answer.

  a How can someone adjust the settings?

  b How can the NCC teams predict a flight's arrival time?

  c How is power provided to the trainers?

  d How much power can six megawatts provide?

e What advantage do offshore turbines have over onshore turbines?

f What help is available for people who do not want to go shopping?

g What information does oven technology give?

h What is the NCC compared to?

i Where are the turbine components built?

j Where can you find 'connected food' technology?

k Which screen provides information about aircraft positions?

l Who is most likely to buy the product?

WORD TIP

internal (adjective) = existing or happening inside a person, place or thing

inside = 1 (preposition/adjective/adverb) in or into a place; 2 (noun) the inner part or space of something OR the <u>outside</u> of a part of the body

Complete the exercise in your **Workbook**.

See Student A text, Appendix 2

3 Carefully re-read your text and find the answers to your three questions. Then identify **at least two things** in the text that you find particularly interesting.

4 Join up with your three partners and tell them the answers to your questions. Then tell them what you found interesting in your text. Try not to refer back to the text.

5 Decide which of the other three texts you would now like to read. Give reasons to your group.

213

D Language focus: compound subjects

1 A *compound subject* consists of more than one noun, which can include pronouns, noun phrases and noun clauses, before the main verb. The individual parts of a compound subject are usually joined by words such as *and, or, either/or, neither/nor.*

Look at these examples from the texts in this unit. Identify the elements of the compound noun and the main verb in each one.

a The sporting purpose of the neon blue light on the shoe's instep is unknown …

b … some aerial wind turbines are much smaller …

c … but the new, brightly-coloured, hands-on appliances with embedded Wifi are too amazing to resist.

d In much the same way as NASA's Mission Control monitors all aspects of its space exploration …

2 Choose a different text to the one you read earlier in Section C. How many more examples of compound subjects can you find? In each case, identify the elements of the compound noun and the main verb.

3 Continue with the other two texts and do the same thing. Then share your answers with your partners.

4 When the word *and* is used to join the elements of the compound subject, the following verb is always plural.

Example: *Both the scheduling team **and** the flight despatcher team **operate** 24 hours a day.*

However, sometimes the compound subject is followed by a singular verb, if certain joining phrases are used.

Example: *The scheduling team* ***as well as*** *the flight despatcher team* ***operates*** *24 hours a day.*

The scheduling team ***alongside*** *the flight despatcher team* ***operates*** *24 hours a day.*

Neither *the scheduling team* ***nor*** *the flight despatcher team ever* ***stops*** *work.*

Either *the manager* ***or*** *his assistant* ***works*** *late every day.*

BUT:

Neither *the scheduling team members* ***nor*** *the flight despatcher team members ever* ***stop*** *work.*

Either *the manager's team members* ***or*** *his assistant's team members* ***work*** *late every day.*

Why is this?

5 Choose the correct form of the verb:

a Eating, sleeping and reading **is/are** enjoyable activities.

b Chocolate and strawberry **is/are** my favourite flavours of ice cream.

c Neither the president nor her assistant **have/has** replied to my question.

d Mum as well as Sharon **enjoys/enjoy** chocolate ice cream.

e Either the boots by the door or the flip-flops in the living room **is/are** John's.

f Neither Marcos nor Carole **lives/live** in that house.

g Wind and rain as well as snow **cause/causes** problems at airports.

h Either you or your brother **are/is** going to go first.

i Either the chicken or the fish in the freezer **needs/need** to be thawed for dinner tonight.

Complete the exercises in your **Workbook**.

E Listening and speaking

1 Look at this example role-play card from a speaking examination. Which of the five prompts do you think are the least and most challenging to answer. Why?

Technology

Technology is constantly changing and its impact on people increases every day.

Discuss this topic.

Use the following prompts, in the order given below, to develop the conversation:

- technology you could not live without
- skills you need to use technology effectively
- what you think the greatest technological development is, and why
- positive and negative effects of technological advances on our lives
- the suggestion that technology destroys privacy.

You may introduce **related** ideas of your own to expand on these prompts.

Remember, you are not allowed to make any written notes.

2 🔊 CD2, Track 16 Listen to **six** different students responding to the **five** prompts, but in the wrong order. Which response matches which prompt? Which response does **not** fit? Why not?

Olaf …

Aisha …

Tom …

Mari …

Pedro …

Maryam …

3 🔊 CD2, Track 17 Now listen to the five students who responded to the prompts. Which of the following **six** phrases could be added to what each student says? Which one does **not** fit? Listen again and match each phrase to the correct student.

a I think the only people who worry about privacy are criminals.

b It seems like there's an app for everything and anything you might want to do.

c Just think of how we use it every day. What's not to like about technology?

d Of course, if a new technology comes along then perhaps we need to learn how to use it.

e So technology is not a new idea. It's been around for centuries.

f We all have one, in fact we've all had one for so long that we probably can't remember life without one. It's just normal to have one.

4 🔊 CD2, Track 17 Listen to the five students again, this time responding to the prompts in the correct order. You will hear each student saying something **extra** about their prompt. As you listen, decide which student …

a believes that all information is open to everyone

b can only see the positive side of technology

c thinks that new technology is not difficult to understand

d welcomes recommendations from friends

e would find it difficult to live their daily life.

5 Read the audioscript in Appendix 3 to check your answers.

LANGUAGE TIP

Notice the *key introductory phrases* the speakers use in order to give their opinions. Practise using these phrases when you speak to each other to develop your fluency in English.

But I believe that …, And the great thing is …, I can't think of …, What's not to like about …?, The point nowadays is that …, I don't have a problem if …, I don't even think that … .

6 Look at these exam-style follow-up questions to the five responses. Discuss each one with your partner and give a suitable response. Try to use some of the expressions from the Language Tip in this and other units.

a What might you do to survive without your phone?

b Tell me about the specific skills you need to use a mobile phone.

c Describe your favourite app to me.

d What would you do if there was a power cut?

e Which people in society might need to have secrets from others?

215

F 💬 Speaking

1 In Section F in Unit 15 you looked at several areas used when assessing spoken language. Which ones can you and your partner remember? Make a list.

2 Complete the gaps in the following criteria using appropriate words from the box.

> ideas   intonation   meaning   questions   simple   structures   vocabulary

  a The candidate uses a range of ... accurately and consistently.
  b The candidate uses ... structures securely.
  c Shades of ... are achieved and some sophisticated ... are communicated.
  d The candidate uses a restricted range of ....
  e Pronunciation and ... are generally clear.
  f The candidate makes an attempt to respond to ... and prompts.

> **TOP TIP**
> Note that in this part of the IGCSE speaking test, you can start the conversation. Remember that you must use the prompts in the order they appear on the role-play card, and you must use all of them.

G 😃 Watch, listen and talk

1 ▶ You are going to watch an IGCSE student talking about **Technology**. The student is responding to the same prompts that you have already seen in Section E. Which, if any, of the criteria from Activity F2 could apply to the student? Why?

2 ▶ Now watch a second student responding to the same prompts. Do you think they perform better or worse than the first student? Why? Which, if any, of the criteria from Activity F2 could apply to the student? Why?

H 📖 📝 Reading and writing

1 Work with your partner. Look at these pictures and answer the questions.

216

a What can you see in each picture? Do not worry if you are not sure. Make a guess!

b Have you ever seen one for real? Have you ever used one?

c When do you think these technologies were in common use?

d Which of the technologies you use today will be the first to disappear? Why?

2 Match the words in the two columns to make a list of ten great technological inventions.

1	mobile	a	oven
2	microwave	b	connectivity
3	global positioning	c	music
4	personal	d	system
5	digital	e	mouse
6	computer	f	phone
7	internet	g	control
8	remote	h	computer
9	digital	i	conferencing
10	video	j	camera

a Which of the ten do you think is the greatest? Why? Which do you think is the least great? Why?

b Which ones do you think make your own life easier and convenient? In what ways?

c Reduce the list from ten to five. What criteria are you going to use to do this?

d Reduce the list to three. How easy or difficult is it to choose?

e What do you think is missing from the list? Give reasons.

f Read the following article about technological inventions. Write a summary of the ways in which technology has made our lives easier and more convenient. Your summary should be about 100 words long. You should use your own words as far as possible.

Ten greatest technological inventions

1 Since the age of modern man began roughly 200 000 years ago, the world has seen a progression of innovation and invention. From primitive developments, such as the wheel and paper, to today's high-tech gadgets that would blow the mind of any Neanderthal, there's certainly no shortage of impressive developments that have changed the way we live and work. In modern times, a handful of technological wonders that started out as novelties, have become indispensable to our daily routines.

2 Communication has always been the key to success, from wars to relationships. The comparison between today's mobile phones, which offer instantaneous and untethered communication, to the old-fashioned paper-and-pen process is nothing short of incredible. So it's not just for making calls that these phones are good for; they offer total computer access at your fingertips.

3 Though humankind got along just fine without microwaves before they were developed in the late 1940s, the invention has been a major game changer in terms of food preparation and the office break room. Not only have microwaves modernised the way we eat, they've also made meals far more convenient, which really means quicker, to prepare.

4   Thanks to the Global Positioning System (GPS), and its integration in just about everything tech-related, most of you will never get lost again. And we're not talking just about those vehicle dashboard displays. Most smart phones probably have GPS apps guiding the way. According to most sources, GPS was originally developed in 1978 by the U.S. military.

5   No list of the 'greatest technologies ever invented' is complete unless it includes the personal computer (PC). The magazine *Popular Mechanics* reports the first general purpose computer was a 30 ton monster invented in 1947. Though an incredible machine, it was far too large for any home. The invention of the PC happened in the 1970s and revolutionised the entire world.

6   Music has graced the world with its presence for thousands of years, but digitising music has improved sound quality and sharing ability. Digital music also cuts back on waste, and it's only a matter of time before CDs, records and cassette tapes become obsolete.

7   The computer mouse is one technology that often gets overlooked and taken for granted. Back when early computers were the size of a house, they could only be manipulated through hundreds of tiny buttons and sliders. The mouse, so named because

of its tail-like cord and round body, was invented in 1964 by Douglas Engelbart, a radar technician from the Stanford Research Institute.

8   Compared to inventions that have existed for hundreds of years, such as the microscope or telescope, the internet is still in its infancy. However, the internet has arguably changed the world more than most other inventions. The internet was invented in the late 1960s and made available to the public in the 1990s. Since then, it has improved both communication and information dissemination and changed daily life for virtually everyone on Earth.

9   Like the microwave, remote controls aren't necessary to humankind's survival. With that said, they're certainly convenient. They have been around since 1955 and we take them for granted today in the way they wirelessly change the TV channel or run through your slideshows, without making you move from your couch or podium. It is undeniably impressive.

10 Digital cameras are loved by many because they capture sentimental moments and personal adventures. They come in handy for recording such memories, but they also play a significant role in news dissemination and recording history in general. While film-based cameras paved the way for their digital descendants, today's high-tech cameras and integrated phones eliminate long processing times and allow us to share pictures instantly.

11 The idea of video conferencing may not seem like a big deal in today's tech-saturated world, but consider how science-fiction-like the idea was even 100 years ago. Today, talking face-to-face, without actually being face-to-face, is commonplace, with just a mouse click, through a digital camera and across the internet.

Adapted from: http://smallbusiness.chron.com

218

REFLECTION

How well do you think you can do each of these things now?

Give yourself a score from 1: Still need a lot of practice to 5: Feeling very confident about this

In this unit you:	1	2	3	4	5
watched a video of students talking about technology, and discussed what they said					
talked about different technologies					
read about technologies and discussed with your partner					
watched and listened to students taking part in a speaking role-play, and assessed their performance					
read about ten great technologies and wrote a summary					

Now set yourself a **personal goal** based on your scores for Unit 20.

Exam focus

Speaking, Part 2, topic card

Look at this exam-style role-play card. Work with your partner and discuss how you might respond to each of the prompts.

1 In pairs, role-play a speaking exam. Then change roles.

Life in 100 years' time

How we live a hundred years in the future will be very different from life today.

Discuss this topic.

Use the following prompts, in the order given below, to develop the conversation:

• any books you have read or films you have seen about life in the future

• what you think life will really be like in one hundred years' time

• ways in which life might get better or worse in the future

• whether humans will have reached another planet and whether or not this would be a good development

• whether there will be greater harmony or more conflict between nations.

You are free to consider any other related ideas of your own.

Remember, you are not allowed to make any written notes.

- As part of your IGCSE assessment, you will take the speaking exam. Many exams will begin with a few questions, so that you can get used to each other's voices and to make you feel more relaxed. These questions will focus on your home and family life, school and perhaps your hobbies and interests as well. You are not being assessed in this part of the exam.
- Here are some examples of topic cards that may form part of the assessed part of the exam. You will be given time to think about the topic on the card and you may ask if you are unsure about anything. You are not allowed to make any written notes. When you are ready, you will have a conversation for a few minutes based on the topic.
- Remember, the topics in the speaking test will be very general and it is not a test of your knowledge about a topic. The important thing is how you use English: your vocabulary and the structure of your sentences, for example.

Card 1
Childhood memories

Many people have lots of memories from when they were young.
Discuss the topic of childhood memories.

The following ideas **must** be used in sequence to develop the conversation:
- your earliest memory
- other events that you remember clearly
- things that have affected you later in your life
- whether people are more likely to remember good or bad things
- false memories – why some people remember things that didn't actually happen.

You are free to consider any other **related** ideas of your own.
Remember, you are not allowed to make any written notes.

Card 2
The clothes I like

Everyone likes wearing different clothes for different reasons.
Discuss the topic of 'the clothes I like'.

The following ideas **must** be used in sequence to develop the conversation:
- whether you follow the latest fashions
- what your parents think of what you wear
- whether there are any types of clothes that you would not wear
- the influence of famous people on young people's choices
- whether young people's friends' opinions are important.

You are free to consider any other **related** ideas of your own.
Remember, you are not allowed to make any written notes.

Card 3

Changes in lifestyle

There have been many changes in the way people live in your country since the time your grandparents were teenagers.
Discuss the topic of changes in lifestyle.

The following ideas **must** be used in sequence to develop the conversation:
- things you have, but your grandparents did not have
- your idea of a healthy lifestyle today, compared to your grandparents' lifestyles
- standards of living; income and possessions
- the way that teenagers behave
- opportunities to travel and knowledge of the world.

You are free to consider any other **related** ideas of your own.

Remember, you are not allowed to make any written notes.

Card 4

Climate change

We are seeing more and more evidence that the climate in many parts of the world is changing – sometimes with disastrous results.
Discuss the topic of climate change.

The following ideas **must** be used in sequence to develop the conversation:
- things you already know about climate change
- the effect of climate change on you and where you live
- some examples of disasters caused by these changes
- steps taken in your country to deal with the effects of climate change
- what might be done on a worldwide basis.

You are free to consider any other **related** ideas of your own.
Remember, you are not allowed to make any written notes.

Card 5

Preparation for work

The education you have had so far (and any further education or training you intend to take) will prepare you for the world of work.
Discuss the topic preparation for work.

The following ideas **must** be used in sequence to develop the conversation:
- subjects you are studying that might help you in a job
- skills you have developed from your hobbies that might be useful later on
- whether some of your subjects seem to have little to do with your intended career
- whether part-time work while young people are still studying might be a good idea
- other aspects of life that may help young people when they enter the world of work.

You are free to consider any other **related** ideas of your own.
Remember, you are not allowed to make any written notes.

Card 6

Studying abroad

Nowadays, many young people spend some time studying away from their home country.

Discuss the topic of studying abroad.

The following ideas **must** be used in sequence to develop the conversation:

* what you might learn from the experience of a different country
* some of the problems you may have living and learning in a different country
* difficulties of settling down after a period away from home
* how study abroad might be an advantage in finding employment
* some of the problems of studying in a different education system.

You are free to consider any other **related** ideas of your own.

Remember, you are not allowed to make any written notes.

Card 7

Road accidents and road safety

There are more and more worries about the number of people who are injured in accidents on roads.

Discuss the topic of road accidents and road safety.

The following ideas **must** be used in sequence to develop the conversation:

* your experiences of road accidents
* your opinion about why accidents happen
* who are most likely to have accidents – pedestrians, cyclists, motorists
* some consequences of road accidents
* some steps that might be taken to reduce the number of accidents.

You are free to consider any other **related** ideas of your own.

Remember, you are not allowed to make any written notes.

Card 8

Watching sport

Some people like to take part in sports, others prefer to be spectators.

Discuss the topic of watching sport.

The following ideas **must** be used in sequence to develop the conversation:

* sports that you go to see or would like to see
* your thoughts about extreme sports and what young people think about them
* what it is about sport that makes it interesting to watch
* the difference between watching on television and actually being there
* whether some sportsmen and women get paid far too much money.

You are free to consider any other **related** ideas of your own.

Remember, you are not allowed to make any written notes.

Card 9

Happiness

We all like to be happy, but what does that mean to each of us?
Discuss the topic of happiness.

The following ideas **must** be used in sequence to develop the conversation
- happy moments you have had in your life
- what might make you unhappy
- how you would define happiness
- what might make someone unhappy
- the idea that as we get older we expect to be less happy
- whether it is true that 'Happiness is a state of mind'.

You are free to consider any other **related** ideas of your own.
Remember, you are not allowed to make any written notes.

Card 10

The police

A police force is necessary to enforce the law, but how strict should it be?
Discuss the topic of the police.

The following ideas **must** be used in sequence to develop the conversation
- any experience you have had with the police
- what you would do if you were head of the police force
- the characteristics needed to be a good police officer
- reasons why the police might be criticised
- how much power the police should have.

You are free to consider any other **related** ideas of your own.
Remember, you are not allowed to make any written notes.

Card 11

Young children

Some young children need to be constantly busy and require a lot of attention.
Discuss the topic of young children.

The following ideas **must** be used in sequence to develop the conversation
- your experience of being with young children
- activities you think young children enjoy
- the challenges of being a teacher of young children
- how young children might be treated differently in different societies
- situations where young children have to 'grow up' very quickly.

You are free to consider any other **related** ideas of your own.
Remember, you are not allowed to make any written notes.

The texts in this appendix relate to different activities in the coursebook. The activity will tell you when to refer to this appendix. Remember: you only need to read your text. Your partner/ the rest of the group will read theirs.

Texts for Student A

Reading texts: Instructions in Unit 5D and E

TEXT 5A: Hiking with huskies in Finland

[1] On husky-trekking tours, every hiker will get their own husky and a local guide to show the way through the forests. Hikers will be provided with special husky-trekking equipment: a shock- absorbing lead between the hiker and the dog, and a comfortable hiker's waist belt.

[2] The lakeside hotel accommodation is a perfect combination of wilderness and wellness, hiking and huskies, outdoor life and relaxation. As a highlight of the tour, the huskies invite you to spend the last evening at their home, as a thank-you for keeping them company!

[3] Hiking with huskies is more strenuous than normal hill walking as the dogs are particularly eager to study the surroundings. Mostly they follow the trail but sometimes they also like to study what can be found deeper in the forests. As the dogs have better senses than us, they also help us to see and hear better what is happening in the natural environment around us.

[4] To participate on this tour you need to be reasonably fit. Husky-trekking is more intensive and physically more demanding than normal hill walking. For the tour you should wear normal hiking shoes or sturdy trainers and suitable outdoor clothing. It is also good to have a small daypack and a water bottle. While in most places it is possible to drink natural water from streams and springs, it is advisable to also take a water bottle with you.

Adapted from: www.responsibletravel.com

STUDENT A (ask Student B)

a Where is the Mediterraneo Marina Park?

b Tell me four animals I can see.

c What is the job of the specialist trainers?

d What special clothing do I need?

e What are the main differences between the pool and the deep seawater experiences?

The SQ3R Method (A): Instructions in Unit 10C

A: QUESTION – Help your mind engage* and concentrate*

Turn the boldface heading for each section into as many questions as you think will be answered in that section. The better the questions, the better your comprehension is likely to be. When your mind is actively searching for answers to questions, it becomes engaged in active learning.

Adapted from: www.ucc.vt.edu

*See the **WORD TIP (Unit 10, Section C)**

Reading texts: Instructions in Unit 12C

TEXT 1: British Virgin Islands

Situated in the western hemisphere, the British Virgin Islands are the perfect destination for both sailing and diving. Positioned right at the top of the Caribbean island chain, this group of 36 small islands is characterised by steep green hills and white-sand beaches. Around them lie the clear blue waters of the Sir Francis Drake Channel. This stunning environment is perfect for a wide range of water sports, which is why we offer our widest variety of adventure training programmes here.

Reading texts: Instructions in Unit 15C

Ginger – part of nature's pharmacy

[1] It is not pretty to look at, but the pink flesh enclosed in the brown, wrinkled skin has been adding flavour to food and drink for well over 2,000 years. Ginger or ginger root is the rhizome (below the ground) of the plant *Zingiber officinale*, consumed as a delicacy, medicine, spice or food ingredient.

[2] Ginger has an interesting history. It was widely used in ancient China, and it is known to date back to the 6th century BCE. It was introduced to the Mediterranean region some time before the 1st century CE, probably by Arabs who were travelling the Silk Road, an important trade route, carrying spices, silk and a variety of other luxuries from China to India and the Middle East and beyond. In 1585, Jamaican ginger was the first oriental spice to be grown in the New World and exported back to Europe.

[3] Ginger produces clusters of white and pink flower buds which bloom into yellow flowers and as a result of its aesthetic appeal and the adaptation of the plant to warm climates, it is often used as landscaping in gardens around subtropical homes. It is a perennial plant, which means that it does not die, returning each year with its leafy stems growing to about one metre in height. Traditionally, the rhizome is gathered when the stalks wither; it is immediately scalded using boiling hot water and scraped to prevent further growth.

[4] Young ginger is juicy and fleshy with a very mild taste, and it has a range of different uses. It is often pickled in vinegar and eaten as a snack or just cooked and used as an ingredient in many dishes. It can also be brewed in boiling water to make ginger tea, to which honey is often added. Mature ginger rhizomes are fibrous and nearly dry. The juice from ginger roots is often used as a spice and is a common ingredient of many cuisines for flavouring dishes such as seafood, meats and vegetables. Powdered dry ginger root is typically used as flavouring for recipes such as gingerbread, biscuits and cakes.

From 'Ginger' in Horus, Egypt Air's in-flight magazine, January 2015

[5] Apart from its uses in cooking, ginger also has wide applications in medicine and healthy living. Ginger contains chemicals that may reduce feelings of sickness, as well as inflammation. Researchers believe the chemicals work primarily in the stomach and the intestines, but they may also work in the brain and nervous system. The majority of studies have shown that using ginger as a dietary supplement can have a positive impact on stomach problems, as well as in reducing muscle inflammation due to too much exercise. Furthermore, high blood pressure and severe headaches can also be alleviated through using ginger extracts and powders. If used in reasonable quantities, ginger has few negative side effects.

Reading texts: Instructions in Unit 20C

STUDENT A: The perfect thing for anyone going at a rate of knots

[1] Self-lacing trainers have arrived, not long after Marty McFly wore a pair in *Back to the Future Part II*. Nike has unveiled the HyperAdapt 1.0 trainer, featuring an 'adaptive lacing' system that automatically tightens the shoe the moment its wearer steps in. The trainers are powered by an **internal*** battery that lasts for about two weeks between charges.

[2] The sporting purpose of the neon blue light on the shoe's instep is unknown, but it looks a bit like the one from the Nike Mag trainers worn by Marty McFly in the 1989 film. McFly, who was played by Michael J Fox, put on a pair of self-tightening Nike Mag trainers after travelling forward in time.

[3] Nike has pitched the trainers squarely at athletes, promising that they would reduce slippage caused by loose laces, thereby sharpening their wearer's concentration. Senior executives did not dare to suggest that their target market was actually people who could not be bothered to tie up their shoelaces.

[4] The self-tightening system is activated when the wearer's heel hits a sensor **inside*** the shoe, which instantly measures their weight and foot position. A series of motorised pulleys then pull together a mesh of filaments around the foot, tighter or looser where required. Plus and minus buttons on the side of the shoe allow the wearer to tighten and loosen their fit. Holding down the minus button for more than two seconds fully loosens the shoe so that it can be removed.

[5] A study by scientists has found that we are hard-wired to be lazy, or at least, to conserve energy, as our caveman ancestors had to do. The research found that over time participants strapped into leg braces that caused them to strain would unconsciously adapt their walking gait to the most economic possible. Nike said that the HyperAdapt 1.0 trainers would learn the best fit for their owners' feet after being worn two or three times. After a while they would gather biometric data that would be relayed to other 'smart' clothing and wearable technology.

*See the **WORD TIP (Unit 20 Section C)**

Adapted from: www.thetimes.co.uk

Texts for Student B

Reading texts: Instructions in Unit 5D and E

Text 5B: Swimming with Dolphins at the Mediterraneo Marine Park

[1] There are many places in the world where you can swim with dolphins, from Australia to Hawaii. The Mediterraneo Marine Park on the island of Malta provides a wonderful location where dolphins, parrots, sea lions and iguanas are abundant. The park invites everyone, young and old, to experience an innovative way of learning more about animals, and at the same time provide you with a memorable holiday.

[2] Offering you a comprehensive dolphin experience, our specialist trainers will ensure you are fully confident and ready before you enter the dolphin pool. Safety is of paramount importance for everyone during the pool experience so you will be attached to a trainer or guide with a safety line at all times, and a net will separate you from the dolphins. Because the water where you swim with the dolphins is shallow, you do not need to be a strong swimmer. However, we supply you with floatation aids to guarantee safety.

[3] For those who are more adventurous, try a customised deep sea excursion on board one of our dolphin boats, which will take you out to sea to find and swim alongside completely wild dolphins. We will supply you with a wetsuit and a mask, but remember to bring your own swimming costume to wear under the wetsuit. As always, our trainers and guides will be with you all the time. However, you must be an experienced swimmer as this exciting opportunity takes place in deep seawater. And there are no nets!

STUDENT B (ask Student A)

a What special equipment do I need for the husky-trekking tour?

b Where is the hotel?

c Tell me three characteristics of huskies

d How different is husky-trekking to normal hill climbing?

e What special clothing do I need?

The SQ3R Method (B): Instructions in Unit 10C

B: READ – Fill in the information around the mental structures you've been building

Read one section at a time with your questions in mind, and as you read look for the answers within the section. Recognise when you need to make up some new questions, in order to clarify something, or to help you take your understanding deeper. Don't pretend to understand something if you really don't!

Adapted from: www.ucc.vt.edu

Reading texts: Instructions in Unit 12C

TEXT 2: The Leeward Islands of the Caribbean

Situated in the western hemisphere, the Leeward Islands are scattered from the Virgin Islands, southwards to Antigua. The best-known islands of this group include St Kitts, Nevis, St Barts and St Martin. Although they cover a small geographic area, the islands reveal great geological and cultural diversity, with a variety of customs, languages and currencies. Some islands are green and mountainous, others are dry and flat. This adventure programme offers longer-distance sailing for both beginners and experienced sailors, and you'll have many opportunities for exploring!

Reading texts: Instructions in Unit 15C

Honey – nature's oldest food

[1]   Exactly how long honey has been in existence is hard to say because it has been around since as far back as we can record. Cave paintings in Spain from 7000 BCE show the earliest records of beekeeping. However, <u>a number of</u> honey bee fossils date back about 150 million years. The earliest record of keeping bees in hives was found in the sun temple erected in 2400 BCE near Cairo, Egypt, and the bee featured frequently in Egyptian hieroglyphs, often symbolising royalty.

[2]   A thick, golden liquid produced by industrious bees, honey is made using the nectar of flowering plants and is saved inside the beehive for eating during times of scarcity. But bees are not the only ones with a sweet tooth. Humans, bears, badgers and other animals have long been raiding the winter stores of bees to harvest their honey. In fact, until sugar became widely available in the 16th century, honey was the world's principle sweetener, with ancient Greece and Sicily among the best-known historical centres of honey production. The ancient Egyptians used honey as a sweetener, as a gift and even as an ingredient in medicine. Honey cakes were baked by the Egyptians and the Greeks and used as offerings. Greek recipes books were full of <u>a range of</u> sweetmeats and cakes made from honey, and cheeses were mixed with honey to make cheesecakes. The Greeks viewed honey as not only an important food, but also as a healing medicine, while the Romans used honey as a gift and included it extensively in cooking.

[3]   Beekeeping flourished throughout the Roman Empire, and elsewhere honey continued to be of importance. This was particularly true in Europe until around the 16th century when the arrival of sugar from further afield meant honey was used less. By the 17th century, sugar was being used regularly as a sweetener and honey was used even less.

[4]   Honey's colour, taste, aroma and texture vary greatly depending on the type of flower a bee frequents. But the benefits of honey go beyond its wonderful taste. A great natural source of carbohydrates which provide strength and energy to our bodies, honey is known for its effectiveness <u>in a variety of</u> areas, instantly boosting performance and endurance, and in reducing muscle fatigue in athletes. Its natural sugars play an important role in preventing fatigue during exercise. The glucose in honey is absorbed by the body quickly and gives an immediate energy boost, while the fructose is absorbed more slowly, providing sustained energy over a period of time.

[5]   Scientific tests show that the various types of honey differ in <u>the amounts of</u> vitamins and minerals they contain because every honey sample is made up of a different mix of nectars. Depending which plants bees are visiting, honey can take on different levels of certain nutrients and beneficial chemicals. Each flower has a varied vitamin and mineral content, so the bee is really filling her larder with a balanced diet just as we do with our grains, beans, vegetables and dairy.

Adapted from: www.livescience.com
www.benefits-of-honey.com
www.honeyassociation.com
www.motherearthliving.com

Reading texts: Instructions in Unit 20C

STUDENT B: A clean solution to energy needs

[1] The future is definitely beyond the horizon, with massive wind turbines out at sea and even airborne wind turbines above the clouds providing a clean solution to the world's energy needs. While Europe has always been at the forefront of wind energy technology, the United States has finally joined the party.

[2] Deep-water turbines are extremely large, and each one alone can generate six megawatts of power – that's enough energy for six thousand average households for a year. Their height is twice as high as the Statue of Liberty, with a diameter that doubles the size of a 747 Jumbo jet's 60m wingspan. On the other hand, some aerial wind turbines are much smaller, with a diameter of around 12 metres.

[3] The clean energy company *Deepwater Wind* is building a wind farm of fifteen mega turbines to the south of Rhode Island in the state of New England, USA. Eventually, there could be as many as 200 such turbines, providing a significant proportion of southern New England's electricity needs. The turbine parts are manufactured in France and assembled on site, with great attention being given to ensure that clean energy is beneficial for everyone and everything, including the whales which inhabit the waters around Rhode Island.

[4] Underwater noise is being controlled and all noise-producing activities will cease during the spring when the whales are present in the Rhode Island area. Furthermore, company boats will travel more slowly to create as little noise as possible. There has been worry among the fishing community, but the *Deepwater Wind's* turbines will be up to 1.6 kilometres apart, providing plenty of room for fishing boats. Birds, too, are likely to be unaffected by the offshore turbines as studies show that migratory birds tend to fly near the coast and not out at sea where the turbines would be.

[5] Offshore wind turbines have the advantage over onshore turbines in that they can be much bigger and therefore produce more energy. Transporting turbine parts over land to onshore sights is complex, involving high costs and time, whereas offshore turbine components can be transported on barges out to sea. This is a much cheaper and time-efficient solution.

Adapted from: 'Down to business: The future is beyond the horizon' in *Royal Wings*, Royal Jordanian in-flight magazine, May/June 2016

Texts for Student C

The SQ3R Method (C): Instructions in Unit 10C

C: RECITE – Retrain your mind to concentrate and learn as it reads

After each section, stop and recall your questions and see if you can answer them from memory. Don't cheat! But if can't answer them, look back at the text again (as often as necessary) for help. However, don't move on to the next section if you can't provide the answers from the previous one.

Adapted from: www.ucc.vt.ed

Reading texts: Instructions in Unit 12C

TEXT 3: Galapagos and Ecuador

Situated in the western hemisphere, the Galapagos archipelago – comprising more than 100 islands – was formed about 4 million years ago. Separated from South America by the Pacific Ocean, this group of islands is an extremely important biological area. Among the amazing animals you can see here are giant tortoises, penguins, iguanas and sea lions. Our adventure is shared between the mainland of Ecuador and the Galapagos islands. The programme includes eco-tours of the rainforest, white-water expeditions and community service projects.

Reading texts: Instructions in Unit 20C

STUDENT C: Smart kitchen knows what's in the fridge

[1] The experience is familiar to anyone who regularly cooks at home: you're at the supermarket buying everything you need for the next meal, but you can't remember if you have butter at home. So what do you do? To buy or not to buy? And now that you think about it, you did buy butter the last time you were at the supermarket, didn't you? And once you get home and look for the butter, you find out that you haven't got any.

[2] But what if you could actually see the contents of your fridge from the supermarket aisle? Wouldn't that be something? In fact, the technology is already here in the form of kitchen appliances with 'connected food' technology built in to fridges and ovens. There are even some options to 'upgrade' non-wifi equipped fridges and ovens, but the new, brightly-coloured, hands-on appliances with embedded wifi are too amazing to resist.

[3] Once you have the appropriate app downloaded into your smart phone, you will receive a live feed from inside your fridge. Apart from showing what is already there, the technology will tell you what you can make with those ingredients by pulling data from an online store of thousands of recipes. The app will even help you to place an order for missing items, just in case you cannot be bothered to make the trip to the supermarket yourself.

[4] The oven technology can 'sense' what is inside the oven and tell you how to cook it. It provides information on the correct cooking time and the right temperature, depending on the food's weight, the oven model and even the altitude of the place where the kitchen is located. There is even technology which allows family members or friends to gather round a screen, choose a recipe and then make it together.

[5] And for those who want some non-human company, you can install cameras in your kitchen ceiling, and the technology will enable you to watch yourself putting carrots on a cutting board. The app will tell you that yes, those are carrots, and will play back a video of you chopping the carrots while also giving you carrot recipes from the online store.

Adapted from: 'Smart kitchen knows what's in fridge', in *Gulf News*, 31 May 2016

Texts for Student D

The SQ3R Method (D): Instructions in Unit 10C

D: REVIEW – Refine your mental organisation and begin building memory

When you've finished reading the entire chapter using the preceding steps, go back over the questions you created for every heading. Check if you can still answer them confidently. If you can't, look back at the chapter and refresh your memory, check what you remember, and then continue reading the subsequent chapters.

[Adapted from: www.ucc.vt.edu]

Reading texts: Instructions in Unit 12C

TEXT 4: Australia

Situated in the eastern hemisphere, Australia is the sixth largest country in the world. Here you can find the world's biggest coral ecosystem: the Great Barrier Reef. Stretching roughly 2,000 kilometres, the reef is the only living organism that can be seen from outer space and is the ideal setting for many of our adventure activities. Our Australian Expedition will take you from Sydney in the south to Cape Tribulation in the north. Along the way, you'll enjoy diving, trekking, sailing, surfing and community service.

Reading texts: Instructions in Unit 20C

STUDENT D: The problem solvers

[1] When you have 200 000 passengers travelling an average of 530 daily flights through the Emirates hub in Dubai, keeping the network in perfect running order is not an easy task. That's where the NCC, Emirates' Network Control Centre, and the beating heart of the airline's entire operation, comes into play, playing a crucial role in the smooth running of the airline.

[2] In much the same way as NASA's Mission Control monitors all aspects of its space exploration, the NCC manages every flight, every departure, every arrival, and every single movement of its fleet. Inside the airline's nerve centre is a 60+ strong team of highly specialised individuals, all monitoring, coordinating and problem-solving on a daily basis. Made up of 15 different departments, each has its own distinct area of specialism. For example, there are crew scheduling teams who focus timetabling crew for different flights, while the team of flight despatchers arrange flight plans and choose the best routes on any given day. A team of engineers, each trained on specific aircraft types, is able to recommend the best possible repair solution.

[3] But despite the need for different departments, nothing is achieved in isolation, with all the teams working together, using their different skillsets to develop the best approach to each situation. It is the responsibility of everyone to ensure that flights stick to schedules as closely as possible, no matter what happens.

[4] The NCC relies on a number of key pieces of technology to help ensure that flights operate on time. For example, using the latest radar technology, the teams can predict the exact time an aircraft will land, taking into consideration wind speed, the flight path and even the aircraft's optimal speed.

[5] The focal point for the entire department is the giant floor-to-ceiling radar screen, which shows vital information such as aircraft holding patterns and which runways are in use. A second screen shows all current aircraft positions, delivering a complete picture of the entire Emirates network at any given moment in time, and ensuring the highest level of connectivity for its passengers.

Adapted from: 'The problem solvers', in *Open Skies*, Emirates in-flight magazine, May 2016

Appendix 3: Audioscript of accompanying CD

Unit 1: E Speaking
Activity 1   CD1, Track 2

Maria: Hi Christos, how are you?

Christos: Hey Maria, I'm really great, what about you?

Maria: Everything's fine! <u>Why don't we go</u> to the shopping centre later? I want to see if I can get some new trainers.

Christos: Yes, we could do that, but <u>I'd rather go</u> at the weekend. Can you wait until then?

Maria: I suppose so, but why?

Christos: Well, I get paid for my part-time job tomorrow, so I'll have some money to spend.

Maria: Fair enough! So <u>let's go</u> at the weekend instead. But what are we going to do today?

Unit 3: F Speaking
Activity 1   CD1, Track 3

Anna: <u>To my mind,</u> fast-food restaurants are here to stay.

Terry: <u>If you ask me</u>, people are starting to realise how unhealthy fast food is.

A: But it's so convenient! <u>In my opinion,</u> people are not going to give that up.

T: <u>Know what I think?</u> People are lazy and will always take the easy option!

Unit 4: C Listening Activities 2 and 3
CD1, Track 4

Speaker 1

Well, of course, we had booked everything well in advance, because in Britain these services get full very early, and we didn't want to be disappointed. Anyway, we got to the terminus in central London in plenty of time and we stood on platform 13E for Edinburgh.

It was a beautiful summer's day. There was me, my wife Julia and the three children. They were still quite young then: three, six and eight, I think. We were supposed to leave at 8.30 in the morning and, as it got closer to our departure time, we all began to get quite excited. By 8.30, we had started to get a little bit anxious because the platform was completely empty, apart from us five with all our luggage. At 9.00, Julia told me to go and find out what was happening, so off I went to the booking office to make enquiries. And yes, you can guess what was wrong – we were 12 hours early! Our departure time was 8.30 p.m., not a.m. I had misread the time on the tickets.

Speaker 2

They call it an airport, but it's really just a field. My sister had booked me a flight as a treat for my 13th birthday, which was May 20th, three years ago, and I must admit that I was absolutely dreading it! I've never really enjoyed flying, and the thought of going up in the air for 30 minutes in a basket really didn't appeal to me. I couldn't understand how the thing was driven and steered, and I think that's what put me off. But once we got up in the air, at 9 o'clock in the morning, it was spectacular – the most beautiful views of the hills, fields and villages below, with the sun sparkling on the river. We didn't want to come down!

Speaker 3

I had investigated all the different options available to me and, in the end, this was by far the cheapest, at only $275. Of course, it wouldn't be nearly as fast as going by plane, but the cost was far less and I would be able to see something of the countryside. Some friends had travelled the same route

the previous year and had said how brilliant it had been, so I wasn't really worried. What they hadn't told me was how uncomfortable these vehicles are when you've been in one for almost two days. It's very difficult to sleep, and there are no toilets or washing facilities, so you've got to hang on until the scheduled stops, usually every four to five hours. When I finally arrived in the south of Spain, after nearly 48 hours on the road, I slept for over 19 hours!

Speaker 4

We set off in the afternoon, as the sun was starting to drop, and with it the temperature, although it was still incredibly hot and humid. We knew the journey would take about two hours, so we had time to reach the oasis before dark, and before the temperature plummeted. With me was my twin teenage sister, Amelia. She was used to riding horses, so this wasn't as difficult for her as it was for me. Even so, she said that riding without a saddle was very uncomfortable, and I had to agree with her! She also complained about not having a riding hat, but I told her she'd look pretty silly if she did! We moved at a leisurely pace – these wonderful animals won't be rushed – and we had time to be amazed by the beautiful scenery all around us and, as dusk fell, the sky as well. We arrived, made camp, ate and fell into a deep sleep under the stars.

Unit 4: C Listening
Activity 8   CD1, Track 5

For many years, *boda-bodas* have been called Uganda's silent killers. *Boda-bodas*, our country's ubiquitous motorbike taxis, snake through traffic jams, navigate potholed roads and provide much-needed employment for young people. They are also injuring and killing thousands every year, monopolising hospital budgets and destroying livelihoods. Since they appeared on the streets of Uganda in the 1960s, the number of *boda-bodas* has swelled. One recent news report estimated that there were more than 300 000 bikes operating in the capital, Kampala.

As a result, the number of motorbike accidents has increased dramatically. According to the Injury Control Centre, there are up to 20 *boda-boda*-related cases at Mulago National Referral Hospital in Kampala every day and the strain on the country's limited health budget is growing. About 40% of trauma cases at the hospital are from *boda-boda* accidents. The treatment of injured passengers and pedestrians accounts for almost two-thirds of the hospital's annual surgery budget.

While *boda-bodas* are helping to reduce youth unemployment – one recent study estimated that 62% of young people in Uganda are jobless – the impact of a serious injury can be catastrophic for riders and their families. Ali Niwamanya, 25, a *boda-boda* driver, spent three months in Mulago hospital and another five at home recovering after a collision with a car in the capital in September. Niwamanya is now in debt after taking out a 3 million Ugandan shilling loan (that's about 1,200 US dollars) for a new bike.

While the human impact of the *boda-boda* craze is evident in the packed hospital wards, the strain that road fatalities could have on the economy is worrying politicians. The death toll on Uganda's roads is twice the average across the rest of Africa. There were 3,343 road deaths in 2011,

but the World Health Organization believes the figure could be more than double that. Some people are warning that, in the very near future, the death toll from Uganda's roads will be higher than that from diseases such as malaria.

Some measures are being taken to try to halt the problem. Last month, the government announced that more money would be available to improve and maintain roads. Even though road safety measures were not specifically included within the budget, the government is establishing a national agency to run campaigns and manage roads. In Kampala, the Capital City Authority is introducing regulations, including registration of drivers, first-aid training, reflector jackets and helmets, and a monthly fee of 20 000 Ugandan shillings paid by the city's 250 000 motorbike taxis.

Other initiatives are also springing up. The Global Helmet Vaccine Initiative is holding a one-day workshop for 100 riders, part of a national scheme under which it has trained 1,800 *boda-boda* riders in basic road safety. On completion, each participant receives a yellow helmet bearing the slogan: 'Your life is your wealth.'

Adapted from www.theguardian.com

Unit 4: E Speaking Activities 1 and 2
CD1, Track 6

Male teenager: The thing that surprised me more than anything was the number of *boda-bodas* on the roads.

Female teenager: What surprised me most was the number of injuries and deaths.

MT: I couldn't believe how long Ali Niwamanya was in hospital for.

FT: I had no idea about the rate of unemployment.

Unit 4: F Listening Activity 3
CD1, Track 7

A

Woman: Good morning, Mega Music Store, how can I help you?

Gregory: Hi, I'd like to know if I can order something from you.

W: Yes, of course – we can help you with DVDs and MP3 downloads, as well as other software and tablets, and so on.

G: Actually, I don't want any of those; I just want to order a power cable. The product number is CD39 dash 2BK. Can you do that?

W: Certainly. Let me take your details …

B

Here is the weather forecast for tomorrow for your local area. There will be some light rain overnight, turning to sunny spells in the early morning and there will be high clouds by the end of the morning. Heavy showers are forecast for the late afternoon and evening. The top temperature is expected to be 18 degrees Celsius.

C

Marina: Hello, could I have some information about your evening classes, please?

College secretary: Of course. Are you interested in anything in particular, or do you want details of everything we offer?

M: I'm interested in learning a new language. I want to learn Italian!

CS: If you look over there, behind those bookshelves, you'll find leaflets about all our evening classes, or you could use one of the computers to check online.

233

Cambridge IGCSE English as a Second Language

D

Thank you for calling the Health and Fitness Sports Centre, the home of tennis, squash, badminton, futsal and swimming. The Sports Centre management has just introduced new prices for using the tennis facilities, so for non-members a weekend court will now cost $12 an hour, while during the week, the daytime price is $8 and $10 after 6 p.m. For members, the price is $9 at any time during the week, and $11 at the weekend.

Unit 4: Exam focus Listening 1 CD1, Track 8

Question 1

And now for the prices and opening times at the Star Cinema. All tickets are priced at $10 for adults and $6.50 for students and children. Our weekend opening time is two o'clock in the afternoon and on weekdays we open one hour later, at three.

Question 2

Daniela: Do you sell street maps?

Shopkeeper: Well, yes, we do, but I'm afraid we've sold out.

D: Do you know where I can get one?

S: Try the newsagent's on the other side of the park. Or the shop at the bus station will have plenty.

D: Isn't there anywhere closer than the bus station?

S: Let me think ... Oh yes, the supermarket across the road from here.

Question 3

Jason: Excuse me! Sorry to trouble you but I'm completely lost! This is my first day working here and I can't find where I need to go!

Woman: You must be the new part-time helper, right? Don't worry, you'll soon find your way around. This is the staff room. But where do you want to go?

J: I'm trying to find the supervisor's office. I need to give him my contact details.

Woman: Well, you're not too far away. Look, you see the lift over there? Go up to the second floor and when you get out of the lift, turn left and left again at the end of the corridor. The supervisor's office is the first door on the right.

J: Thanks so much.

Question 4

Welcome aboard our city sightseeing bus. First, let me tell you about the tour. We're going to travel through the most historic parts of the city for about an hour, with lots of opportunities for you to take photos, or just admire the wonderful buildings and scenery. Then we'll drop you off near the market place. You can visit the museum, which is very interesting, or why not buy some fruit and cheese from the market and have a snack in the park next to the museum? But please please please come back promptly to the bus after one hour – we can't wait for any latecomers! Now for some safety information ... .

Unit 4: Exam focus Listening 2 CD1, Track 9

1

Adult man: Everything half price before we close today. Fruit, vegetables, lovely flowers, you can get everything you need here, in your local market. Come to the front and take a good look. You won't believe my prices today. Potatoes and carrots for lunch tomorrow, apples and melons, everything 100% fresh and half prices. Yes, madam, what can I get for you?

Adult female: Just some fruit please ... hmmm I'll take a kilo of oranges please.

AM: Certainly madam, no problem. How about some strawberries? They were grown

locally, just down the road. Or some lovely pears?

AF: Yes, they look delicious, but not today thanks. But on second thoughts, I'll take five kilos of potatoes.

2

Hi Fatma, this is Muna. How are you? I don't know if you remember me, but we were in sociology class together during summer school. We were so pleased to see each other in the classroom after meeting at the registration day in April. Anyway, I'll be working in Bahrain next month and I'd love to see you and go for a coffee. I was supposed to be coming in September, but my trip was postponed. So, I'll be coming in November instead. Can you let me know if you have any free time? Hopefully, we'll meet again soon.

3

Teenage girl: Hi, Ali, how are you? Last time I spoke to uncle Fahad he said you were going away with your school basketball team.

Teenage boy: Yeah, we were supposed to go for two weeks but it was cut short.

TG: So when did you get back?

TB: In the end the trip was just one week, which was kind of disappointing.

TG: I suppose so, but did you win your matches?

TB: We played two warm-up matches, which we lost, and six competitive matches. We won four of those, which wasn't bad I suppose. We didn't win the competition cup, but we all got a medal for taking part.

TG: Excellent! Well done!

4

Adult male: Hello, do you have a table for three, please? I have a young baby so perhaps somewhere not too noisy? We didn't make a reservation.

Adult female: No reservation? For three, let me just check … Unfortunately, we are fully booked but I think I might have a table for two somewhere. We can add a highchair for the baby, if that's ok?

AM: It depends where the table is …

AF: Just there, by the window.

AM: Hmmm it might be too cold there for the baby. Do you have anywhere else?

AF: As I said sir, we are fully booked, so that's all I can offer you at the moment, unless you can wait until after eight o'clock.

**Unit 5: C Listening Activity 2
CD1, Track 10**

Chen Wen: Hello everyone, my name's Chen Wen, and today we are very lucky to be talking to someone who has an <u>amazing job</u>! Please welcome Wang Yanghua, an aerial tourism helicopter pilot based in Guilin, Southern China.

Wang Yanghua: Hello, Chen, thank you for inviting me

CW: So, aerial tourism? What on earth is that?!

WY: Well, it's basically holiday sightseeing, but from a helicopter. Instead of seeing things from the ground, I take tourists and holidaymakers up in a helicopter, and we look at things from above.

CW: That's certainly a different way of doing things. Tell us how you became interested in flying. Is it something that you've always wanted to do?

WY: Actually, no. As a teenager I wanted to be a doctor.

CW: So how did you become a pilot?

WY: Well, I was at the cinema a watching a film, and at some point there was a <u>dramatic scene</u> with helicopters flying over cities and forests …

CW: … and that made you want to become a pilot?

WY: To be honest, it just suddenly hit me that flying helicopters was what I wanted to do. Strange, but true! I got my full licence seven years ago.

CW: What is a <u>normal workday</u> for you?

WY: Well, it depends very much on the time of year, because obviously the weather impacts greatly on when I can fly, and to which sights. But on a summer's day I need to be at the airfield a couple of hours before that day's sightseers are ready to board the helicopter, so usually I'm there around seven in the morning.

CW: Where exactly do you take the tourists?

WY: We are very lucky in this part of China to have such <u>stunning scenery</u>. Guilin offers breath-taking lakes and rivers, as well as rolling hills, and <u>spectacular views</u>.

CW: Do sightseers ever want to avoid nature and look down on cities instead?

WY: Certainly they do. I have a colleague, who flies in Beijing, and she only does city sightseeing tours. She tells me that the most <u>popular attractions</u> are the Beijing National Stadium, known as the Bird's Nest, and, of course, the Great Wall of China.

CW: Describe how different it is to see something from a helicopter

WY: Well, firstly, <u>ground-level sightseeing</u> is usually static. It's **stationary***. People get off the coach or out of the car and stand in front of something and take a photo or two, or a couple of selfies. Often

people sit and admire something and really only see a building or a statue from one <u>static angle</u>. But when you're in a helicopter, sightseeing becomes more dynamic …

CW: Which means?

WY: The angle of view and speed are constantly changing because, obviously, the helicopter is constantly moving. What you see is a panorama, from east to west and north to south, and if you close your eyes for a few seconds, when you open them again the view will be completely different.

CW: So if you blink you may miss something?!

WY: Yes! Secondly, how high or low the helicopter is flying …

CW: … its altitude?

WY: Exactly. Altitude impacts hugely on how we see something.

CW: What else is different?

WY: Well, at ground level, it's usually very difficult to know what other things are around the sight you are looking at. But from the air, you can see the building or lake or whatever it might be, in a context. And that of course helps us to appreciate its size and shape in relation to other things.

CW: Finally, Wang, what's the most interesting thing you've ever seen from a helicopter?

WY: You know something? Every time I fly, I see things differently, so something which may not have struck me as being very interesting on one day could look completely different on another. So, every day is fascinating in some way or another. Every day I see something which amazes me.

235

CW: As I said at the start, you really do have an amazing job! I definitely know what my next holiday activity is going to be! Wang Yanghua, aerial tourism helicopter pilot, thank you so much, and fly safely!

WY: Thank you!

Unit 5: F Reading and Speaking Activity 2   CD1, Track 11

For anyone wanting a winter holiday, the area around Dali, in the province of Yunnan in southern China, offers many attractions, such as beautiful islands and delightful mountain scenery, as well as wonderful wildlife. One example of this can be found near Xiao Putuo island in Erhai Lake, where thousands of snow-white seabirds take to the air whenever food is thrown at them. As you know, birds often fear humans, but this event really happens. Some of the birds even fly toward the food held out by visitors and take it from their hands. The whole scene is breath taking, with blue water and sky, white clouds, and snow-capped mountains in the distance.

Erhai (meaning *ear-shaped*) Lake is the second largest freshwater lake in the region, covers an area of 257 square kilometres and has an average depth of 11 metres. The lake is an important food source for the local people, who are famous for their amazing method of fishing. They train cormorant birds to catch fish who then return them to fishmongers!

Xiao Putou island, where Erhai Lake is found, is covered with lush green leaves and flowers, and the recent building of several hotels along the lake's shores make this an increasingly popular place for tourists to visit. Locals can rent you a small boat to visit both the island and the lake. Nearby

Cangshan Mountain is another natural attraction, with almost 95% of it covered by forest. Along with the complex landscape of the mountain, the forest makes walking difficult for novices. Up to 200 people lose their way each year, and have to be rescued, so a professional guide is essential if you want to go walking in the area. If you insist and really want to explore the mountain, but are looking for an easier option, a 45-minute cable car ride will transport you to the top, which is 4,000 metres above sea level.

This ride is a thrilling experience during the winter time. You will be amazed by the green mountain landscape at lower levels, which gradually changes to a white blanket of snow as you slowly travel upwards. Then, as the cable car reaches higher levels, it can get quite shaky if the weather is windy.

Another attraction near the lake are the hot springs at Eryuan, which is in fact the original source of the water in Erhai Lake. There are 200–300 hot springs open to the public, attracting many winter visitors from Taiwan, Thailand, Myanmar, Hong Kong and Japan, as well South Korea. Improved transport links are planned to increase tourism, and there are currently 15 domestic air links connecting the region with major cities.

Major events, such as the six-day shopping festival, encourage locals and tourists to buy herbal medicine, agricultural products, and clothes, as well as food and gift items. As many as 30 000 people visit the festival every year. Another spectacular event is the annual

singing fair, which attracts nearly 100 000 people.

Unit 5: G Speaking Activity 3 CD1, Track 12

EXAMINER: Hello. What's your name?

STEFANOS: Stefanos

E: How do you spell your family name?

S: ALEXANDROU

E: Which town do you live in, Stefanos?

S: Nicosia

E: Thank you. Describe how you travelled here today.

S: Car

E: How many brothers and sisters do you have?

S: None

E: Tell me what you enjoy doing in your free time.

S: Playing on my computer

E: Thanks, Stefanos. Talk to me about your favourite subjects at school.

S: Science

E: OK. And what career would you like to follow?

S: I want to be a doctor

E: Thank you. What did you do last weekend?

S: I visited my grandparents

E: And what are your plans for next weekend?

S: I don't know

E: Thank you very much, Stefanos

Unit 5: G Speaking Activity 8 CD1, Track 13

EXAMINER: Hello. What's your name?

MARIA: Hi. I'm Maria

E: How do you spell your family name?

M: Actually it's quite easy: CHRISTOU

E: Which town do you live in, Maria?

M: I live here in Nicosia, well, just outside actually

E: Thank you. Describe how you travelled here today

M: <u>Well</u>, my mum drove me

E: How many brothers and sisters do you have?

M: I don't have any.

E: Tell me what you enjoy doing in your free time

M: <u>To be honest,</u> I don't have much free time but I like watching TV

E: Thanks, Maria. Talk to me about your favourite subjects at school

M: <u>Hmm,</u> I like everything but my favourite subject is English

E: OK. And what career would you like to follow?

M: <u>So far,</u> I have no idea but maybe teaching

E: Thank you. What did you do last weekend?

M: <u>Let me think.</u> OK, I had an exam at school so I did some studying

E: And what are your plans for next weekend?

M: <u>Next weekend?</u> I don't know. Maybe I'll go shopping with some friends

E: Thank you very much

Unit 5: Exam focus Listening
CD1, Track 14

Volcanoes are feared for their mighty power, but also highly prized for the fertile soils on their slopes. They are also admired for their beauty, and create excitement in our imagination. Today I'm going to talk to you about five of the world's most jaw-dropping volcanoes, from Asia's Mount Fuji in Japan all the way across the world to Crater Lake in the USA, stopping off to admire Mount Bromo in Indonesia, Africa's Virunga National Park in the Democratic Republic of Congo, and of course Europe's Mount Vesuvius in Italy along the way. Ready?!

First, Mount Fuji – but what can I say? It's stunning! For many Japanese, it's a lifelong ambition to make the arduous hike to the summit of this volcano. For everyone who completes the 3776-metre trek, there's a red badge as a reward, but to be honest, the mystery and beauty of this legendary mountain is best appreciated from a distance. The perfectly cone-shaped top of Mount Fuji rises in splendour above the surrounding low-lying plains, and on a clear day you can see it from some of Tokyo's skyscrapers, 133 kilometres away! Some of the most outstanding views are from the windows of the famous high-speed bullet train as it passes the town of Fuji, and not a step of hiking is required.

In eastern Java there is a wonderful landscape of volcanoes – the Bromo-Tengger-Semeru National Park. Here the volcanoes sit within dramatic highlands, creating spectacular scenery. The park is home to Indonesia's highest volcano, Mount Semeru, but many visitors prefer to climb the more accessible Mount Bromo, which also guarantees hikers a grandstand seat of sunrise. This is the best time to view the splendid colours of the volcano's enormous crater (that's the bowl of the volcano).

Moving westwards to Africa we find the continent's first national park, Virunga, in the Democratic Republic of Congo. Virunga National Park is also a national heritage site, famous for its gorillas, but its main attraction is for admirers of volcanoes. Mount Nyiragongo volcano features the world's largest lava lake – yes, you heard correctly, a lake of lava – where boiling hot rock bubbles like a fizzy drink and hot gases blow into the atmosphere. Virunga borders Rwanda's Volcanoes National Park where more fiery marvels can be seen.

Next stop is Italy, where perhaps you wouldn't expect to see one of the world's most amazing volcanoes. However, Mount Vesuvius, surrounded by bubbling hot springs and still occasionally making rumbling noises, sits very close to the city of Naples, one of Italy's largest cities. Suburbs of Naples, as well as agricultural fields, rise up the slopes of the volcano, and nearby are two famous and stunning archaeological sites: the ruins of the Roman town of Pompeii and the less well-known town of Herculaneum. Both towns were completely devastated by a massive eruption nearly two thousand years ago. You can go to the top of mainland Europe's only active volcano for fabulous views into the crater and out to sea across the Bay of Naples. Something not to be missed is a visit to the Observatory where you can get some background information into volcanology research.

Finally, to the USA, where our fifth and last volcano is in the state of Oregon's only national park: Crater Lake. This is surely one of America's most beautiful landscapes, but visitors see none of it until they drive to the edge of the crater and then the lake, inside the crater, appears dramatically, shimmering in different shades of peacock blue. All around it are cliffs and pine forests where plenty of wildlife runs around. Many visitors just drive around the scenic Rim Road, but a hike provides a more rewarding encounter with this astonishing landscape.

So there you have it. Five amazing volcanoes to explore and admire. Which one is first on your bucket list?!

Unit 6: E Speaking Activities 2 and 3   CD1, Track 15

1 I reckon you should use a louder alarm clock.

2 Why don't you get someone to wake you up?

3 How about using two alarm clocks?

4 If I were you, I'd go to sleep earlier.

5 I suggest you have an afternoon nap.

6 You'd really better change your habits.

7 I would strongly advise you to set your alarm earlier.

8 My advice would be to get a new alarm clock.

9 It might be a good idea to ask you parents to help you.

10 You might try sleeping with the window open

Unit 7: F Listening and Speaking Activity 3   CD1, Track 16

Baruti Ngwani: Welcome to this week's show. Today we're going to talk about careers and, in particular, one career which some of you may believe is only for men: working for NASA, the National Aeronautics and Space Administration in the USA! My guest is Kagiso Abaka, a careers advisor for NASA, based here in Joburg. Welcome!

Kagiso Abaka: Hi, Baruti.

BN: So, what does a young woman need to do in order to work for NASA?

KA: The same as a young man, of course! For anyone who likes finding out how things work, solving puzzles and problems, or creating and building things, then why not consider a career in science, technology, engineering or maths? Within NASA, women work in all of these areas, and there is information available on careers and how you can prepare for them.

BN: Interesting …. But what is an engineer? What does an engineer actually do?

KA: Good question! Engineers are the people who make things work, using power and materials. Engineers have moved the world into skyscrapers, high-speed cars, jets and, of course, space vehicles. They make our lives interesting, comfortable and fun. Everything in our daily lives relies heavily on the work of engineers: computers, television, satellites ….

BN: Is there just one type of engineer, then?

KA: No, there are many types, including aerospace, chemical, civil, computer, electrical, industrial, mechanical, and so on. Obviously each type specialises in a particular area.

BN: Hmmm, I see. So is an engineer a scientist?

KA: Not really. Scientists are knowledge seekers, who are always searching out why things happen. They are inquisitive, which means that they are always asking questions. Nature, Earth and the universe are what fascinate the scientist. The scientist questions, seeks answers and expands knowledge.

BN: What career options are available for people like this?

KA: There's an amazing variety. Careers are available in both the life and physical sciences.

BN: For example?

KA: For example … becoming a biologist, medical doctor or nutritionist would all require studies in life sciences, whereas a job as an astronomer, chemist, geologist, meteorologist or physicist would all involve studying the physical sciences.

BN: OK, I see. I've also heard about technicians. What do they do? Is it different from engineers and scientists?

KA: Technicians are an important part of the NASA team. They work closely with scientists and engineers in support of their research. Their skills are used to operate wind tunnels, work in laboratories, construct test equipment, build models and support many types of research.

BN: Most of our listeners are still at school, studying hard, so what should their focus be, if these types of careers are interesting to them?

KA: Well, obviously, education is a critical requirement. Mathematics and science are the basis for most NASA careers and the decisions you make in school can affect your future career possibilities.

BN: And after high school?

KA: It can seem like a long journey, but a career as a scientist or engineer requires four to seven years of college study after high school. A bachelor's degree requiring four years of study is the minimum necessary. Colleges and universities also offer graduate programmes where students can obtain master's and doctoral degrees. The master's programme usually takes two years. An additional two to four years is needed to earn a doctorate.

BN: And for anyone who likes the idea of a career as a technician?

KA: Well, technicians typically earn a two-year Associate of Science degree. Some may continue for two additional years and obtain a bachelor's degree in engineering technology. Others may earn a bachelor's degree in engineering or one of the physical sciences.

BN: So for those of you who want to think about a career with NASA, it may seem a long way off, but study hard and who knows? One day one of you might be walking on the moon!

Adapted from http://spaceflightsystems.grc. nasa.gov

Unit 9: C Listening Activity 1
CD1, Track 17

Pablo Selles: We are very lucky to have in our studio today Janine Mesumo, who works as a careers advisor at an international school in Madrid. Her main role is to advise students who have recently completed their IGCSEs, AS and A Levels on what they should do next. Part of this is giving them advice on writing their first CV. Have I got that right, Janine?

Janine Mesumo: Absolutely, Pablo. Actually, a great deal of my time is spent in helping students draw up their CV, which can be quite problematic when you haven't yet had any work experience.

PS: What areas should first-time CV writers include?

JM: I think the key here is not to try to include too much. Prospective employers need to be able to get a quick overview, rather than a detailed biography of someone's life – that can come at the interview. However, there needs to be enough information, so that the employer can decide whether or not to call the applicant for an interview.

PS: Hmm, I see. So what information would you say is essential?

JM: Start with personal details: name, address, contact details. You'd be surprised how many people forget to put their telephone number and email address on their CV! Then, education and qualifications. Some people recommend combining these two areas; so, for example, you might say '1999–2001, International School, Madrid, six IGCSEs in Maths, English …', and so on, rather than listing the qualifications in a different section.

PS: That's an interesting idea – I like that! What comes next?

JM: Well, this is where some students become rather worried, because usually the next section is work experience.

PS: But often students don't have any work experience!

JM: Exactly, and so they worry about leaving a blank. But as a school- or college-leaver, nobody is going to expect you to have an employment history, so there really is no need to worry. However, it is worth mentioning weekend or after-school jobs, or any work for charities, or voluntary work.

PS: OK, and after that? What about hobbies and interests?

JM: Yes, it is important to include leisure interests, but a common mistake is simply to list things, for example: 'reading, football, music'.

PS: So what should our listeners do?

JM: Instead of simply giving a list, explain in what way these things interest you or what skills you have developed through them. For example, if you put reading, give details about what you like to read …

PS: … and if you list music, what types of music you like listening to.

JM: Exactly, but also, music might mean playing an instrument, so give that information as well. Or if you're the captain of a sports team, include that information as it demonstrates leadership skills.

PS: Any other sections that need to be included?

JM: Well, two really. The first should include any skills which have not been mentioned before, such as IT skills, proficiency in other languages (don't just put 'French'!), and details of any organisations or clubs which you belong to. And finally, give the names, addresses and contact details for two referees.

PS: Which are what?

JM: A referee is a person who would be willing to write about you in a positive way! Always check with the person before you put their name on your CV.

PS: Janine, we're coming to the end of our time. Thank you very much for a very informative chat. If any listeners would like more information on writing their CV, just go onto our website and you'll find everything you need.

Unit 9: E Listening Job Interview 1
Activity 3   CD1, Track 18

Interviewer: Good morning, Miss Gupta. Please take a seat.

Abha Gupta: Thanks.

Int'er: Did you have any problems getting here?

AG: Nope, I found the address very easily. I checked it out yesterday.

Int'er: I see. Now, you've just left school with four IGCSEs. Is that correct?

AG: Yeah.

Int'er: And the subjects?

AG: Oh, right, err, let me think now … Science, English, Art and Music.

Int'er: Thank you. Which of those was your favourite subject at school?

AG: I didn't really like any of them. The teachers were not very interesting. I must've been really lucky to pass them.

Int'er: And which school did you attend?

AG: The new one, behind the park at the start of the motorway.

Int'er: I see. Now, tell me something about your interests, the things that you do in your free time.

AG: Well, not much really. I like riding my bike. That's why I think this job would be good for me.

Int'er: Because you like riding a bike?

AG: Er, yeah. The job's to do with sport, isn't it?

Int'er: Yes, Miss Gupta, it is. Have you had any work experience yet – for example a weekend job?

AG: Well, yes, I had a job with my brother washing cars. We used to do it in our free time. We got loads of money to spend on clothes and DVDs, or for going to the cinema and other things.

Int'er: What personal qualities do you think you could offer us here at Winning Sports?

AG: Well, like I told you, I like sports, especially riding my bike,

and every weekend I go to the match, if they're playing at home, of course. What else do you want to know?

Int'er: I think that's all for the time being, Miss Gupta.

AG: Is that it?

Int'er: Yes, thank you very much, Miss Gupta. That's all. Goodbye.

AG: Did I get the job?

Int'er: I'll be in touch. Goodbye.

Unit 9: E Listening Job Interview 1 Activity 4 CD1, Track 19

Int'er: Did you have any problems getting here?

Int'er: Now, tell me something about your interests, the things that you do in your free time.

Int'er: Have you had any work experience yet – for example, a weekend job?

Int'er: What personal qualities do you think you could offer us here at Winning Sports?

Unit 9: E Listening Job Interview 2 Activity 1 CD1, Track 20

Part A

Lan Huang: Hello, have a seat. My name's Lan Huang. And you are … Mr Hairilombus Papachristofer *[hesitantly]*, is that correct?

Bambos: Hello, pleased to meet you. Actually, the pronunciation is Haralambous Papachristoforou. Most people call me Bambos, for short. I'm Greek, on my father's side.

LH: Really? How interesting! Did you have any trouble finding our office, ummm … Bambos?

B: Not at all, Ms Huang. I came yesterday to make sure I knew exactly how to find you, and to

check how much time I would need. And today I used Google maps on my smartphone, just in case. I arrived two hours early!

LH: That shows good initiative! Now, what is it about the job that interests you?

B: Well, first of all, I visited your website when I saw the advertisement, and discovered more about the format of *Teen Weekly*, and that really interested me.

LH: It did? Why?

B: Basically, I just love writing. Ever since I was a child, I've been writing stories and trying to write poems too. I've also won three writing competitions.

LH: Congratulations! Is there anything else that demonstrates your love for writing?

B: Well, I've been editor of our online school webzine for two years, and I also publish my own monthly blog.

LH: Excellent! Now, obviously our readership is teenagers, young people who are still at school. What do you think are the main interest areas for your age group?

B: I guess for many teenagers, myself included, the most interesting topic is celebrity gossip and stories about film stars and musicians, sports people, important people – where they are, what they are doing, and so on. But not just gossip. I think many teens are interested in their society and culture, as well as global issues like the environment.

LH: Good. Anything else?

B: Well, for many teenagers, becoming an adult is a scary thought, and they often want to discuss their future education and careers.

LH: Thank you, Bambos. Now, is there anything you would like to ask me?

B: Well, yes, Ms Huang, I have some questions. I made a note on my phone – can I check them?

LH: Please, go ahead …

**Unit 9: E Listening Job Interview 2
       Activity 4   CD1, Track 21**

Part B

Bambos: OK, firstly, what is the commitment in terms of time? I assume it's a part-time position, as I'm still at school?

Lan Huang: Yes, of course. It's very part-time, so only 20 hours per month.

B: Great. Secondly, would I be able to work from home?

LH: Absolutely! In fact, we prefer you to do that. We would probably need you here for a meeting once every two to three months.

B: Perfect. Umm … thirdly, the advertisement mentions 'competitions'. What type of things do you ask your readers to do for these?

LH: Good question! To be honest, this is a new idea and something that we want the successful applicant for the job to consider.

B: Really? That's awesome. OK, finally, is the salary paid weekly or monthly?

LH: As it's a part-time job, based on monthly hours, the company pays at the end of each calendar month.

B: Thank you. That answers all my questions.

LH: Thank you, Bambos. It was a pleasure meeting you.

Unit 9: F Listening

**   Activity 6   CD1, Track 22**

SPEAKER 1 – female adult

I was terribly nervous before my first job interview, so it's not really surprising that I didn't get the job! It was all my

fault*. I was very late, and when I did finally arrive I was hot and bothered and I looked a complete mess. Very unprofessional. Also, I had dropped my interview notes on the bus so I couldn't remember the questions that I wanted to ask. My advice of course is to be prepared, and don't copy my example, because that will only end in disaster!

SPEAKER 2 – male adult

If you go online you'll find pages and pages of advice about how to prepare for a job interview, and, to be honest, you can waste loads of time trying to find the perfect strategy. But in my experience the **drawback*** is that they all really give you the same advice, which is simply: relax and be yourself! Easier said than done I think. However, no matter how well you have prepared yourself, if on the day you appear nervous and try to pretend to be someone else, you are definitely not going to do very well.

SPEAKER 3 – female adult (older)

I'm quite old now so I don't think I'll be attending any more job interviews! But during my life I've been to a few, and in the latter part of my career, up until about three years ago, I was the one doing the interviewing. I must've done over a hundred. It was interesting being the one asking all the questions, and watching the interviewee squirming in their seat when I asked a difficult question! Having said that, I think I was a good interviewer because I always remembered my own days in the hot seat!

SPEAKER 4 – male teenager

I've only had one job interview so far, for a part-time job in a supermarket. Even though the job was only stacking the shelves at weekends, I spent hours preparing for the interview, going online, trying to find the best strategies for doing well. I even got my parents and friends to do practice interviews with me. In the end, the interview only lasted about five minutes, and I

was actually very disappointed, even though I got the job!

SPEAKER 5 – female teenager

I haven't had a face-to-face interview yet, but I did do an internet interview last year. It was for a part-time tele-sales job. Basically, the job was to phone people and try to sell them a different product each week, like make-up, or some other cosmetics. The interview wasn't difficult. It was an internet call and there was no video, so I've never actually seen the people who employ me, which is a bit strange. But I got the job and it's ok for now, but not something I want to do for the rest of my life.

SPEAKER 6 - male adult (older)

Since a very early age I worked with my dad in his carpenter's workshop, along with one of my dad's brothers. When my dad and his brother retired, I took over running the place, and stayed there until I myself retired, five years ago now. So, you may not actually believe this, but I have never had a job interview in my whole life! Does that make me very lucky or have I missed out on something special? I can't say it's something I've ever worried about actually.

*See the **Word Tip** (Unit 9, Section F)

**Unit 9: Exam focus
       Listening   CD1, Track 23**

Joshua (teenage male): Good morning, Mrs Karima. Thank you for finding time to speak to me today.

Mrs Karima (adult female): Hello, Joshua, it's good to see you outside the classroom!

J: Mrs Karima, can you give us some advice about what we need to do in order to find our first job?

Mrs K: Well, with no or little real-world work experience, you may be concerned that you won't qualify for many jobs, or that there aren't many jobs available. However, your grades, school activities, club memberships and volunteer activities can demonstrate qualities that employers look for. A part-time job can be a first step into the working world.

J: The problem is that we don't have enough time to work during term time, especially when exams are getting close.

Mrs K: I appreciate that, Joshua, and of course you are right – studying must come first. But when the holidays arrive, you really should try to work. You can take on more hours and take on more responsibilities that will help you establish job experience.

J: Why is getting a part-time summer job so important?

Mrs K: Summer jobs often open doors for jobs during other parts of the year. Be sure to keep in touch with previous employers, as that may help you get hired again. Part-time jobs for teenagers can also lead to full-time employment and even future careers. Some jobs for teens may even include on-the-job training that will help you get started in your new position, or even start to develop a career.

J: How important is it to have a CV ready?

Mrs K: Even if you've never worked before, you should start to develop a résumé or CV. You can highlight your achievements at school or college, club memberships and social activities that demonstrate characteristics beneficial in a future job. You'll definitely be one step ahead of most of your friends when you walk into an interview with a résumé which includes your current skill set.

J: So, Mrs K, let's say I'm interested in a job I've seen advertised. What should I do to be ready?

Mrs K: Most teen jobs will require you to go through at least a brief interview before you are hired. You should dress neatly, be well-groomed, and be prepared to tell someone why you want the job. Most employers will understand that you're just trying to make some extra money. But if you can explain how getting this job will help you develop yourself, or even benefit others, then you'll be ahead of the game.

J: That also makes a lot of sense. What other things should I tell the interviewer?

Mrs K: Be ready to explain what skills you have that will allow you to perform this job successfully. For example, are you the one whose friends are always asking for computer help, or do you organise and run a club or committee at school, or are you just really good with people? Highlight your strengths and explain why you are their best choice for this job.

J: But doesn't that make me sound like a big head?

Mrs K: Absolutely not! People in interviews who sell themselves are much more likely to be offered a job. Something else to remember is that jobs for teens are primarily part-time, and may only allow you to work as many hours as you are legally allowed to. In some cases, you can only work up to sixteen hours per week, or a maximum of 70 hours in any one month. If you are slightly older, an 'A' level student, it's eighteen and 80 hours. Make sure you understand the requirements of the job and that the employer knows how much time you are willing and available to work.

J: I hadn't thought of that. What's your final suggestion?

Mrs K: It's worth remembering that employers like to re-hire teens with a good work history. A part-time summer job or holiday job may be temporary work, but it could lead to bigger and better things! So, always try to leave on good terms with your employers, so that they can provide a good reference for you to use in your next job search.

J: Mrs K, thank you for talking to us.

Mrs K: You're welcome, Joshua.

**Unit 10: E Speaking
          Activity 4   CD1, Track 24**

Fatima: OK, Abdullah, let's do some practice for our speaking exam.

Abdullah: Good idea, Fatima. You go first – what's your presentation about?

F: Come on, Abdullah, you should know by now that we don't have to do a presentation or give a speech in the exam.

A: Really? I thought that's what we have to do. So what is it then?

F: We have a discussion with the examiner about a topic. It lasts about 10 to 15 minutes, I think.

A: Great! I'm going to talk about fast-food restaurants and I guess you would choose animals or becoming a vet.

F: Unfortunately, we don't get to choose our topic, Abdullah. The examiner has a set of topic cards and we have to talk about the one he or she chooses for us.

A: But what if I don't know anything about the topic? I won't be able to say anything! Fatima, that's mean!

F: But it's not a test of knowledge about the topic. The topic is just to give us something to talk around. We are being tested on how well we can communicate in English.

A: OK, fair enough. What happens when we see the topic card? Can we make written notes?

F: No, but there are some ideas on the topic card which we can use and we have a couple of minutes to prepare. We should use that time properly, to think and plan for the discussion.

A: And then what happens? We start talking about the topic, right?

F: Yes, that's right. The examiner will ask us some questions, too, about the topic.

A: Do I lose marks if I get the answers wrong?

F: No, Abdullah, there are no right or wrong answers – the examiner just wants to hear you speaking in English. Try to use expressions like: *In my opinion … , I believe … , On the other hand … , On the whole … ,* and so on.

A: Hmmmm, so answering with 'yes' or 'no' is probably not a good idea, right? We need to use 'because' as much as possible.

F: Right! We need to explain ourselves with more ideas and reasons.

A: What happens if I don't understand something? Maybe the examiner will think I'm not very good.

F: Come on, Abdullah! Just tell the examiner if you don't understand, or you could ask them to give you an example, or say something like: *Do you mean … ?,* or ask the examiner to repeat something

A: Like: *Sorry, could you say that again, please?*

F: Exactly!

A: OK, so let's have a look at one of these topic cards, then, so we can practise.

F: There are plenty in the back of our Coursebook, Abdullah …

Unit 10: G Listening
Activity 3   CD1, Track 25

Speaker 1

My home country, Nigeria, can be very hot at times, but nothing like the temperatures here in Dubai. I'm not sure I will ever get used to it! Thank goodness that everywhere has air conditioning, but even that doesn't help in the really hot summer months, when it is almost impossible to be outside during the heat of the day. At least the heat forces me to stay indoors to study, and that's the real reason why I'm here – to study and get my degree. I just wish I'd chosen somewhere a little cooler!

Speaker 2

Dubai is so cosmopolitan – it doesn't matter what you like or what you want to do, you can find it here somewhere. It's impossible not to be active doing something every minute of every day because there is just so much to entertain you. My biggest problem is making a choice! When I've done enough studying, it's time to think about which shopping mall to meet my friends at, or which café to go to for some much-needed relaxation. Now that's a challenge!

Speaker 3

My family told me that, in this digital age, I would never be apart from them when I came on my own to study in Dubai. Yes, we chat online every day, and send each other instant messages constantly, and I'm forever downloading photos of my sister's new twin babies, but it's not true – I am alone, and I miss them so much. I've made some friends, it's true, but at the weekends I don't go out much. I just think about my family and how much I miss them all.

Speaker 4

I thought studying here in Dubai would be much easier than back home in Sweden, but you know something? I've never studied so much in all my life! We have so much to read and so many assignments to complete every month, and there always seems to be yet another quiz or test to prepare for. I know it will all be worthwhile in the end, don't get me wrong, and I'm not afraid of hard work, but I'm still young and I want to enjoy this experience as much as possible. There never seems to be enough time for anything apart from studying. And do you know something? I haven't even been to the top of the Burj Khalifa yet, and I've been in Dubai for nearly two years!

Speaker 5

My reason for choosing Dubai as a place to study is mainly because of its location. I thought about a college in Europe, probably the UK, because obviously I speak English, but I decided against it. Not only is it difficult and expensive to travel outside Europe from there, but also the weather is awful! I'm from Brazil, remember?! So, now that I'm here in Dubai, it's easy to travel either east or west. I've already been to Egypt, but next trip I want to go east, maybe to the Maldives, or perhaps further. I'm not sure yet, but the sky is the limit!

Speaker 6

I tried at high school to start learning Arabic because I find the language and culture so incredibly interesting, but I failed miserably. It was so difficult to find a good teacher and to meet up with other people trying to learn Arabic so that we could practise together. I almost gave up. But then my dad suggested that I could combine learning Arabic with studying abroad, and that's how I ended up here in Dubai. At first I didn't want to leave home and, unfortunately, being in an international university means that nobody here uses much Arabic. But at least there are plenty of good teachers readily available, and there are plenty of opportunities to practise. An excellent choice I think! Now I love living and studying in Dubai, and my Arabic has really improved.

Unit 11: F Speaking, Listening and Writing Activity 3   CD1, Track 26

Male teenager: I really do believe that Maha is a special type of hero. Just think about what she has done so far in her life, and how much she has sacrificed in order to provide for other people. All that time living abroad after she had studied for so many years in Alexandria. I think that is real sacrifice and dedication, which is why she is now so successful and admired by so many people. Look at all the awards and prizes she has won, and I'm sure that she will continue to win many more. For me, Maha is definitely a hero.

Female teenager: I absolutely don't agree with you! All Maha has done is to be a successful businesswoman, but you make it sound as if she is the only such person on the planet! Yes, she has done some amazing things, but I expect she has made a considerable amount of money too, and for me that doesn't make her a hero, far from it. I'm happy that she is providing things that people need, homes to live in and places to go to for shopping and entertainment, but I don't believe she's done something heroic.

Unit 12: D Listening Activity 5   CD1, Track 27

Kigongo Odok: Hello, my name is Kigongo Odok. Welcome to another edition of Youth Uganda. Today I am very happy to welcome to our local studio Namono Alupo, who works for WAGGSS, the World Association of Girl Guides and Girl Scouts.

Namono Alupo: Thank you so much for inviting me, Kigongo!

KO: Namono, I've heard about something called World Thinking Day, which takes place every year in February, am I right?

NA: Yes, on February 22, to be exact.

KO: To be honest, I know absolutely nothing about it! What's it all about? What actually happens on World Thinking Day?

NA: Well, the whole idea is to get our members thinking about important international issues, and to connect with the worldwide network of girl guides and girl scouts. In recent years, we have had record numbers of our members celebrating WTD in 90 countries. We also produce an activity pack, and last year more than 53 000 were downloaded in four different languages: English, French, Spanish and Arabic.

KO: Wow, that's an incredible achievement, but who exactly are your members?

NA: All age groups, from young children to adults, including adolescents …

KO: And an adolescent is …?

NA: Good question! Neither children nor adults are adolescents: they are young people in the years when everything about themselves is changing very quickly.

KO: Definitely a difficult transition period. And how else can you judge the success of WTD, apart from what you have already told me?

NA: Hmmm, let me think … Well, we also sold 100 000 badges, but, to be honest, nowadays it's all about social media, and we know that 14 319 of our members uploaded profile pics during their WTD involvement.

KO: So on a typical WTD, what do your members actually do, apart from upload selfies?!

NA: We want people to be inspired by the history and impact of our global movement, and to take action and speak out on the issues we most care about.

KO: For example?

NA: We want to make a global difference by fundraising for projects around the world. The activity pack gives our members ideas on how to do this, and invites them to explore and celebrate the meaningful connections that make our lives better. Sometimes neither a parent nor a school teacher is available to help young people do these things, and this is when WAGGGS can get involved.

KO: And who exactly do you want your members to connect with?

NA: That's a good question, and an important one. Connections could be with the people closest to us, to a place we care about, or to a Girl Guide or Girl Scout friend on the other side of the world.

KO: And how do they do this?

NA: Well, the activity pack, which I've already mentioned, contains various activities which our members are encouraged to participate in. Each activity has a different objective, for example, connecting with a community and helping to bring about change, or learning about the WAGGGS Cabana World Centre in Mexico or the Sangam World Centre in India.

KO: So is there any sort of challenge involved?

NA: Yes. The activity pack encourages members to make four special connections, and in doing so they collect four puzzle pieces. Then they put together their puzzle, and share their connections with the world.

KO: And I guess the connections are the ones you described earlier? With the people closest to us, ummm and to a place we care about, and …?

NA: … to a Girl Guide or Girl Scout friend on the other side of the world.

KO: Now it all makes sense! How can our listeners find out more information?

NA: They can find out more by visiting our website, which is www.wagggs. org, and follow the links for World Thinking Day. From there you can download the activity pack to your PC or tablet, and there's a special printer-friendly version to save paper and ink. You can also check where your local WAGGGS group meets and easily connect with them.

KO: Excellent! Thanks very much for talking to us today, and good luck with the next WTD

Loosely based on information from: www.waggggs.org

Unit 13: F Listening
Activity 3 CD1, Track 28

Hello everyone. My name's Ajeet and I'm a motorcycling enthusiast. Today I'm going to talk to you about one of my heroes, Nelson Suresh Kumar, now sadly no longer with us, and his Himalayan adventure, riding the Khardung La, the world's highest motorable road.

Welcome to the geography of superlatives: the highest mountains, the deepest gorges, and some of the greatest displays of biodiversity on the planet. Travelling across the Himalayas is truly an adventure and a treat for adrenaline junkies like me and Nelson. Even more so for those who decide to do it on two wheels, again like us. While we motorcycle riders are often misjudged as reckless daredevils, a majority will tell you that we are passionate motoring enthusiasts who live for the joy of the ride.

Before leaving his native India, Nelson rode his motorcycle across the entire country. But he didn't stop there. In 2008, he arranged, and successfully completed, a ride from Argentina to Alaska, making him the only Indian to do a Pan-American solo ride over that distance. And it was a feat that further fueled his passion.

During his 91-day ride from South America to North America, he decided to make his hobby a business. Once back in Dubai, his residence at the time, he partnered with a few of his friends to start a motorcycle touring company and began organising motorcycle tours in India, Nepal and Bhutan, and then in Thailand, Sri Lanka and South Africa.

One of the most popular rides is the Himalayan Mot Adventure – a ride to Khardung La in Leh, Ladakh, the highest motorable pass in the world. This mountain pass is a gateway to the famous Siachen Glacier, the second-longest glacier in the world's non-polar areas, and the location of the world's highest battlefield.

This route has the most beautiful valleys along with numerous mountain passes. It is also one of the most remote and thinly populated areas in the world. The route to Leh is accessible only for four months in a year, from June to September, since the entire area is covered in snow for the rest of the year.

The route goes like this: start in Chandigarh and then head through Shimla. Then get off the highways and onto smaller narrow roads to Kalpa. The next day, ride through the Spiti Valley and visit the Moon Lake Villages of Nako and Tabo, and Buddist monasteries *en route*. The route continues through the Moree Plains. After a stop at the Leh Palace,

the riders continue on to Khardung La, reaching a height of more than 5,000 metres above sea level.

You have paved roads, gravel, mountain tracks and about 30 water crossings, riding in mud, slush and snow, through deserts, valleys and lakes. Nelson rode half of the world, but nothing compares to this place.

Sometimes riders do not stop at Khardung La, and travel as far as the Nubra Valley in Jammu and Kashmir, about 100 kilometres from Leh. This valley is a site worth seeing due to the sand dune deserts at 5,000 metres above sea level. The Nubra valley has white sand that resembles sugar, and travellers can see the extremely rare and critically endangered double-humped Bactrian camels as well.

When people asked Nelson to describe how it felt to complete the ride to the top of the world, he could only reply that he had ridden motorcycles all over the world, and this place was entirely different from any place he had ever seen. Truly amazing. I can guarantee anybody that this is the ride of their lifetime. Because Nelson told me himself.

Adapted from Gulf Life.

Unit 14: B Speaking and Vocabulary
Activity 8 CD2, Track 2

Paramedics provide an immediate response to emergency medical calls. They are usually the first senior health-care professional on the scene, and they are responsible for assessing the condition of a patient and providing treatment and care prior to hospital admission. A paramedic will attend emergencies, including minor injuries, sudden illness and casualties arising from road and rail accidents, criminal violence, fires and other incidents. They are usually in a two-person ambulance crew, with the other crew member being an ambulance technician or emergency care assistant who helps them. Some will work alone, however, using an emergency response car, motorbike or bicycle to get to a patient.

Adapted from www.prospects.ac.uk

Unit 14: C Listening
Activity 3   CD2, Track 3

John: Dr Mary, what can you tell us about Florence Nghtingale's early years?

Dr Mary Winterson: Well, Florence Nightingale was born in Italy on 12th May 1820 and was named Florence after her birthplace. Her parents, Fanny and William, were wealthy and spent a considerable amount of time touring Europe.

J: How did she do at school? Did she get good grades?

MW: Yes, she did. As a schoolchild, Florence was academic and rarely had problems with her studies. She was attractive and the expectation was that she would marry and start a family.

J: But that didn't happen, did it?

MW: No, it didn't. Florence had different ideas. As a teenager she became involved in the social questions of the day, making visits to homes for sick people in local villages, and she began to investigate hospitals and nursing.

J: How did her parents react to this?

MW: Not very well, I'm afraid! Her parents refused to allow her to become a nurse as, in the mid-19th century, it was not considered a suitable profession for a well-educated woman. Because of the conflict which arose between Florence and her parents, it was decided to send her to Europe with some family friends, Charles and Selina Bracebridge.

J: Not such a bad punishment! Where exactly did they go?

MW: The three of them travelled to Italy, Greece and Egypt, returning to England through Germany in July 1850. While in Germany, they visited a hospital near Dusseldorf, where Florence returned in the following year to undergo a three-month nurse training course. This enabled her to take a post at a clinic in London in 1853.

J: Wasn't Britain at war around this time? With Russia?

MW: Yes, you're absolutely right. In March 1854, Britain was at war with Russia. While the Russians were defeated in the autumn of that year, British newspapers criticised the medical facilities for the soldiers wounded during the fighting. In response to the criticism, the government appointed Florence Nightingale to oversee the introduction of female nurses into British military hospitals in Turkey and, on 4th November 1854, she arrived in Scutari with a group of 38 nurses.

J: What an amazing story! What happened when they got to Scutari?

MW: Well, initially, the doctors did not want the nurses there because they felt threatened but, within ten days, many more casualties arrived and all the nurses were needed to cope with this sudden influx of wounded soldiers.

J: So the doctors were forced to accept the female nurses? Were the nurses successful?

MW: Yes! The introduction of female nurses in military hospitals was an outstanding success, and the nation showed its gratitude to Florence Nightingale by honouring her with a medal in 1907. Throughout her life, she continued tirelessly to campaign for better conditions in hospitals and for improved health standards.

J: When did she die?

MW: She died on 13th August 1910, having been a complete invalid herself and totally blind for 15 years. She was a national heroine. Her far-sighted reforms have influenced the nature of modern health care, and her writings continue to be a resource for nurses, health managers and planners.

J: Yes, she was certainly an inspiring woman.

Unit 14: F Speaking and Listening
Activity 5   CD2, Track 4

Marianna Milutinovic: Today we welcome Alvaro Solomou, one of the 1200 relief workers with the Red Cross, the ICRC, who is going to talk to us about the ICRC's approach to giving assistance. Welcome to the programme, Alvaro.

Alvaro Solomou: Hello, Marianna, and thank you for inviting me.

MM: Alvaro, can you tell us about how the ICRC assists victims of famine and drought and other natural disasters?

AS: Well, we should remember that, all too often, natural disasters happen in areas where there is already some other sort of problem, such as an economic crisis, or a period of political instability. Put the two together and the people involved become even more insecure and desperate.

MM: I imagine that different contexts also create extra problems, don't they?

AS: Yes, geographic context, as well as ethnic, political and economic, all translate into different needs and, therefore, the response the ICRC makes must be adapted to suit the context.

MM: How is that done?

AS: We use what is called the 'Assistance Pyramid'. This establishes that preference must be given in any relief situation to the foundations of the pyramid – in other words, to food, water and essential goods – before anything else is done.

MM: What about health care? Isn't that a priority?

AS: Hygiene and medical care take second and third places in the pyramid. Obviously, if a person is starving and thirsty, it does not matter how good the health care is.

MM: I see. Does the ICRC only assist when there is a crisis?

AS: No, not at all. In fact, in recent years, it has been the policy to provide help in developing countries once a crisis has passed, or even before one has occurred.

MM: How is that actually done?

AS: Well, for example, the ICRC assistance programmes have been extended, so that they now include seed and tools distribution, and the provision of veterinary care. The ICRC identifies priorities in a region, in order to provide the best possible assistance.

MM: Going back to the issue of water for a moment, isn't it true that millions of people across the world have difficulties gaining access to water? What can the ICRC do about this?

AS: Oh yes, that's absolutely true and, of course, in many places the water that is available is actually extremely unhealthy and may carry waterborne diseases, such as cholera and typhoid. The ICRC has a programme of assistance, which includes construction, engineering and providing access to water, along with hygiene and environmental protection, thus ensuring that water is clean and safe to use.

MM: Is it dangerous working for the ICRC?

AS: Well, in any crisis situation there are dangers, but all of us are strongly motivated by humanitarian work, and hopefully we can all cope with the stress and the pressures which are bound to exist.

MM: Alvaro, thank you for giving us such an interesting insight into the work of the ICRC.

Unit 14: Exam focus
Listening   CD2, Track 5

Part A

The world's transport crisis has reached such catastrophic proportions that road-traffic accidents now kill more people each year than malaria. I predict that by 2030, 2.5 million people will be killed on the roads in developing countries each year and 60 million will be injured. Even today, 3,000 are killed and 30 000 seriously injured on the world's roads every day.

These are really frightening statistics, but, of course, it isn't only road-traffic accidents which concern me. Air pollution from traffic claims 400 000 lives each year, mostly in developing countries, and some 1.5 billion people are exposed every day to levels of pollution well in excess of World Health Organization recommended levels.

We need to be aware of this because the damage being caused to people now, and especially youngsters, will follow them through until later life, and directly affect not only their health, but also their economic potential, and the health budgets of already strained national administrations.

Research shows us that the problems of the world's poor are multiplied by the car. It's a simple basic fact. Deaths and injuries take place mainly in developing countries and mainly to pedestrians, cyclists, bus users and children. The poor suffer disproportionately. They experience the worst air pollution and are deprived of education, health, water and sanitation programmes because the needs of the car now soak up so much national income. Advances in vehicle, engine and fuel technology are more or less irrelevant in Asian and African cities, where the growth of car and lorry numbers is dramatic and where highly polluting diesel is widespread.

Fortunately, I can report that in certain places, such as in parts of South America, something is being done. Transport budgets have been reallocated to improve the quality of life of poorer citizens and the results have been staggering. Bicycle- and pedestrian-only routes were planned, and cars were banned from certain areas. Parks were built on derelict land and car-free days implemented. This policy was radical and has improved the quality of life for the poor. This needs to be repeated all over the world.

Part B

Male teenager: Didn't that guest speaker give an interesting talk about traffic problems yesterday? It will really help us with that school project we have to do this term.

Female teenager: Yes, she was very interesting and she gave me some good ideas for our project too. I've already done some research.

MT: Since yesterday morning? Wow, that was quick!

FT: Well, I found out from my aunty, who's a police captain, that in the UK, the number of people killed in road accidents has fallen dramatically since 2000.

MT: Really? By how much? Maybe we can use the data?

FT: Well, in 2000, 3,409 people died, including pedestrians, cyclists, motorcyclists and all vehicle users, but last year that had dropped to less than 1,800.

MT: That's incredible! That's nearly a 50% drop. I read somewhere that the annual death rate from road accidents in the UK is about five per 100 000.

FT: So for every 100 000 people, five die? That doesn't seem very high, even though, of course, it should be 0. I know that in some countries in Africa, it's more than 40 per 100 000.

MT: I think we could design a graph for our project – a line graph – showing how the death rate from road traffic accidents has changed over the past ten or 15 years.

FT: And we need to make it clear that nearly half of people killed are pedestrians, cyclists or motorcyclists – my aunty told me they are called 'vulnerable road users'.

MT: So they are more at risk because a car or a lorry gives you more protection. And we know that in South America even more 'vulnerable road users' are killed …

FT: … Yes, I spoke to the speaker yesterday and she told me the figure is nearer to 70%.

MT: I think we could put some focus on the effectiveness of bicycle- and pedestrian-only routes, and what happens when cars and other vehicles are banned from certain roads.

FT: Good idea. I know that locally more and more people are using their bikes to get to and from school and work, using the new cycle paths …

MT: … and that new pedestrians-only area downtown has really increased the number of shoppers. Banning cars has to be the way ahead.

FT: I agree. Well, I think we have enough to be going on with. Let's Skype later and discuss how to proceed. Bye!

MT: Great, talk later …

Unit 15: E Listening and Speaking Activity 3 CD2, Track 6

Adam: I believe that health and fitness is a business like any other, and people have to profit from it.

Hana: Obviously a healthy lifestyle makes you feel better. But in my opinion a healthy lifestyle can also be expensive.

Mustafa: Healthy living is only for young people in my country, as far as I'm concerned.

Sara: Some of my school friends have a healthy lifestyle. They are very keen on sports and play in different school teams.

Miska: It seems to me that if you are really interested and involved in something I think it can become stressful and dangerous.

Layla: To be honest, I don't think I have a particularly healthy lifestyle nowadays. I guess that I'm too busy at school, doing homework, and helping out at home.

Unit 15: E Listening and Speaking Activity 5 CD2, Track 7

Layla: To be honest, I don't think I have a particularly healthy lifestyle nowadays. I guess that that I'm too

busy at school, doing homework, and helping out at home. But I know that I should do more. The longer you wait, the more difficult it gets to change. In addition, and having said that, I think my diet is pretty healthy, and I play sports at school and walk everywhere. It could be worse!

Sara: Some of my school friends have a healthy lifestyle. They are very keen on sports and play in different school teams. They all say how much they enjoy it, and they never seem to be bored with nothing to do. Furthermore, they quite often ask me to join in, but I fear that I won't be as good as them and make a fool of myself.

Hana: Obviously a healthy lifestyle makes you feel better. But in my opinion a healthy lifestyle can also be expensive. I think the key is moderation. If you do the right amount, it is obviously very beneficial, but too much could cause an injury. So it's probably not a bad idea to programme your healthy lifestyle, by firstly including both physical and mental activity, and secondly introducing a balanced diet.

Miska: It seems to me that if you are really interested and involved in something I think it can become stressful and dangerous. This type of lifestyle can take over everything you do, and I think that can be risky and cause you to worry. Is it worth it? I don't think so. There's no need to be extreme about living in a healthy way. I'm young. I want to enjoy my life!

Adam: I believe that health and fitness is a business like any other, and people have to profit from it. I think that when you pay for something, it's up to you to make sure you are getting good value for money. There are cheats and people who want to make more and more everywhere, and the health and fitness scene is no different. I'm afraid there's nothing you can do about it.

**Unit 16: D Listening
          Activity 3   CD2, Track 8**

The other unmentioned risk here has to do with the fact that media usage is often a **sedentary** activity. Children spend more than 60% of their waking day sitting down, and by some estimates children sit for an average of 8.5 hours a day. Furthermore, activity levels are thought to decline steeply after the age of eight, especially among girls. Researchers decided to study a small group of pre-tween girls (aged seven to 10 years) to determine if sitting is as **detrimental** to their health as it appears to be to adults. At the start of the study, all of the girls had healthy functioning **arteries**. However, after sitting for three hours, playing on tablets or watching movies, there was a '**profound**' negative change in functioning arteries by up to 33% in the girls. This is alarming since a *1%* decline is known to increase heart disease risk by 13% in adults.

Fortunately, there were also some more encouraging findings. The girls' artery function had returned to normal a few days later when they returned to the laboratory for tests. And when the sitting time was interrupted by a gentle 10-minute cycling session, no decline was recorded. Still, no one knows what effect sitting for hours, day after day, has on kids' health, so it is best to encourage kids to stay active.

Not surprisingly, researchers have found that higher cellphone use was linked to reduced physical activity and fitness. According to the authors, cellphone use may be able to **gauge** a person's risk for a multitude of health issues related to an inactive lifestyle.

Depending on the research you read, back problems are also a possibility, In a UK study involving ten year-olds, up to 10% may already have **precursors** to bad backs, and 9% of the kids showed worsening **back disc** problems with at least one disc. The researcher connected this to carrying heavy school books, watching TV, and playing video games, but texting may also play a significant role.

Adapted from: http://articles.mercola.com

**Unit 18: C Listening
          Activity 2   CD2, Track 9**

Thomas Sampson: Welcome to our weekly programme on health issues for young people. Today I have with me in the studio Dr Maria Bealing, a dental expert. Hello, Dr Bealing.

Dr Bealing: Hello, Thomas, and thank you for inviting me.

TS: Dr Bealing, people have been chewing gum since the ancient Greeks used the bark from mastic trees as a breath freshener. And today, gum is chewed for many more reasons, such as when we feel hungry, or to get a nicotine hit if you're trying to give up cigarettes. But is chewing a stick of gum actually harmful to the body?

DB: Well, the moment a person unwraps a piece of gum and tosses it into their mouth, the brain is alerted that the digestive process is about to begin, and bells start ringing up there! During what's called the cephalic stage …

TS: Sorry, the what?

DB: The cephalic stage … c-e-p-h-a-l-i-c … this is when the body anticipates the arrival of food and …

TS: Sorry to interrupt again but how does the brain know that food is on its way?

DB: Through the senses: we either see the food, in a cupboard or in the supermarket fridge, or smell it in a restaurant, or hear someone chopping it up in the kitchen, or hear a gum wrapper being opened, and so on.

TS: OK, I understand.

DB: And then the brain releases saliva to help us chew whatever is coming.

TS: That's why we use the expression 'mouth-watering'? It means that our saliva, the juices in our mouth, is ready to receive food?

DB: Exactly. And this gets our stomach juices excited too. But because no real substance is ever delivered, some people argue that gum chewing tricks the brain, which upsets the stomach.

TS: I've heard that people can lose weight through gum-chewing. Is that correct?

DB: Scientific studies haven't successfully proven that gum can stave off hunger and lead to weight loss. Chewing gum jump-starts the digestive process and so it may, in fact, increase hunger, and this may, in turn, lead to weight gain.

TS: So are there any benefits in gum chewing?

DB: Well, researchers have found a benefit. Recent studies have shown that chewing gum during a task can increase cognitive function. In other words, chewing while doing can help some people concentrate.

TS: I must admit that I'm a bit of a gum-chewer, so should I stop, or can I carry on?

DB: My advice, if you really want to chew, is to try sugarless gum, but only after a meal. The saliva it helps to produce will clean your teeth and the minty or fruity flavour of the gum will sweeten your breath and possibly satisfy a sweet tooth.

TS: Thank you doctor, that sounds very sensible to me!

**Unit 19: D Speaking and Listening
Activity 6   CD2, Track 10**

Speaker 1 male teenager

I've never been a really big fan of current fashion trends. Money of course is an obstacle for someone like me, so even if I want to be fashionable, I can't necessarily pay the prices that are demanded. So I think we should just wear what we feel happy in, and not worry so much about having all the latest gear. In any case, something fashionable today is out of fashion tomorrow, and clothes from the past often become popular again. Who can keep up with it?

Speaker 2 female young adult

For me the word fashion is a nightmare word! It makes me think of so many negative things. The way fashion controls people's lives is awful, and of course nowadays fashion is not just about clothes, but about the latest Ferrari or Lamborghini and watches and restaurants and even pets and the latest pair of trainers! People who only care about how much something costs, and how good they look, rather than anything else in life, are not in my circle of friends.

Speaker 3 male young adult

I don't understand all the negativity about trying to be fashionable. What's wrong with wanting to look and feel and smell great? Of course you need money, but tell me something that doesn't need money in today's world. I'm still studying right now and don't have a job yet and not much money, so I'm not in a position to buy the latest sunglasses and all the other things that I want. But as soon as I get my first wages after a couple of years, I'm going straight to the shopping mall!

Speaker 4 female adult

Something I learned at art college was that fashion is an incredibly complex subject, which is very difficult to define and really understand. Of course fashion has different meanings for different people, but fashion ultimately is a joining of not just art but also building design and engineering and even in many cases science and having an understanding of how the world works. Now in my job I'm seeing that anything can be fashionable: it depends on how people view whatever it might be.

Speaker 5 male young adult

Fashion is not an option for me, it's an absolute must, and being 'in' is probably the most important thing that I think about every day. I don't care about the cost – I will find a way to buy whatever it is that I need in order to look my best. Cars and watches and trendy restaurants and furniture do nothing for me, but clothes and hair styles are the things that drive me every day. Work is great, but how I look and feel come first.

Speaker 6 female adult

Personally I have no interest whatsoever in fashion and alternative styles of clothes and so on. But my kids do and their demands can be very difficult to deal with, from the financial side. It's so difficult to say no when children ask for something that all their friends have or are wearing. Obviously there has to be a limit, but big businesses and advertisers are incredibly clever at making people and especially children feel inferior if we don't have something that others do.

**Unit 19: E Listening Activities
4 and 5   CD2, Track 11**

The introduction of school uniforms in state schools is not a new subject. Schools have a long history of using school uniforms to create an atmosphere of pride, loyalty and equality among the student population. There has always been an image of professionalism associated with having students wear a uniform. It provides for a more business-like approach to learning, removing some of the distractions normally encountered when children feel they should possess the latest designer fashions, or follow the latest trend sweeping the nation at any given time.

School uniforms also tend to involve students more and make them part of a 'team' at the school. This is not so as to erase their individuality, but to include everyone on the same level, as far as image and dress are concerned.

Another important factor in the use of school uniforms has been cost. With fashions constantly changing from year to year, and even from season to season, parents have always felt the pressure from their children to provide them with the latest peer-pleasing designs. Uniforms reduce the cost of keeping up, since they remain the same – day after day, year after year. And their cost, in relation to fashion merchandise is very appealing over the long term.

Wearing a uniform at school, as opposed to wearing the latest fashions, may also help the child avoid ridicule, embarrassment or abuse from others that can be caused when the 'have-nots' are compared with the 'haves'. Uniforms assist in avoiding such conflicts by removing the chance for confrontation over clothing, at least during the child's time at school.

The debate will continue. But more and more people in education – students, parents, teachers and administrators – are convinced that mandatory school uniforms lead to success. They point out that pupils in private schools, who achieve impressive academic results, have traditionally worn uniforms. As a result, most state schools have also adopted a school-uniform policy – and the trend seems set to continue.

Adapted from www.communityonline.com

Unit 19: E Listening
Activity 6   CD2, Track 12

Jan (teenage male): I don't have a problem wearing school uniform. At least when I get home I can take it off and change into something more comfortable.

Cheryl (teenage female): Fair enough, but don't you think we look like penguins at school, everyone wearing the same clothes?

J: But that's the whole point, isn't it? 'Uniform' means the same, so at school there is no difference between us. Don't you know anyone whose parents can't afford to dress them in fashionable clothes at school? With school uniform, nobody has to worry if they look different.

C: But why should we be forced into wearing clothes that we don't like? Why don't they just give us some guidelines about what we can and can't wear? Wouldn't that be better? For example, no jeans, or everyone has to wear a white shirt or blouse?

J: Come on! You know as well as I do that everyone would soon find a way round the guidelines, and the teachers would find it impossible to know what is acceptable and what isn't.

C: Yes, I suppose you're right. On the other hand, if they treat us like penguins then they shouldn't be surprised if we behave like one! I think we're old enough to know what is acceptable and what isn't, in terms of school clothes.

J: Maybe, but that brings me back to my original point. What about those kids who are just going to show off in their new fashions, and the kids who can't really keep up? You know it will happen. Then we may get bullying and kids laughing at each other just because of their clothes.

C: Well, we certainly don't want any fights or confrontation over something like our clothes. Maybe the school should allow us all to vote and make a decision?

J: No way would we agree to wearing a uniform! But I would certainly vote for it. In any case, it makes me feel part of the school community, and I'm actually very proud of my school and my badge. Aren't you?

C: I guess so, but not wearing a uniform doesn't make me less proud than you, does it?

J: No, but we should feel proud to show off which school we go to, and one way to do that is by wearing a uniform. And another thing I've heard …

C: What's that?

J: Well, in schools where students have to wear a uniform, there's evidence that they achieve better academic standards!

C: Well, in that case …

Unit 19: Exam focus Listening
Activity 1   CD2, Track 13

Extract 1

V1: Good morning. May I help you?

V2: Yes, please. I need to buy this book for history at college.

V1: Do you want the book with or without the answer key?

V2: Well, the version without the answer key, please, as I think it'll be cheaper?

V2: Yes, it is cheaper. And we'll give you a free promotional history magazine with it as well.

V1: Ah, okay thank you … and since we weren't told about the book with the answer key, I definitely won't take it, thank you.

Extract 2

V1: Excuse me! I'm trying to find my way to the restaurant. Which floor is it on?

V2: Actually there are two in this store. It depends if you want to just have a coffee or sit and have a meal?

V1: Hmmm, I'm not sure. Maybe I should look for my friend in both.

V2: Well then, you need to go to the third floor if you arranged to eat a meal or on the ground floor for the café. The escalator is there on your left and you should find both of them without any problem.

Extract 3

V1: Do you keep going to the same old places for coffee with your friends? Are you bored of the same old faces, the same old flavours of coffee? Yes? Then why not try 'Coffee Cup' a new place to go, with fresh new coffee flavours and a large outdoor seating area where you can relax with friends? Try our new promotional coffees with coffee beans from as far away as Jamaica and Cuba! The coffee beans are specially selected for you, because we know what you like best!

Extract 4

Ok children, listen to the schedule for today because we don't want any of you getting lost or being late like last time. The bus will be here in about 60 minutes to take us to the sports centre. When we get there you can choose your programme: either activities in the swimming pool or in the gym. But remember you're not allowed to play on the outdoor playing fields. We'll have about four hours at the gym with a break mid-way when we can go to the café for something to eat and drink. The bus to go back will be here at about two o'clock, just in time for your parents to meet you at school.

Unit 19: Exam focus Listening
Activity 2   CD2, Track 14

Good morning everyone. Today we're going to talk about one of my favourite topics: cats, or at least the domesticated cat, which is the one many of us have living in our homes and gardens. We now know that the domesticated cat has been a part of human lives for about 12 000 years. Archeologists found the skeleton of a cat on the eastern Mediterranean island of Cyprus in an area that is now named the Near East, but was formerly known as Mesopotamia. This particular cat had been deliberately buried alongside a human, most probably its owner, and would suggest that a special bond had existed between the human and the animal, many thousands of years ago.

Studies have shown that the domesticated cat descended from the African wildcat, and it shares its ancestry with lions and tigers from about 10–15 million years ago. These large cats in their turn have their ancestors from the region around west Asia.

Domesticated cats became an important addition to society when humans began to settle down, around 10 000 years ago, when more permanent living settlements were built. Because humans were not moving around so much, searching for food, crops like wheat and barley needed to be stored, and where there are crops, there are mice. So the cat became more of a friend when humans realised how the cat could control the mice which were eating the crops.

The cat gradually became invaluable domestically due to its hunting skills, and since it was now living in close proximity with humans, it stated adapting its characteristics to its new environment. It started to fit in: living with and appealing to humans, and so the process of domestication began.

One country where the cat has played a dominant role and where initially it was thought they originated from, is Egypt. But the domestic cat has actually only been part of Egyptian culture and tradition for the past 4,000 years or so. Egyptian culture was famous for its admiration of the cat through various humans during history commonly portrayed as a cat, or a woman with a cat's head. The word 'cat' itself comes originally from a North African word *'quattah'*. This word was then adapted by most European countries in various different forms such as *'katze'* in German, *'gatto'* in Spanish and of course *'cat'* in English.

Today, not surprisingly, the cat is the most popular pet in the world for both men and women. Studies have shown that neither gender has a greater preference for cats. In the United States alone there are about 90 million domesticated cats and that accounts for 34% of Americans having a pet cat lying around somewhere in their home. The worldwide population of cats exceeds 500 million although unfortunately not all of them live the comfortable life of a pet. However, the cat has made a place for itself in our hearts.

Unit 19: Exam focus Listening
Activity 4   CD2, Track 15

Alfonso Fiore: Today I have the great honour of speaking to writer and fashion expert, Valentina Santini, winner of three World Fashion awards so far. Valentina has four homes, but we are meeting in her home in Florence, the only one located in Europe, to find out what the word fashion means to her. Is it just the shoes and clothes that we see in magazines, or is it something else, something difficult to define? Judging by the look of your home Valentina, you most definitely have an eye for everything that is tasteful and fashionable. It's a real pleasure to meet you!

Valentina Santini: The pleasure is all mine. I'm a great fan of your magazine, and of course of your writing.

AF: Thank you! To begin with, can you explain to us what fashion actually means?

VS: Well, as someone once said: "Fashion fades, only style remains the same". I think the most important thing to remember when talking about fashion, whether you're referring to clothes, furniture, accessories or even food, is that it is constantly evolving and changing, just like the sea. This is how it differs to style, which is more personal, individual, more like a pond which doesn't move.

AF: So, when we use the word fashion, we don't just mean the clothes that start off on the runways of fashion houses and which eventually end up in clothes shops?

VS: Absolutely not. Of course, the fashion industry, as you yourself know, is massive, and the major sector is indeed the clothing industry. But we mustn't forget aspects of it such as makeup, hair trends and furniture, which are just as important.

AF: I see. Since we're talking about furniture, would you say that the pieces you currently have in your home are in fashion?

VS: As with clothes, there isn't just one or ten or even one hundred fashion styles for furniture, nor indeed for interior design in general. In fact, there are hundreds, going back thousands of years, and from all over the world. The list is endless! I would say this house is quite fashionable at the moment, and I feel very comfortable in my surroundings.

AF: I would expect that from a fashion expert such as yourself. Can you tell me a little about fashion and makeup?

VS: Social media is probably one of the main reasons that makeup today is so huge in our society. I mean, if you visit Pinterest, Instagram, YouTube, or any other social medium, you can find thousands of makeup tutorials, methods, makeup trends, and so on. It's come to the point where if you want to be fashionable, then you need to be able to keep up with this whole online bubble which is the fashion world.

AF: What would you say defines something as fashionable?

VS: As I said before, fashion is constantly changing. What makes it change are the great fashion houses whose job it is to design new and wonderful items. The reason that high-end fashion brands are the inspiration for the fashion world is not just because of the quality they offer and their celebrity status, but it's also because they are constantly raising the stakes. They are creating items that change every season, they **create** fashion, and everyone else just follows: celebrities, music and film stars. Everyone. For something to be considered "fashionable" in today's society, it needs to follow the guidelines exhibited by these fashion houses.

AF: Do you agree with this? If that's the case, then we would be buying new furniture every few months just so we can consider ourselves to be in fashion.

VS: Perhaps that's a little extreme, but I have met people who do this. It's a vicious circle, I won't deny it, but it isn't all bad. In fact, I know for certain that the shirt you are currently wearing is from a very high-end and expensive fashion house!

AF: Guilty as charged!

VS: It's not a crime to love fashion, whether that love is for a pair of trainers or a designer sofa or a fast car. The best thing to remember is that if you love fashion, let it guide you, but not control you. A truly fashion-conscious person knows that you take fashion and you make it your own. In that way, it is **you** who defines fashion, and you don't let yourself be defined by it.

AF: I absolutely agree with you and really, it's been wonderful speaking to you Valentina; a real eye-opener! Thank you so much for your time!

VS: It's my pleasure.

© Emily Lucantoni

Unit 20: E Listening and Speaking
Activity 2   CD2, Track 16

OLAF: I can't think of any negatives! Technology is only positive.

AISHA: I don't have a problem if people know about me. I've nothing to hide anyway.

TOM: My age group was born with technology and we've grown up with it, so we don't need special skills.

MARI: My grandparents used different types of technology, but they still had it.

PEDRO: My phone. No need to even think about it.

MARYAM: There are so many amazing technologies, but for me all the smart apps take my breath away.

Unit 20: E Listening and Speaking
Activity 4   CD2, Track 17

Pedro: My phone. No need to even think about it. We all have one, in fact we've all had one for so long that we probably can't remember life without one. It's just normal to have one. If you took my phone away from me, I just wouldn't be able to operate normally. Life would be meaningless!

Tom: My age group was born with technology and we've grown up with it, so we don't need special skills. Of course, if a new technology comes along then perhaps we need to learn how to use it. But I believe that we can easily transfer our skills from one technology to another – we're not stupid, are we?

Maryam: There are so many amazing technologies, but for me all the smart apps take my breath away. It seems like there's an app for everything and anything you might want to do. And the great thing is that everyday day a new app comes along, or friends make you aware of an app that they've tried and enjoy using.

Olaf: I can't think of any negatives! Technology is only positive. Just think of how we use it every day. What's not to like about technology? The point nowadays is that everything involves technology to some extent, so it's impossible for life to continue without it.

Aisha: I don't have a problem if people know about me. I've nothing to hide anyway. I think the only people who worry about privacy are criminals. I don't even think we have any idea of who knows what about us because nothing is secret in the 21st century.

253

Acknowledgements

I am very grateful to the following: Muhammad Muavia Bashir (Buraimi, Oman) for his insightful feedback and support with early drafts of this new edition; Akis Panayi (Nicosia, Cyprus) for his comments on early units; Stavros Zenonos (Nicosia, Cyprus) for his ideas and suggestions on vocabulary issues; Emily Lucantoni (Nicosia, Cyprus) for her writing of various texts; James Frith and his team at Cambridge University Press for immense support and encouragement during all stages of the production of this new edition.

The authors and publishers acknowledge the following sources of copyright material and are grateful for the permissions granted. While every effort has been made, it has not always been possible to identify the sources of all the material used, or to trace all copyright holders. If any omissions are brought to our notice, we will be happy to include the appropriate acknowledgements on reprinting.

Text

Unit 1 excerpts from website Cambridge BID: Loving Cambridge, www.cambridgebid.co.uk, reproduced by permission; Unit 2 adapted from article 'How Much Pocket Money Is Enough' by Admin, April 2011 from www.financialized.ca, reproduced by permission; Unit 3 adapted from article '13 Things Your Fast-Food Worker Won't Tell You' by Michelle Crouch, originally published in *Reader's Digest*, Copyright © 2012 by Trusted Media Brands, Inc., reproduced by permission, all rights reserved; Unit 3 adapted from article 'McDonald's takes on pizza for Italy growth spurt' by Francesca Landini, from Reuters.com, 9 January 2013 © 2013 reuters.com, all rights reserved, reproduced by permission and protected by the Copyright Laws of the United States, the printing, copying, redistribution, or retransmission of this Content without express written permission is prohibited; Unit 3 adapted from 'Hopitality with dates', Ahlan Wasahlan, November 2013; Unit 3 adapted from article 'Marketing the Mollusc' by Dr Karen Millson in *Tribute*, reprinted with kind permission of Apex Media; Unit 4 adapted from www.garda.ie An Garda Siochana; Unit 4 adapted from think.direct.gov.uk courtesy of the Department for Transport; Unit 5 adapted from article 'Hiking with huskies holiday in Finland' from www.responsibletravel.com, reproduced by permission; Unit 6 adapted from article 'Why teenagers can't get up in the morning' by Fiona MacRae, 30 August 2006, from *Daily Mail Online*, reproduced by permission; Unit 6 adapted from article 'Reading from a tablet before bed may affect sleep quality' by Kathryn Doyle, from Reuters.com, 11 March 2016 © 2016 reuters.com, all rights reserved, reproduced by permission and protected by the Copyright Laws of the United States, the printing, copying, redistribution, or retransmission of this Content without express written permission is prohibited; Unit 7 adapted from www.chemistscorner.com; Unit 7 adapted from article 'Females in Athletic Training' by Michelle Matt, 16 November 2015, from www.livestrong.com, Demand Media, Inc.; Unit 7 adapted from article 'Indian camel breeders lament Pushkar Fair's downfall' by Charlotte Turner, 15 November 2013, Agence France Presse, reproduced by permission; Unit 8 adapted from www.vocabulary.co.il; Unit 9 adapted from bestcareerlinks.com; Unit 10 Study Less, Study Smart: The best ways to retain more in less time by Patrick Allan - http://lifehacker.com/study-less-study-smart-the-best-ways-to-retain-more-1683362205 Lifehacker is part of the Gawker Media Group Copyrighted 2016. Gawker Media. 125821:1116PF; Unit 10 adapted from 'SQ3R - Reading/Study System' from http://ucc.vt.edu/academic_support/study_skills_information/sq3r_reading-study_system.html, Cook Counseling Center, Virgnina Tech, reproduced by permission; Unit 11 – adapted from 'The ten strangest Olympic sports' by Lateef Mungin, courtesy CNN; Unit 13 excerpt from 'Helen Keller Biography' by Tejvan Pettinger, Oxford, www.biographyonline.net, reproduced by permission; Unit 14 adapted www.nhscareers.nhs.uk; Unit 15 'Ginger' article from *Horus* (in-flight magazine of Egypt Air), January 2015; Unit 15 adapted from 'High Intensity Exercise: Can less really be more?' *Wings of Oman* (in-flight magazine of Oman Air), May 2016; Unit 15 adapted from article 'Is Gardening Good Exercise?' by Marie Iannotti, Courtesy of About.com / © Maria Iannotti, reproduced by permission; Unit 16 adapted from article 'Teens Spend a "Mind-Boggling" 9 Hours a Day Using Media, Report Says' by Dr. Mercola, 16 December 2015, http://articles.mercola.com/sites/articles/archive/2015/12/16/teens-media-usage.aspx, reproduced by permission; Unit 17 adapted from article 'Earning from Waste', 17 February 2016, reproduced by permission of Apex Media; Unit 17 by Sophie Yeo, RTCC, www.rtcc.org; Unit 17 adapted from 'A dangerous thirst', *The Times*, August 2001; Unit 17 adapted from article 'The Environment' by Christina Hartje-Dunn from Palo Alto Medical Foundation, www.pamf.org, reproduced by permission; Unit 18 adapted from 'Saving through science' by Jessica Gliddon in Etihad's in-flight magazine, September 2013; Unit 19 adapted from 'Fast fashion to ethical couture' in *Oman Daily Observer*, April 2016; Unit 20 adapted from article 'Self-lacing trainers the very thing for anyone going at a rate of knots' by James Dean, *The Times*, 18 March 2016, reproduced by permission; Unit 20 adapted from article 'Down to business: the future is beyond the horizon' by Candice Turner, *Royal Wings* May/June 2016, reproduced by permission; Unit 20 adapted from 'The Kitchen of the Future knows what's in your fridge' by Deena Shanker, Bloomberg News, The YGS Group Used with permission of Bloomberg Business Copyright © 2016. All rights reserved; Unit 20 adapted from 'The problem solvers' in *Open Skies* (Emirates in-flight magazine), May 2016; Unit 20 adapted from 'Ten Greatest Technological Inventions' by Wendy Gould http://smallbusiness.chron.com/10-greatest-technological-inventions-40511.html#page1, *reproduced by permission of Demand Media, Inc.*

Images

Cover image Mark Wragg/Getty Images Part 1 opener Hans Neleman/Getty Images; U1B(1) Tooga/Getty Images; U1B(2) Poncho/Getty Images; U1B(3) Daniel Grill/Getty Images; U1B(1) Blend Images – Kidstock/Getty Images; U1B(2) arabianEye/Getty Images; U1D(1) Cambridge School Dictionary, Cambridge University Press; U1F(1) teekid/Getty Images; U1EF(1) Maremagnum/Getty Images; U2B(1) Donaldson Collection/Getty Images; U2B(2) Stu Forster/Getty Images; U2B(3) Jeff Overs/Getty Images; U2B(4) NBC/Getty Images; U2B(5) Tristan Fewings/Getty Images; U2C(1) Eric Audras/Getty Images; U2E(1) JGI/Jamie Grill/Getty Images; U2F(1) Hero Images/Getty Images; U2F(2) DRB Images, LLC/Getty Images; U2F(3) Yuri_Arcurs/Getty Images; U2F(4) Carol Yepes/Getty Images; U3B(1) Bernhard Winkelmann/Figarophoto/Getty Images; U3B(2) gmevi/Getty Images; U3B(3) Jackson Vereen/Getty Images; U3B(4) Philip Wilkins/Getty Images; U3B(5) Jamie Garbutt/Getty Images; U3C(1) Lew Robertson/Getty Images; U3C(2) Andrew Bret Wallis/Getty Images; U3EF(1) Klaus Vedfelt/Getty Images; U3EF(2) DEA/P. INGALDI/Getty Images; U3EF(3) Abid Katib/Getty Images; U3EF(4) Alexandra Grablewski/Getty Images; U3EF(5) Freer Law/Getty Images; U4B(1) Gavin Hellier/Getty Images; U4B(2) Frank Bienwald/Getty Images; U4B(3) Peter John Dickson/Getty Images; U4B(4) Charles Bowman/Getty Images; U4C(1) Barbara Gonget/G&B Images/Alamy Stock Photo; U4C(2) Charles Bowman/Alamy Stock Photo; U4F(1) Doug Menuez/Forrester Images/Getty Images; U5B(1) Bernard van Dierendonck/LOOK–foto/Getty Images; U5B(2) Michel Setboun/Getty Images; U5B(3) Shadrack/Getty Images; U5B(4) Barry Winkiler/Getty Images; U5B(5) Paul McGee/Getty Images; U5B(6) Mike Hill/Getty Images; U5B(7) Oleksiy Maksymenko/Getty Images; U5F(1) Peter Stuckings/Getty Images; Part 2 opener Thomas Koehler/Getty Images; U6B(1) Lonnie Duka/Getty Images; U6B(2) Jeff Pachoud/Getty Images; U6B(3) Kristian Sekulic/Getty Images; U6B(4) Roy Mehta/Getty Images; U6B(5) Education Images/Getty Images; U6C(1) Andrew Fox/Getty Images; U6E(1) Randy Faris/Corbis/VCG/Getty Images; U6EF(1) Yui Yu Hoi/Getty Images; U6EF(2) Superb Images/Getty Images; U7B(1) Sean Murphy/Getty Images; U7B(2) Hero Images/Getty Images; U7B(3) Thomas Barwick/Getty Images; U7B(4) Tyler Stableford/Getty Images; U7B(5) Aping Vision/STS/Getty Images; U7B(6) Simon Ritzmann/Getty Images; U7B(7) Christoph Wilhelm/Getty Images; U7B(8) Tom Merton/Getty Images; U7B(9) John Lamb/Getty Images; U7B(10) StockRocket/Getty Images; U7B(11) World Perspectives/Getty Images; U7B(12) Fuse/Getty Images; U7EF(1) Dennis MacDonald/Alamy Stock Photo; U7EF(2) Anil Ghawana/Alamy Stock Photo; U8B(1) Andre Brands/EyeEm/Getty Images; U8B(2) Ariel Skelley/Getty Images; U8B(3) Hero Images/Getty Images; U8B(4) koosen/Getty Images; U8B(5) Gary Ombler/Getty Images; U8B(6) Kemzo Tribouillard/Getty Images; U8B(7) Matthias Kulka/Getty Images; U8C(1) Maskot/Getty Images; U8C(2) Sam Hofman/Getty Images; U8F(1) Asbodels/Getty Images; U9B(1) Blend Images – Kidstock/Getty Images; U9B(2) PamelaJoeMcFarlane/Getty Images; U9B(3) Jason Edwards/Getty Images; U9B(4) Ralf–Finn Hestoft/Getty Images; U9B(4) Miles Kemp/Getty Images; U9E(1) PaulPaladin/Getty Images; U9E(2) Rich–Joseph Facun/Getty Images; U10B(1) Photo Alta/Eric Audras/Getty Images; U10B(2) Ariel Skelley/Getty Images; U10B(3) AntonioGuillem/Getty Images; U10B(4) FatCamera/Getty Images; U10B(5) seb_ra/Getty Images; U10C(1) Floren Kopp/Getty Images; U10EF(1) GCShutter/Getty Images; Part 3 opener Boris Austin/Getty Images; U11B(1) dpa picture alliance/Alamy Stock Photo; U11B(1) Guinness World Records; U11B(2) Guinness World Records; U11C(1) lazyllama/Shutterstock.com; U11D(1) Bettman/Getty Images; U12B(1) ullstein bild/Getty Images; U12B(2) EyesWideOpen/Getty Images; U12B(3) Dorling Kindersley/Getty Images; U12B(4) Cultura RM Exclusive/Adie Bush/Getty Images; U12B(5) Joshua Dalsimer/Getty Images; U12D(1) TP/Alamy Stock Photo; U12E(1) Alex Mita/Getty Images; U12E(2) DEA/W.Buss/Getty Images; U12E(3) Andrew Caballero–Reynolds/Getty Images; U12E(4) Heritage Images/Getty Images; U12E(5) PhotoStock–Israel/Getty Images; U13B(1) Alexander Hassenstein/Getty Images; U13B(2) Archive Photos/Getty Images; U13B(3) Leon Neal/Getty Images; U13B(4) Justin Sullivan/Getty Images; U13C(1) Keystone/Getty Images; U13D(1) GraphicsArtis/Getty Images; U14B(1) Caiaimage/Robert Daly/Getty Images; U14B(2) Hemant Mehta/Getty Images; U14B(3) Mike Powell/Getty Images; U14C(1) Print Collector/Getty Images; U14E(1) CandyBoxImages/Getty Images; U14E(2) Massoud Hossaini/Getty Images; U14E(3) AFP/Getty Images; U15B(1) Mango Productions/Getty Images; U15B(2) The Washington Post/Getty Images; U15B(3) Maria Stenzel/Getty Images; U15B(4) loonger/Getty Images; U15B(5) technotr/Getty Images; U15B(6) Image Source/Getty Images; U15B(7) Lilly Roadstones/Getty Images; U15C(1) Bruno Crescia Photography Inc/Getty Images; U15C(2) Lew Robertson/Getty Images; U15H(1) Mike Harrington/Getty Images; U15H(1) Mint Images – Oliver Edwards/Getty Images; Part 4 opener Rafe Swan/Getty Images; U16C(1) Clarissa Leahy/Getty Images; U16F(1) Neidring/Drentwett/Getty Images; U16F(2) Niels Busch/Getty Images; U16F(3) Rafael Elias/Getty Images; U16F(4) Johner Images/Getty Images; U17B(1) Hindustan Times/Getty Images; U17B(2) iuoman/Getty Images; U17B(3) Nebojsa Markovic/Getty Images; U17B(4) Kevin Schafer/Minden Images/Getty Images; U17B(5) AFP/Getty Images; U17C(1) Bloomberg/Getty Images; U17C(2) Bloomberg/Getty Images; U17F(1) Dariush M/Shutterstock; U17EF(1) Getty Images; U18B(1) Matt_Collingwood/Getty Images; U18B(2) Ian Hooton/SPL/Getty Images; U18B(3) George Clerk/Getty Images; U18B(4) annhfhung/Getty Images; U18D(1) Zomi/Getty Images; U18F(1) Maya Kovacheva Photography/Getty Images; U18F(2) Getty Images; U19B(1) feedough/Getty Images; U19B(2) PG Pictures/Alamy Stock Photo; U19B(3) Ron Berg/Getty Images; U19B(4) Roger Bamber/Alamy Stock Photo; U19C(1) Hoang Dinh Nam/Getty Images; U19D(1) Hoxton/Martin Barraud/Getty Images; U19D(2) Arabian Eye FZ LLC/Getty Images; U19D(3) Shestock/Getty Images; U19D(4) PeopleImages/Getty Images; U19D(5) Robert Daly/Getty Images; U19D(6) Mango Productions/Getty Images; U20B(1) The Washington Post/Getty Images; U20B(2) Altaeros Energies; U20B(3) Chesky_W/Getty Images; U20B(4) Erik Tham/Getty Images; U20H(1) Mark Hamilton/Getty Images; U20H(2) Brand X Pictures/Getty Images; U20H(3) ruig/Getty Images; U20H(4) Harry Todd/Getty Images; U20H(5) Kritina Lee Knief/Getty Images.